glish

e Neo-Classic Theory of Tragedy in England during the Eighteenth Century. By CLARENCE C. GREEN. Cambridge, Mass.: Harvard University Press; London: Humphrey Milford, Oxford University 34. pp. 11s. 6d.

at the neo classic theory of drama went out of fashion in e eighteenth century is well known, but there

HARVARD STUDIES IN ENGLIS

VOLUME XI

THE NEO-CLASSIC THEORY OF TRAGEDY IN ENGLAND DURING THE EIGHTEENTH CENTURY

BY

CLARENCE C. GREEN

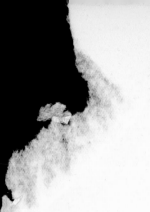

LONDON : HUMPHREY MILFORD

OXFORD UNIVERSITY PRESS

THE NEO-CLASSIC THEORY OF TRAGEDY IN ENGLAND DURING THE EIGHTEENTH CENTURY

By

CLARENCE C. GREEN

Cambridge, Massachusetts

HARVARD UNIVERSITY PRESS

1934

C

PRINTED AT THE HARVARD UNIVERSITY PRESS

CAMBRIDGE, MASS., U. S. A.

To

CAROLYN PALMER GREEN

PREFACE

THOSE who know the history of dramatic theory are doubtless aware of the gap that the following essay attempts to fill. Butcher, Saintsbury, Spingarn, and others have told with varying degrees of fullness the story of the rise of the neo-classic theory of tragedy, but their accounts are scattered through books dealing with a multitude of other subjects, and are to be read only with the expenditure of an excessive amount of energy and time. My introductory chapter simply retells the familiar story in compendious form. It lays no claim to originality. The story of the decline of the theory in eighteenth-century England, on the other hand, although a number of books and partial studies deal more or less directly and exclusively with the subject, has received neither unified nor complete treatment. The main body of my essay draws together a mass of widely dispersed material, much of which has been previously handled by others. Its object is to supply the student of the drama with a unified and reasonably complete history of the defeat of the neo-classic forces at the hands of the eighteenth-century critics.

For setting my feet in the right path at the outset of my journey through the centuries I wish to thank Professor John Tucker Murray. To the kindly interest of Professors Chester Noyes Greenough and James Buell Munn I owe the appearance of the essay in this series. The care and editorial acumen of Professor Hyder Edward Rollins are responsible for my having avoided many an ignorant blunder. As editor and teacher he has been an educational influence that I shall not forget. In conclusion I wish to express my thanks to the Harvard University Press for its excellent work on the proof, and to the librarians and assistants of the Harvard College Library for their ever-cheerful helpfulness.

C. C. G.

CAMBRIDGE, MASSACHUSETTS
September 1, 1934

CONTENTS

PART I

PART II

PART I

INTRODUCTION

INTRODUCTION

The Development of the Neo-Classic Theory of Tragedy to 1699

TODAY we "do not go back to Aristotle so much for the right answers as for the right questions," says Mr. F. L. Lucas,[1] referring to the *Poetics*. In the sixteenth and seventeenth centuries, however, critical theorists — both those who did and those who did not go back to the source — commonly believed that the oracle at Stagira invariably gave right answers. Some theorists were almost religiously devoted to the "best of critics." When, in 1692, Dacier,[2] for example, finds Minturno objecting on high theological grounds to Aristotle's contention that the misfortunes of a very virtuous man should be excluded from tragedy, he is moved to pious indignation — "as if," he exclaims, "Theology and Holy Scripture could ever be contrary to the sentiments of Nature, on which this judgment of Aristotle is based!" Aristotle is Nature, Nature Aristotle — this was all that many a trustful critic knew or felt that he needed to know.

Conformity to the "rules of Aristotle," not the capacity for giving pleasure, Chapelain[3] writes in 1638, is the cri-

---

1. *Tragedy* (New York: 1928), pp. 10–11.

2. *La Poétique d'Aristote, traduite en françois avec des remarques* (Amsterdam: 1692), pp. 186–187. Compare the *Poetics*, XIII, 2, in S. H. Butcher, *Aristotle's Theory of Poetry and Fine Art, with a critical text and translation of the Poetics* (4th ed., London: 1927); and A. S. Minturno, *De Poeta Libri Sex* (Venice: 1559), III, 182–183.

3. "L'Exorde" to *Les Sentimens de l'Académie Françoise sur la Tragi-Comédie du Cid*, ed. Georges Collas (Paris: 1912), p. 87.

terion of a play's excellence, and if some "regular" dramas
fail, their failure is not the fault of the rules, but of the authors, whose "sterile genie n'a peu fournir à l'Art matiere
qui fust assez riche." Great minds as well as small expressed an intermittent faith in the rules. Even Dryden,[1]
whose plays were never marked by great "regularity,"
early in his career as a dramatist took pleasure in at least
claiming to have observed the rules in *Secret Love* (1668), in
the prologue to which he writes:

> He who writ this, not without pains and thought,
> From *French* and *English* theatres has brought
> Th'exactest rules, by which a play is wrought.
>
> The Unities of Action, Place, and Time;
> The scenes unbroken; and a mingled chime
> Of *Johnson's* humour, with *Corneille's* rhyme.

Nevertheless, it is by no means true, as there is danger of
implying, that every neo-classic critic, to borrow a phrase
applied by Saintsbury [2] to Rymer, was "Puck-led by the
Zeitgeist into a charcoal-burner's faith in 'the rules.'" The
"intense stupidity" of Rymer was not a gift of the Time-
spirit, nor is common sense peculiar to our own age. Alexandre Hardy (1626),[3] the first master of Corneille, considered it not only wrong but impossible to confine "une
Tragedie dans les bornes d'une Ode, où d'une Elegie."
Boileau and Rapin, says Mr. A. F. B. Clark,[4] combined
"a general orthodoxy with a saving sense of the 'grace
beyond the reach of art.'" And Corneille, the practising

1. *Essays of John Dryden*, ed. W. P. Ker (Oxford: 1926), I, 109.
2. *A History of Criticism* (London: 1900–1904), II, 392.
3. *Le Théâtre d'Alexandre Hardy* (Paris: 1624–1628), III, sig. a5.
4. *Boileau and the French Classical Critics in England, 1660–1830* (Paris: 1925), p. 275.

dramatist, whose words are quoted by Dryden,[1] observed
that "'tis easy for speculative persons to judge severely;
but if they would produce to public view ten or twelve
pieces of this nature [*sc.* tragedies], they would perhaps
give more latitude to the rules than I have done, when, by
experience, they had known how much we are bound up
and constrained by them, and how many beauties of the
stage they banished from it."

The English were constitutionally restive under the curb
of the rules, and English taste, even before the reign of law
had been fully established, made a wry face at classic
frigidity. "The English comment on the classic drama,"
writes Mr. Lucas,[2] "is Pepys' entry on Jonson's *Cataline*:
'A play of much good sense and words to read, but the
least diverting that ever I saw any. And therefore home
with no pleasure at all, except in sitting next to Betty
Hall.'" At a later time (1693) Dryden,[3] in a characteristic
passage, summed up the contrast between French classic
and English romantic taste as follows:

As little can I grant, that the French dramatic writers excel
the English. Our authors as far surpass them in genius, as our
soldiers excel theirs in courage. 'Tis true, in conduct they surpass
us either way; yet that proceeds not so much from their greater
knowledge, as from the difference of tastes in the two nations.
They content themselves with a thin design, without episodes,
and managed by few persons. Our audience will not be pleased,
but with variety of accidents, an underplot, and many actors.
They follow the ancients too servilely in the mechanic rules, and

1. *An Essay of Dramatic Poesy* (1668), in *Essays*, ed. Ker, I, 75–76; see Corneille, *Des Trois Unités*, in *Oeuvres de P. Corneille*, ed. C. Marty-Laveaux (Paris:
1862), I, 122.
2. F. L. Lucas, *Seneca and Elizabethan Tragedy* (Cambridge, England: 1922),
p. 104.
3. "Dedication" to *Examen Poeticum*, in *Essays*, ed. Ker, II, 7.

we assume too much licence to ourselves, in keeping them only in view at too great a distance. But if our audience had their tastes, our poets could more easily comply with them, than the French writers could come up to the sublimity of our thoughts, or to the difficult variety of our designs. However it be, I dare establish it for a rule of practice on the stage, that we are bound to please those whom we pretend to entertain; and that at any price, religion and good manners only excepted.

Many Renaissance dramatists and critics believed that the rules were derived directly from the *Poetics*, but today it is hardly necessary to repeat that those who held this belief were for the most part wrong. The percentage of neo-classic ideas on dramatic subjects that were drawn unadulterated from the *Poetics* was very small. Of the remaining ideas some originated in the *Poetics*, but were later distorted, some went back to the *Ars Poetica* of Horace, and some sprang from the general rationalism of the Enlightenment. Any study of the neo-classic rules, however, must continually revert to the *Poetics*, since it was the chief source of misconception. Giraldi Cintio, in his *Discorso sulle Comedie e sulle Tragedie*,[1] written in 1543, tells us that it was customary in the schools of his day to study the relative merits of a Greek and a Senecan play on the same subject in the light of Aristotle's *Poetics*. Apparently, then, the systematic inculcation of erroneous interpretation began early.

Much of the subsequent confusion in neo-classic dramatic theory arose from Aristotle's definition of tragedy:[2] "Tragedy, then, is an imitation of an action that is serious, complete, and of a certain magnitude; in language em-

1. *Scritti Estetici*, ed. G. Antimaco, in *Biblioteca Rara* (Milan: 1864), LIII, 6.
2. *Poetics*, VI, 2.

bellished with each kind of artistic ornament, the several kinds being found in separate parts of the play; in the form of action, not of narrative; through pity and fear effecting the proper purgation of these emotions." Modern scholarship, perhaps the modern temperament as well, makes it fairly easy for us to know what Aristotle meant by some parts of his definition, but our ancestors encountered difficulties that forced them into a rich variety of misinterpretations. "But after all," writes Butcher,[1] "it contains only two real difficulties. The one lies in the clause concerning the 'several kinds of embellishment.' Fortunately, however, Aristotle has interpreted this for us himself; otherwise it would doubtless have called forth volumes of criticism. The other and more fundamental difficulty relates to the meaning of the *katharsis*. Here we seek in vain for any direct aid from the *Poetics*." Butcher, it is clear, leaves us only one "real" difficulty, but so far as neoclassic theory is concerned, it seems to me, there are two difficulties. The second one emerges in Mr. Lucas's analysis of the definition:[2] "Aristotle states in due logical order, first, what tragedy is and represents; secondly, the form it employs; thirdly, the manner in which it is communicated; and, lastly, the function it fulfills." The second difficulty resides in that part of the definition that states "what tragedy is and represents," resides specifically in the word "imitation." This word leads us to a consideration of the *rationale* of neo-classic tragic theory.

Lisideius, in Dryden's *Essay of Dramatic Poesy* (1668),[3] it will be recalled, defines a play as "*a just and lively image of human nature, representing its passions and humours, and*

1. *Aristotle's Theory of Poetry and Fine Art* (4th ed., 1927), pp. 242–243.
2. *Tragedy*, pp. 13–14.   3. *Essays*, ed. Ker, I, 36.

the changes of fortune to which it is subject, for the delight and instruction of mankind," and the other parties to the dispute finally agree that the definition is a fair one. Probably most theorists of the seventeenth century would have given their assent. Now it will be noticed that the two cruxes that appeared in Aristotle's definition reappear in Dryden's. For Aristotle's "imitation of an action" we have Dryden's "image of human nature," and for Aristotle's "purgation of the emotions of pity and fear" we have Dryden's "for the delight and instruction of mankind."

The first of these two pairs of phrases is perhaps the most baffling in the whole range of critical theory. In one respect Aristotle's "imitation of an action" and Dryden's "image of human nature" mean the same thing: they are both specific variations of the formula, "imitation of nature." In another respect it is impossible to say what they have in common, for the paradox is that the meaning they share is almost hopelessly ambiguous. In other words, if we assume that each writer when he used his particular phrase was thinking that tragedy must represent the "natural" facts of human life, or, in Dryden's phrase, "human nature," we are confronted with the necessity of deciding whether they meant the same things by "natural" and "nature." Or consider the following passage from a contemporary of Dryden's: "Nothing can please in a Play but Nature," says John Dennis [1] in 1718, "no not in a Play which is written against the Rules; and the more there is of Nature in any Play, the more that Play must delight." It is not fair, we may feel, to expect Aristotle

1. "*To* Walter Moyle," in *The Select Works of Mr. John Dennis* (London: 1718), II, 532.

and Dryden to mean the same thing — though it is in one sense perfectly fair. We no doubt feel that it is less unfair to expect the meanings of Dryden and Dennis to be identical, while simultaneously entertaining the conviction that it is somehow unwise to expect their meanings to be *exactly* the same.

The ground of this conviction is the indubitable fact that seventeenth and eighteenth-century writers obviously did use the word "nature" in different "senses," as we say. In these writers, says Ker,[1] "'Nature' means whatever the author thinks right; sometimes it is the reality that is copied by the artist; sometimes, and much more commonly, it is the principles of sound reason in poetry; and sometimes it is the Ideal." According to Mr. P. H. Frye,[2]

it has been pointed out that by their own confession nature was nothing but a paraphrase for the imitation of their classics. . . . Or worse, their pretended deference for nature has been treated as an empty formula to which they themselves never thought of attaching any significance, unless it were as a cover for their artificiality. More suggestively, however, Leslie Stephen [3] has observed that the natural, after all, is nothing more or less than the usual.

Mr. Frye [4] himself believes that "the only kind of nature that they knew or cared anything about was human nature." It is unnecessary to examine each one of these so-called "meanings" on its historical merits, for it can easily be demonstrated that in the strict sense of the word they are not "meanings" at all. "Nature," for example, can-

1. *Essays of John Dryden*, I, xxiv–xxv.
2. "Dryden and the Critical Canons of the Eighteenth Century," *Nebraska University Studies*, VII (1907), 30.
3. See Stephen, *English Literature and Society in the Eighteenth Century* (New York: 1907), p. 75, for a statement to this general effect.
4. P. 32.

not *mean* "the principles of sound reason in poetry," because if it did, the writer who "imitated nature" would have been "imitating the principles of sound reason in poetry," which surely is nonsense. Ker's statement is intelligible only when it is interpreted as saying that the writers referred to held the theory that Nature is "reasonable" and that good poetry is characterized by the same reasonableness.

The general significance of this demonstration may be made clearer by the use of an analogy. Jones and Smith may disagree with each other because, through the ignorance of one or both, they are using the same name for different objects; so that Jones says that X has four legs, and Smith that X has six legs, when, as a matter of fact, X may really be something with only two legs. The confusion arises because Jones should say Y, and Smith should say Z. This is the sort of confusion that some scholars believe the neo-classic writers to have been guilty of — guilty, that is, of using "nature" as the name of totally different things. On the other hand, Jones and Smith may disagree because, although they are talking about the same thing, they hold different theories concerning its predicates; so that Jones says that X is regular, and Smith that X is irregular. There may be confusion here, too, but the confusion, if there is any, will be due, not to the fact that they are not both talking about X, but to the fact, perhaps, that they are both using "regular" in a private way, as they were privately using X in the first analogy. But there may be no confusion of this sort at all: they may both mean the same object by X and the same quality by "regular," and yet disagree about the "regularity" or "irregularity" of X. It is this kind of disagreement, as I see it, that is to be found among the seventeenth and eighteenth-century writers. For some of them said that Nature is "regular," and some as stoutly maintained that it is "irregular." There is no reason, however, for assuming that they meant different things by "nature." They simply held different theories about it.

Anyone who discusses these theories, of course, must continually speak of the "meanings" of the word "nature," as does Professor A. O. Lovejoy in the following passage, but the peculiar sense in which the word had different meanings should be kept clearly in mind. "Nothing," writes Professor Lovejoy,[1]

. . . is more needful, especially for the student of the literature and philosophy of the seventeenth and eighteenth centuries, than a thorough understanding of the diversity of meanings of the word ["nature"], at once the most sacred and most protean in the vocabulary of those periods. What is requisite is, of course, not a mere list of lexicographer's definitions, but such an analytical charting of the senses of the term as will make clear the logical relations and (what is historically still more important), the common confusions between them, the probable semasiological development of one out of another, and the doctrines or tendencies with which they are severally associated. To read eighteenth-century books (in particular) without having in mind such a general map of the meanings of "nature" is to move about in the midst of ambiguities unrealized; and it is to fail to observe an important causal factor in certain of the most momentous processes of change in opinion and taste. For "nature" has, of course, been the chief and the most pregnant word in the terminology of all the normative provinces of thought in the West; and the multiplicity of its meanings has made it easy, and common, to slip more or less insensibly from one connotation to an-

1. "'Nature' as Aesthetic Norm," *Modern Language Notes*, XLII (1927), 444.

other, and thus in the end to pass from one ethical or aesthetic standard to its very antithesis, while nominally professing the same principles.

In the article from which this passage is quoted Professor Lovejoy [1] makes "an analytical enumeration of the purely aesthetic uses of the term — *i. e.*, its meanings in the formulas that art should 'imitate' or 'follow' or 'keep close to Nature.'" The enumeration includes seventeen senses, ranging all the way from strictly neo-classic senses to their opposites. The neo-classic senses of the word, according to Professor Lovejoy,[2] are as follows:

1. The universal and immutable in thought, feeling, and taste; what has always been known, what everyone can immediately understand and enjoy.
2. "Nature" as the generic type, excluding the differentiae of species and individuals.
3. Intuitively known principles or standards of "taste" . . . whereby that which is objectively and essentially (*i. e.*, "by nature") beautiful is recognized.
4. Uniformity.
5. Simplicity.
6. Economy of means in achieving a given end.
7. Regularity: nature as "geometrizing."

From these theories concerning "nature" and the "natural" it followed [3] that a work of art may be said to "imitate nature"

a. When it has "universal aesthetic validity," or the "capacity for being immediately understood and enjoyed by all men

1. Pp. 444–445.
2. Pp. 445–447.
3. P. 448: "*Implied Desiderata in Works of Art* (if they are to 'accord with Nature' in one or another of the above senses)." See "*Implied Desiderata*" *o, g, p, h, i.* The "above senses" are the seventeen already referred to.

(whose 'natural' taste has not been corrupted)." This is "often construed" as implying the "depiction of general types, only, not of individuals."

b. When, as a frequent implicate of *a*, the work of art adheres "to standards of 'objective' beauty."

c. When it adheres "to rules and precedents, or [imitates] models, of which the 'conformity to nature' (*i. e.*, their universal validity, and appeal to that which is immutable in human nature) has been shown by their general and long-continued acceptance."

d. When it is characterized by "simplicity, *i. e.*, sparseness of ornament and avoidance of intricacy in design."

e. When it is characterized by "symmetry, balance, definiteness and regularity of form."

By synecdoche the predicates of "nature" came to stand for "nature" itself. Consequently it is hard to tell what neo-classic writers mean when they say that art ought to "imitate nature." The same writer has different predicates in mind at different times, so that it is possible for him to seem to contradict himself from page to page when he is not really doing so at all, since the same object may have different, though it cannot have contradictory, qualities. The disagreement among different neo-classic writers is likewise often more apparent than real, though there were, of course, real disagreements too. The point to be kept in mind is that, although these writers used the word "nature" and the phrase "imitation of nature" in different senses, they really "meant" *something*.

The qualities that the neo-classic writers predicated of "nature" are reducible, I believe, to five, which appear in Professor Lovejoy's chart: universality, typicalness, uniformity, simplicity, and regularity. The fact that "nature" has these qualities indicates why rules for following her are necessary. It is the exception, we say, that proves the rule, which means, not that the exception proves the rule to be true, but that it defines the limits of the rule. Conversely, the rule determines what is to be included within it, and what is not. If a writer happens not to know what constitutes universality, the rules will tell him. But there is another, a more pregnant, reason why the neo-classicist considered rules essential. The "natural," he said, for example, is "universal," not "particular": it is that which excludes exceptions, oddities, queernesses, the things that exist *here* and *now* and nowhere else, and for that reason cannot be generalized into, or subsumed under, a rule. The neo-classicist, it may be said, was therefore congenitally disposed to welcome the rules, because the idea of rules agreed perfectly with his idea of the "natural."

The five qualities that the neo-classicist attributed to the "natural," however, were subservient, as I see it, to one dominant quality — order, or rationality. "Nothing can please in a Play but Nature," says Dennis [1] in the passage already quoted, "no not in a Play which is written against the Rules; and the more there is of Nature in any Play, the more that Play must delight. Now the Rules are nothing but an Observation of Nature. For Nature is Rule and Order it self." The equation could hardly be more explicit. D'Aubignac (1657) [2] makes the equation between Nature and Reason almost equally explicit and just as clear: "In all that depends upon common sense and reason, such as

1. "*To* Walter Moyle," in *The Select Works*, II, 532.
2. *The Whole Art of the Stage* (London: 1684), I, 23. This is a translation of *La Pratique du Théâtre* (1657), ed. Pierre Martino (Paris: 1927). All references are to the translation, though in the text the better-known French title is given.

are the Rules of the Stage, there to take a license, is a crime, because it offends not Custom, but Natural light, which ought never to suffer an Eclipse." Boileau,[1] while not setting up the equation, asserts without equivocation the essential rationality of art:

> Aimez donc *la raison*; que toujours vos écrits
> Empruntent d'elle seule et leur lustre et leur prix.

It is Dennis [2] again who synthesizes the three in a single formula: "*Now Nature, taken in a stricter sense, is nothing but that Rule and Order and Harmony which we find in the visible Creation,*" and "*as Nature is Order and Rule and Harmony in the visible World, so Reason is the very same throughout the invisible Creation. For Reason is Order and the Result of Order.*"

The implications of this passage, it seems to me, are perfectly clear. Reason is the principle of order, the Platonic Idea of order — the universal that manifests itself imperfectly in particulars. It participates, as Socrates would have said, in the "visible," or physical, world, as well as in the "invisible," or mental, world. In the degree to which it does participate in these two worlds, physical and mental "nature" is rational, or orderly, and therefore worthy of imitation. In the degree to which it does not participate, the two worlds are unworthy of imitation. The exceptions to order, the oddities and queernesses of "nature," taken, as Dennis might have said, in a "looser sense," are beyond the pale.

---

1. *L'Art Poétique*, I, 37–38, text and translation in *The Art of Poetry: The Poetical Treatises of Horace, Vida, and Boileau, with translations by Howes, Pitt, and Soame*, ed. A. S. Cook (New York: 1926).

2. *The Advancement and Reformation of Modern Poetry* (London: 1701), sigs. A8ᵛ –a1.

The beauty of this presentation of the matter lies in its simplicity, which would have appealed to the neo-classic mind itself. It shaves away, with Occam's razor, the multiplied distinctions of Professor Lovejoy's chart, which, useful as it is, is more valuable as an exercise in semasiology than as a key to neo-classic theory. It demonstrates, I think, that although the word "nature" was used in a multitude of senses, and the phrase "imitation of nature" in a way meant different things in different writers, and even different things in the same writer at different times, there was a central core of meaning to which those writers clung and to which we, not too precariously, may cling: not only for the obvious reason, already insisted upon, that it was always the *same* entity of which the various qualities were predicated, but because the various qualities themselves were merely "instances" of the *same* universal— rationality, or order.

If this view is sound, it explains why neo-classic writers could so wholeheartedly accept Pope's *cliché*,[1]

> Those RULES of old discovered, not devis'd,
> Are Nature still, but Nature methodiz'd.

It puts in the neatest of nutshells the gist of their doctrine. The rules, they thought, were a formulation of the rationality and order "discovered" *in* "nature."

---

1. *An Essay on Criticism*, I, 88–89, in *The Poetical Works of Alexander Pope*, ed. A. W. Ward (London: 1924). Both Rapin and Dennis preceded Pope in making this observation. In *Reflections on Aristotle's Treatise of Poesie*, translated by Rymer (London: 1674), sig. b3, Rapin says that the *Poetics* "*is nothing else, but* nature *put in method, and* good sense *reduc'd to principles*." In *The Impartial Critick, or Some Observations upon a Late Book, entitled A Short View of Tragedy, written by Mr. Rymer* (1693), in *Critical Essays of the Seventeenth Century*, ed. J. E. Spingarn (Oxford: 1908–1909), III, 194, Dennis writes: "The Rules of *Aristotle* are nothing but Nature and Good Sence reduc'd to a Method."

So long as the neo-classicists remained on logical ground, which was their proper demesne, they were safe, but when they passed over to psychological ground they were in strange territory, where they behaved outlandishly. They tried to prove by logic what logic has nothing to do with. Dryden tries it in a passage on the unity of place in *A Defence of An Essay of Dramatic Poesy* (1668).[1]

Now, there is a greater vicinity in nature betwixt two rooms than betwixt two houses; betwixt two houses, than betwixt two cities; and so of the rest: Reason, therefore, can sooner be led by imagination to step from one room into another, than to walk to two distant houses, and yet rather to go thither, than to fly like a witch through the air, and be hurried from one region to another. . . . So, then, the less change of place there is, the less time is taken up in transporting the persons of the drama, with analogy to reason; and in that analogy, or resemblance of fiction to truth, consists the excellency of the play.

The assumption that imagination must always have reason in its train is without foundation in psychological truth. In his discussion of this passage A. W. Verrall [2] puts his finger precisely upon the weak spot: "The error into which the Renaissance critics are drawn is this: Dramatic imitation means the production in the spectator of a fancy, or a voluntary *delusion* that he is bodily present at the place and time of the supposed action."

Reason, however, did not have all its own way. Thus, Dryden, in his *Apology for Heroic Poetry and Poetic Licence* (1677),[3] the Rymers would have said, is "fanati-

1. *Essays*, ed. Ker, I, 128.
2. *Lectures on Dryden* (Cambridge, England: 1914), p. 134. It is not necessary to conclude with Verrall that the "Renaissance critics" believed that "this is what Aristotle means when he demands 'imitation.'"
3. *Essays*, ed. Ker, I, 186.

cal": "All that is dull, insipid, languishing, and without sinews, in a poem, they call an imitation of Nature: they only offend our most equitable judges, who think beyond them; and lively images and elocution are never to be forgiven." And Sir Robert Howard (1668) [1] confessed that "'tis not necessary for poets to study strict reason, since they are so used to a greater latitude than is allowed by that severe inquisition." But on the whole, especially as the seventeenth century wore to a close, reason carried the day and put fancy in durance.

Seventeenth-century rationalism merely carried to its logical conclusion the venerable Renaissance doctrine of verisimilitude, for which also Aristotelian sanction was claimed, though its origin was really the Horatian *incredulus odi*. To be sure, when Aristotle [2] speaks of Homer as the one "who has chiefly taught other poets the art of telling lies skilfully," he certainly implies that the skilful telling of lies is not only an art but a legitimate one. The Renaissance, however, if it saw the implication, failed to take it seriously. What it did take seriously was his pronouncement [3] that "the poet should prefer probable impossibilities to improbable possibilities." Art, said the neo-classicists, ought to imitate, not truth, such as the truth of history, but things like truth; for truth is full of possible improbabilities, things stranger than fiction, whereas the verisimilar is just sufficiently truthful to be "reasonable" and "natural." It took a considerable meta-

---

1. *Preface to the Duke of Lerma*, in D. D. Arundell, *Dryden and Howard, 1664–1668* (Cambridge, England: 1929), pp. 94–95.

2. *Poetics*, XXIV, 9. Compare Rymer, *A Short View of Tragedy* (London: 1693), p. 92: "Nothing is more odious in Nature than an improbable lye; And, certainly, never was any Play fraught, like this of *Othello*, with improbabilities."

3. *Poetics*, XXIV, 10.

morphosis, such as the changing of Procne into a bird or
Cadmus into a snake *coram populo*, to render Horace in-
credulous,[1] but the Renaissance was much less gullible, and
it built up the whole body of rules to support its doctrine
of verisimilitude. It was the rule of rules, which Boileau
(1673) [2] draws up thus:

> Jamais au spectateur n'offrez rien d'incroyable;
> Le vrai peut quelquefois n'être pas vraisemblable.
> Une merveille absurde est pour moi sans appas;
> L'esprit n'est point ému de ce qu'il ne croit pas.

In view of the insistence upon the natural, the reasonable, and the probable, it is not surprising that seventeenth-century criticism should consist mainly of fault-
finding, for creative writers, hedged about as they were by
minute prescriptions concerning the permissible and the
impermissible, were almost bound to make more misses
than hits, and the critics, who were bent upon testing the
excellence of art by analytic, rational standards, were
equally bound to pass more verdicts of guilt than of innocence. But to this generalization there were notable exceptions. In the criticism of the latter part of the century one
is impressed by the liberality of spirit in some of the writers. There is a growing sense that art cannot be evaluated
exclusively in terms of the rules, that taste can sometimes
detect graces in work that falls short when measured by
the yardstick of the stricter canons of art.[3]

A second and allied movement in the criticism of this
same time may also be mentioned. It was destined to bear
considerable fruit later on, and has come to be known as

1. *Ars Poetica*, ll. 187–188, in *The Art of Poetry*, ed. Cook.
2. *L'Art Poétique*, III, 47–50.
3. Compare A. F. B. Clark, *Boileau and the French Classical Critics in England, 1660–1830*, pp. 390–391.

"historical criticism," or the practise of appraising literature in terms of the taste and conditions of the age in
which it is produced. The romantic revolt in drama that
occurred in France between 1600 and 1630 was partly
the result of the earlier manifestations of this movement,
which were strongest among the critics and playwrights of
Spain, who had stimulated and defended an earlier and
similar revolt in the Spanish drama.[1] "This change in the
drama," writes Juan de la Cueba in his *Ejemplar Poético*
(1606),[2] "was effected by wise men, who applied to new
conditions the new things they found most suitable and
expedient; for we must consider the various opinions, the
times, and the manners, which make it necessary for us to
change and vary our operations." In England Ben Jonson, in the words of Professor Schelling,[3] manifested "a
liberality of spirit and a sense of the need of the adaptation
of ancient canons of art to changed English conditions"
that place him definitely on the side of the angels in this
regard.

During the Restoration period in England, however,
Saint-Evremond, Dryden, and Dennis were the most con-
spicuous proponents of the new enlightenment. In his
essay *De la Tragédie ancienne et moderne* (1672) Saint-
Evremond [4] writes:

It must be acknowledged that Aristotle's *Art of Poetry* is an
excellent piece of work; but, however, there's nothing so perfect

1. Compare J. E. Spingarn, *A History of Literary Criticism in the Renaissance*
(2nd ed., New York: 1908), pp. 232 ff.

2. *Parnaso Español*, ed. J. J. L. de Sedano (Madrid: 1774), VIII, 61.

3. "Ben Jonson and the Classical School," *Publications of the Modern Language Association of America*, XIII (1898), 248.

4. In *European Theories of the Drama*, ed. B. H. Clark (New York and London: 1929), p. 164.

in it as to be the standing rules of all nations and all ages. Descartes and Gassendi have found out truths that were unknown to Aristotle. Corneille has discovered beauties for the stage of which Aristotle was ignorant; and as our philosophers have observed errors in his *Physics*, our poets have spied out faults in his *Poetics*, at least with respect to us, considering what great change all things have undergone since his time.

And Dryden notes, in his *Heads of an Answer to Rymer's Remarks on the Tragedies of the Last Age*[1] — which must be dated shortly after 1678, when Rymer's book was published—that "it is not enough that Aristotle has said so, for Aristotle drew his models of tragedy from Sophocles and Euripides; and if he had seen ours, might have changed his mind." It is not necessary to conclude that Dryden's words were inspired by Saint-Evremond's, as Mr. A. F. B. Clark[2] is inclined to do, for no later than 1671, a year before Saint-Evremond's essay, Dryden[3] had written:

> They, who have best succeeded on the stage,
> Have still conform'd their genius to their age.

This couplet obviously anticipates the thought expressed in the *Heads of an Answer*, which was written some seven years later, and it ought to ease Saintsbury's[4] implied regret that Dryden "never *published* that word of power"— the sentence in the *Heads of an Answer* — "which dissolves all the spells of Duessa." Finally, Dennis, in *The Impartial Critic*[5] of 1693, insisted at length on the difference between the circumstances of Greek and of English drama.

1. *The Works of John Dryden*, ed. Sir Walter Scott and George Saintsbury (Edinburgh: 1882–1893), XV, 390.
2. *Boileau and the French Classical Critics in England, 1660–1830*, p. 292.
3. Epilogue to the second part of *The Conquest of Granada*, in *Essays*, ed. Ker, I, 160.   4. *A History of Criticism*, II, 413.
5. *Critical Essays of the Seventeenth Century*, ed. Spingarn, III, 148–154.

Nevertheless, in spite of the occasional outcropping of the "criticism of beauties" as opposed to the "criticism of faults," and in spite of a minor strain of criticism according to time and circumstance, the general trend of neo-classic criticism was of the rules-good-sense type; so that the seventeenth-century notion of "what tragedy is and represents" is adequately conveyed by the phrase "imitation of nature," or the more or less deliberate attempt by dramatists to make the audience believe that it was "bodily present at the place and time of the supposed action," and that the imitated action represented only what was "natural" and "reasonable," only what was regular, orderly, and harmonious, only that part of crude nature that participates in the rational principle of order. With this restatement of what I take to be the determination of the first crux in neo-classic tragic theory, we may proceed to a determination of the second crux, which appears in the difference between the Aristotelian and the neo-classic conceptions of the function of tragedy.

In his famous definition, as we have seen, Aristotle says that tragedy effects "through pity and fear . . . the proper purgation of these emotions." Later on in the *Poetics* [1] he tells us that the imitation of "actions which excite pity and fear [is] the distinctive mark of tragic imitation." I shall perhaps be readily pardoned for not adding more pages to the already enormous literature centering around this greatly misunderstood doctrine of *katharsis*. As everyone knows, it has been widely and variously misinterpreted. Twining [2] reduced the more probable of

1. XIII, 2.

2. *Aristotle's Treatise on Poetry, translated: with notes on the translation, and on the original; and two dissertations, on poetical, and musical, imitation* (London: 1789), p. 232; compare Butcher, p. 245 n.

the interpretations to two. According to the first, the *katharsis* is homeopathic, for tragedy purges us of the very emotions that it excites, and leaves us in a healthy state of emotional quiescence. According to the second, the *katharsis* is due to "the *moral lesson* and *example* of the drama." An example of the emotional, or medical, interpretation may be found in Minturno (1563):[1] "As the physician drives out poison from our bodies by means of poison, so the tragic poet purges our mind of its impetuous perturbations by the impetuosity of passions expressed gracefully in verse." Milton, in the preface to *Samson Agonistes*,[2] explains the *katharsis* in the same way:

Tragedy, as it was antiently compos'd, hath been ever held the gravest, moralest, and most profitable of all other Poems: therefore said by *Aristotle* to be of power by raising pity and fear, or terror, to purge the mind of those and such like passions, that is to temper and reduce them to just measure with a kind of delight, stirr'd up by reading or seeing those passions well imitated. Nor is Nature wanting in her own effects to make good his assertion: for so in Physic things of melancholic hue and quality are us'd against melancholy, sowr against sowr, salt to remove salt humours.

The last four lines of the play itself[3] repeat the idea:

> His servants he with new acquist
> Of true experience from this great event
> With peace and consolation hath dismist,
> And calm of mind *all passion spent.*

For the Renaissance, however, such passages as the three that have been quoted are rare, and the more popu-

1. *L'Arte Poetica* (Venice), p. 77.
2. Ed. F. A. Patterson, in *The Works of John Milton*, ed. F. A. Patterson and others (New York: 1931–1932), I, ii, 331.
3. Lines 1755–1759. The italics are mine.

lar interpretation of the *katharsis* is the ethical one.[1] All that need be said here is that modern scholars, whether they agree with Aristotle or not, are virtually unanimous in rejecting the ethical view of his meaning. "The theatre," they are sure Aristotle believed, "is not the school."[2] If modern scholarship is right, then, how un-Aristotelian is D'Aubignac[3] when he refers to "the Representations of the Stage, which may therefore properly be called the Peoples School." And how un-Aristotelian also is Racine[4] when, apropos of the moral aim of his *Phédre*, he writes approvingly of the ancients:

Their plays were a veritable school where virtue was of no less importance than with the philosophers. Hence it was that Aristotle laid down the rules of dramatic poetry, and Socrates, the wisest of the philosophers, did not disdain to speak of the tragedies of Euripides. We should like our works to be as solid and full of useful instruction as were those of antiquity.

In England, too, from the time of Sir Philip Sidney,[5] the ethical aim was steady if misdirected. "Delightful teach-

1. Compare Spingarn, *A History of Literary Criticism in the Renaissance* (2nd ed., 1908), p. 81: "Like Milton, Minturno conceived of tragedy as having an ethical aim; but both Milton and Minturno clearly perceived that by *katharsis* Aristotle had reference not to a moral, but to an emotional, effect." See also p. 58: "On the whole, it may be said that at bottom the [Renaissance] conception was an ethical one, for, with the exception of such a revolutionary spirit as Castelvetro, by most theorists it was as an effective guide to life that poetry was chiefly valued. Even when delight was admitted as an end, it was simply because of its usefulness in effecting the ethical aim."

2. Butcher, p. 224.

3. *The Whole Art of the Stage* (1657), I, 5.

4. "Préface" to *Phédre*, in *European Theories of the Drama*, ed. Clark, p. 157.

5. *The Defense of Poesy, otherwise known as An Apology for Poetry* (1595), ed. A. S. Cook (Boston: 1890), pp. 9–11, *et passim*. Compare Butcher, p. 239: "The Aristotelian doctrine as it has been handed down to modern times has again in this instance often taken the tinge of Roman thought, and been made to combine in equal measure the *utile* with the *dulce*. Sir Philip Sidney, for example, who in his *Apologie for Poetrie* repeatedly states that the end of poetry is 'de-

ing" as the end of poetry, dramatic and otherwise, was so venerable a precept by 1609 that Ben Jonson [1] was free to jest about it:

> The ends of all, who for the scene do write,
> Are, or should be, to profit and delight.

Rymer,[2] therefore, is making no innovation when he says (1678): "I am confident whoever writes a Tragedy cannot please but must also profit; 'tis the Physick of the mind that he makes palatable." Nor is Dryden being original when, in the *Heads of an Answer to Rymer* (*ca.* 1678-1679),[3] he bids himself "consider, if pity and terror be enough for tragedy to move; and I believe, upon a true definition of tragedy, it will be found, that its work extends farther, and that is to reform manners, by a delightful representation of human life in great persons, by way of dialogue." And Jeremy Collier [4] is but making a time-worn observation when he writes in 1698 that "the Business of *Plays* is to recommend Virtue, and discountenance Vice; To shew the Uncertainty of Humane Greatness, the suddain Turns of Fate, and the Unhappy Conclusions of Violence and Injustice: 'Tis to expose the Singularities of Pride and Fancy, to make Folly and False-hood contemptible, and to bring every Thing that is Ill under Infamy, and Neglect."

But, just as with the other articles of the neo-classic faith that have been reviewed, here also complete unanim-

---

lightful teaching,' or 'to teach and to delight,' has no suspicion that he is following the *Ars Poetica* of Horace rather than that of Aristotle. The view of Sidney was that of the Elizabethan age in general."

1. The second prologue to *Epicoene; or, The Silent Woman*, in *The Works of Ben Jonson*, ed. W. Gifford and F. Cunningham (London: 1875), III, 332.

2. *The Tragedies of the Last Age* (London: 1678), p. 140.

3. *Works*, ed. Scott and Saintsbury, XV, 383.

4. *A Short View of the Immorality and Profaneness of the English Stage* (4th ed., London: 1699), p. 1.

ity is lacking. It is not surprising, either, that Dryden at one time was on the side of liberalism. "Among the sayings in the *Defence*," [1] writes Ker,[2] "that illustrate the general position of Dryden is the remark on the end of poetry as principally *delight*, and only in the second place *instruction*: 'Delight is the chief, if not the only end of poetry: instruction can be admitted but in the second place, for poesy only instructs as it delights.'" In *The Usefulness of the Stage* (1698)[3] Dennis defended the theatre against Collier on the ground that it promotes human happiness by stimulating pleasurable passions — an argument that is not essentially different from Dryden's. Dryden, then, anticipated Dennis by some thirty years: he answered Collier and himself in advance. But his answer might just as well not have been made, for it went practically unheard. The triumph of didacticism was almost complete.

A natural consequence of the moral interpretation of the *katharsis* was the principle of poetic justice. What could be more instructive, asked the neo-classicist, than the reward of virtue and the punishment of vice? And what, we ask, could be less Aristotelian? Aristotle [4] carefully condemns the tragedy that has "an opposite catastrophe for the good and for the bad." "The pleasure . . .

1. See *A Defence of an Essay of Dramatic Poesy* (1668), in *Essays*, ed. Ker, I, 113.

2. *Essays of John Dryden*, I, li. Later, in the *Heads of an Answer* (*Works*, ed. Scott and Saintsbury, XV, 391), Dryden makes what seems to be a contradictory straddle: "The chief end of the poet is to please; for his immediate reputation depends on it. . . . The great end of the poem is to instruct, which is performed by making pleasure the vehicle of that instruction; for poesy is an art, and all arts are made to profit. [Rapin]." The second sentence, however, may be simply a notation of what Dryden considered Rapin's view.

3. Pp. 1–10.   4. *Poetics*, XIII, 7–8.

thence derived," he says, "is not the true tragic pleasure. It is proper rather to Comedy." The neo-classicist, though he may have thought that he had the support of Aristotle for his doctrine of poetic justice, really deduced it, logically enough, from his belief in the ethical function of poetry. Rymer gave the doctrine its name; D'Aubignac [1] called it "the most indispensible Rule of Drammatick Poems." In 1699 Drake, in *The Antient and Modern Stages Survey'd*,[2] observes that poetic justice "is now become the Principal Article of the *Drama*." Indeed everyone — Corneille, Dryden, and Saint-Evremond among the rest — seems to have accepted the rule with hardly a murmur. Yet it was not to be long before Addison [3] should call it a "ridiculous Doctrine in Modern Criticism."

For the neo-classic mind, then, the chief constituents that went to make up the function of poetry were instruction and delight; but a third element, "admiration," had been added by Minturno in 1559.[4] The poet, properly so called, should not only instruct and delight us, the Renaissance believed, but should also move us to admiration of his hero. It is the poet's business, writes Dryden,[5] "to affect the soul, and excite the passions, and, above all, to move admiration (which is the delight of serious plays)." Saint-Evremond,[6] another of the more level-headed of the seventeenth-century critics, also believed that "we ought, in tragedy, before all things whatever, to look after a great-

---

1. *The Whole Art of the Stage* (1657), I, 5.
2. P. 226.
3. *The Spectator, by Joseph Addison, Richard Steele & Others*, ed. G. G. Smith (London, Toronto, and New York: 1930), No. 40 (April 16, 1711).
4. *De Poeta*, I, 3.
5. *A Defence of an Essay of Dramatic Poesy* (1668), in *Essays*, ed. Ker, I, 113.
6. *De la Tragédie* (1672), in *European Theories of the Drama*, ed. Clark, p. 167.

ness of soul well expressed, which excites in us a tender admiration."

So heavily emphasized, in fact, was admiration that, allying itself with the love-element, it worked, in seventeenth-century tragedy, toward the utter destruction of pity and terror, upon which, of course, Aristotle insists. The heroic plays of the Restoration were specially designed to arouse admiration, so that it is somewhat surprising to discover Addison [1] speaking of it in December, 1700, as a "new passion." He is writing to Bishop Hough concerning a conversation he had had with Boileau in France: "Aristotle, says he, proposes two passions that are proper to be raised by tragedy, terror and pity, but Corneille endeavours at a new one, which is admiration." Addison, it is true, did not mean that Corneille was endeavoring to substitute admiration for terror and pity, but admiration did as a matter of fact tend to effect the substitution. It was inevitable that it should have done so. For, given an heroic ideal like that expressed, for example, in the English heroic plays, all possibility of terror vanishes. Fear, says Aristotle,[2] is aroused "by the misfortune of a man like ourselves"; therefore we cannot fear for Almanzor, a man who never was on sea or land. By the same token the possibility of pity also disappears; for the Aristotelian idea is that, as Butcher [3] puts it, "we pity others where under like circumstances we should fear for ourselves," and no one can imagine himself in the circumstances of Almanzor.

Admiration alone, then, was enough to destroy the

---

1. *The Works of the Right Honourable Joseph Addison*, ed. R. Hurd and H. G. Bohn (London: 1889–1891), V, 333.

2. *Poetics*, XIII, 2.   3. P. 256.

effects of pity and terror, but, as has been said, it had a powerful ally — love. Whereas admiration was a basic psychological foe to the effects that Aristotle considered legitimate for tragedy to produce, love, in seventeenth-century tragedy, was in the nature of a deliberate substitute designed to render tragedy less morbid and nerve-racking. "We were obliged," writes Saint-Evremond (1672),[1] "to mingle somewhat of love in the new tragedy, the better to remove those black ideas which the ancient tragedy caused in us by superstition and terror." Four years earlier Dryden, in *An Essay of Dramatic Poesy*,[2] had put into the mouth of Eugenius a similar defense of "the most frequent of all the passions." And in his *Heads of an Answer to Rymer* (*ca.* 1678-1679) he advanced two other reasons, typical of the time, for introducing the love theme into tragedy: love is, first of all, "heroic," and therefore admirable;[3] and, secondly, it is "the best common-place of pity."[4] It must be admitted that it now seems impossible that admiration of the Restoration variety and pity could both have been effects of heroic love, but the fact that Dryden did not consider them incompatible deserves at least to be recorded. The chances are, however, that Dryden was confusing — perhaps only verbally — the "admirable" qualities of the hero with his purely amorous qualities; in other words, that he did not consider love "fit for tragedy" because it was "heroic" so much as because it was passionate. In any case, love was "the one theme of Restoration drama."[5]

1. *De la Tragédie*, in *European Theories of the Drama*, ed. Clark, p. 166.
2. *Essays*, ed. Ker, I, 54.
3. *Works*, ed. Scott and Saintsbury, XV, 383.   4. XV, 390.
5. Margaret Sherwood, *Dryden's Dramatic Theory and Practice* (Boston, New York, and London: 1898), p. 10.

As the century wore on, however, nearly everyone took his turn at denouncing the misuse of the "soft passion." Even Corneille, who set the fashion of the love-play in the *Cid*, at length repented, as did Dryden. Rapin [1] attributes the evil practise to the influence of the women and the Spaniards, and concludes that "'tis to degrade *Tragedy* from that *majesty* which is proper to it, to mingle in it love, which is of a character alwayes *light*, and little sutable to that *gravity* of which *Tragedy* makes profession." Rymer [2] admires the Greeks for not allowing "their Love to come whining on the Stage to Effeminate the Majesty of their Tragedy." In the epilogue to *The Virtuoso* (1676) Shadwell [3] ridicules a typical "love and honour" play as follows:

> . . . A dull Romantick whining Play;
> Where poor frail Woman's made a Deity,
> With sensless amorous Idolatry;
> And sniveling Heroes sigh, and pine, and cry.
>
> Though singly they beat Armies, and huff Kings,
> Rant at the Gods, and do impossible things;
> Though they can laugh at danger, blood, and wounds;
> Yet if the Dame once chides, the milk-sop Hero swoons.

And at the same time Crowne, [4] who was himself addicted to the writing of heroic plays, makes the following admission: "I confess since love has got the sole possession of the stage, reason has had little to do there; that effeminate prince has softened and emasculated us the vassals of the

1. *Reflections* (1674), p. 112.
2. *A Short View of Tragedy* (1693), p. 62.
3. *The Complete Works of Thomas Shadwell*, ed. M. Summers (London: 1927), III, 181.
4. "Epistle to the Reader," prefixed to *The Destruction of Jerusalem* (1677), in *The Dramatic Works of John Crowne* (London and Edinburgh: 1873–1874), II, 237.

stage." The practise at which these criticisms were directed was the result of theatrical opportunism; the criticisms themselves were in the spirit of the strictest neo-
classicism.

It was probably not merely a lucky accident that the
required element of admiration agreed so nicely with what
the neo-classic mind considered the proper character for
the tragic hero, though the connection here is psychological
rather than logical; so that I shall refrain from insisting
too strenuously upon what seems to be the obvious fact
that the neo-classic tragic hero is, shall we say, made to the
order of admiration. However this may be, it is certainly
true that the ideal seventeenth-century hero was different
from Aristotle's. In the *Poetics*, XV, 1-5, Aristotle says
that "in respect of Character there are four things to be
aimed at": goodness, propriety, truth to life, and consistency. By goodness, of course, he means moral goodness, "goodness and badness being the distinguishing
marks of moral differences." [1] By propriety he means that
the character must be made to behave according to the
type he represents, but this prescription should not be interpreted as implying a narrow realism, for, though the
third aim in the creation of character is truth to life, the
tragic poet, imitating, as he does, "persons who are above
the common level," should follow "the example of good
portrait painters," who, "while reproducing the distinctive form of the original, make a likeness which is true to
life and yet more beautiful. So too the poet, in representing men who are irascible or indolent, or have other defects
of character, should preserve the type and yet ennoble
it." [2] And by consistency he means merely artistic con-

1. *Poetics*, II, 1.   2. *Poetics*, XV, 8.

sistency, which is different from either propriety or truth to life. The most important thing, however, that Aristotle says about the tragic hero is that, because tragedy must arouse the emotions of pity and terror, he must be a happy medium between extremes. The phrase "happy medium," nevertheless, requires careful definition. It does not mean that the hero should be colorless or average, as what has been said above indicates clearly enough: he must be "above the common level" of moral character, and though he must be true to life he must be "yet more beautiful." The criterion that determines his mediate position between extremes is his capacity, as we have seen, of arousing the emotions of pity and terror. In "a perfect tragedy," therefore, Aristotle says,[1]

it follows plainly, in the first place, that the change of fortune presented must not be the spectacle of a virtuous man brought from prosperity to adversity: for this moves neither pity nor fear; it merely shocks us. Nor, again, that of a bad man passing from adversity to prosperity: for nothing can be more alien to the spirit of Tragedy; it possesses no single tragic quality; it neither satisfies the moral sense nor calls forth pity or fear. Nor, again, should the downfall of the utter villain be exhibited. A plot of this kind would, doubtless, satisfy the moral sense, but it would inspire neither pity nor fear; for pity is aroused by unmerited misfortune, fear by the misfortune of a man like ourselves. Such an event, therefore, will be neither pitiful nor terrible. There remains, then, the character between these two extremes, — that of a man who is not eminently good and just, yet whose misfortune is brought about not by vice or depravity, but by some error or frailty. He must be one who is highly renowned and prosperous, — a personage like Oedipus, Thyestes, or other illustrious men of such families.

1. *Poetics*, XIII, 2–3. Compare Butcher, p. 317.

Clear as the *Poetics* now seems to us on the subject of the
proper character for the tragic hero, here again the French
and Italian critics of the Renaissance, with a few exceptions, went entirely wrong. Butcher and Spingarn have
traced out the bad linguistics and poor reasoning by means
of which the perversion was effected, and I shall deliver the
curious into their competent hands. Here it is enough to
say that the Aristotelian doctrine was as a matter of fact
perverted. What Aristotle says about the necessity of the
hero's being "above the common level," "highly renowned and prosperous," "illustrious," and so on, was
taken to mean that high rank was a sufficient qualification
for the tragic hero, as well as for the characters of tragedy
in general. Indeed, according to the Renaissance, it was
chiefly the rank of the characters that distinguished tragedy from comedy. Both Butcher and Spingarn agree
that this distinction is un-Aristotelian, "but the fact is,"
Spingarn [1] concludes, "that a similar distinction can be
traced, throughout the Middle Ages, throughout classical
antiquity, back almost to the time of Aristotle himself."

It is only just to record, however, that certain of the
Renaissance critics seem to have been aware of what Aristotle really meant. Jean de la Taille [2] is in perfect accord
with Aristotle when he pronounces against the utter villain and the perfect saint, such as Socrates. Racine,[3] too,
is on the right track:

1. *A History of Literary Criticism in the Renaissance* (2nd ed., 1908), p. 64.
Compare Saintsbury, *A History of Criticism*, II, 61, where he differs from both
Butcher and Spingarn on this point.
2. *Art de Tragédie* (1572), in Pierre Robert, *La Poétique de Racine* (Paris:
1890), p. 351.
3. "Préface" to *Andromaque* (1668), in *European Theories of the Drama*, ed.
Clark, pp. 154–155.

Aristotle, far from asking us to portray perfect heroes, demands on the contrary that tragic characters — whose misfortunes bring about the tragic catastrophe — should be neither wholly good nor wholly bad. He does not want them to be extremely good, because the punishment of a good man would excite indignation rather than pity in the audience; nor that they be excessively bad, because there can exist no pity for a scoundrel. They must therefore stand midway between the two extremes, be virtuous and yet capable of folly, and fall into misfortune through some fault which allows us to pity without detesting them.

Dryden [1] also knows the law, though he realizes the occasional expedience of breaking it:

That the criminal should neither be wholly guilty, nor wholly innocent, but so participating of both as to move both pity and terror, is certainly a good rule, but not perpetually to be observed; for that were to make all tragedies too much alike.

On the whole, however, it was again the perverted and not the pure teaching that ruled; so that the "moral nobility" insisted upon by Aristotle was equated with mere high rank, chiefly recognizable by its starched dignity, its courtly etiquette and decorum. It is obvious that the passage in the *Poetics* [2] in which Aristotle says that characters should be drawn with "propriety" was the starting point for the Renaissance conception of decorum, according to which "the type" should be rigorously preserved. But it was the starting point only in the sense that it gave the initial hint. For Horace lent impetus to the idea in the *Ars Poetica*,[3] where he asserts that the "schoolboy," the "beardless youth," "riper manhood," and "declining

1. *Heads of an Answer*, in *Works*, ed. Scott and Saintsbury, XV, 387; compare Dryden, *The Grounds of Criticism in Tragedy* (1679), in *Essays*, ed. Ker, I, 216.   2. XV, 2.   3. Ll. 156–178.

age" must be sharply distinguished from one another by the poet's description. In Aristotle's *Rhetoric* [1] Horace had found a discussion of similar distinctions, and, failing to note that the discussion was purely rhetorical, or logical, he had borrowed the conclusions and decked them out as an esthetic law. It was this mistake, combined with that of separating the comic and tragic *genres* on the basis of the rank of their characters, that produced the Renaissance doctrine of decorum, which bound the poet never to allow a character to act or speak out of harmony with his type.

How important the conception had become by 1674 is abundantly evident from the following passage in Rapin's *Reflections*: [2]

> Besides all the *Rules* taken from *Aristotle*, there remains *one* mention'd by *Horace*, to which all the other Rules must be subject, as to the most *essential*, which is the *decorum*. Without which the other Rules of *Poetry* are false: it being the most solid foundation of that *probability* so essential to this Art. Because it is only by the *decorum* that this *probability* gains its effect; all becomes *probable*, where the *decorum* is strictly preserv'd in all circumstances.

In the same year Boileau [3] drew up the rule in a couplet:

> Ne faites point parler vos acteurs au hasard,
> Un vieillard en jeune homme, un jeune homme en vieillard.

And the next couplet [4] indicates the almost complete identity between decorum and courtly etiquette:

1. *The Rhetoric of Aristotle, translated with an analysis and critical notes, by J. E. C. Welldon* (London and New York: 1886), II, 12–17.
2. P. 65. Compare Milton, *Of Education*, ed. A. Abbott, in *Works*, ed. Patterson and others, IV, 286: ". . . what the laws are of a true *Epic* Poem, what of a *Dramatic*, what of a *Lyric*, what Decorum is, which is the grand master-piece to observe." 3. *L'Art Poétique*, III, 389–390.
4. III, 391–392. Compare Rymer, *The Tragedies of the Last Age* (1678), p. 43: "Tragedy requires . . . what is great in Nature, and such thoughts as quality and Court-education might inspire."

Étudiez la cour et connoissez la ville;
L'une et l'autre est toujours en modèles fertile.

A particularly amusing restriction upon stage behavior is to be found in Rymer.[1]

If I mistake not, in Poetry no woman is to kill a man, except her quality gives her the advantage above him, nor is a Servant to kill the Master, nor a Private Man, much less a Subject to kill a King, nor on the contrary. Poetical decency will not suffer death to be dealt to each other by such persons, whom the Laws of Duel allow not to enter the lists together.

But if murder and other forms of cruel action, according to the law-makers, were allowable in certain circumstances, they were forbidden the open stage. It is interesting to observe that even this rule lacks the authority of Aristotle,[2] who defines the "Scene of Suffering" as "a destructive or painful action, such as death on the stage, bodily agony, wounds and the like," though it had the support of Greek practice, upon which Horace,[3] the true law-giver in this case, bases his famous dictum:

Non tamen intus
Digna geri promes in scenam, multaque tolles
Ex oculis quae mox narret facundia praesens.
Ne pueros coram populo Medea trucidet,
Aut humana palam coquat exta nefarius Atreus.

During the earlier Renaissance Giraldi Cintio [4] took a liberal view of the matter, declaring that some deaths, provided they are not too violent, may take place on the stage

1. *The Tragedies of the Last Age* (1678), p. 117.
2. *Poetics*, XI, 6.
3. *Ars Poetica*, ll. 182–186.
4. *Discorso sulle Comedie e sulle Tragedie* (1543), in *Scritti Estetici*, ed. Antimaco, in *Biblioteca Rara*, LIII, 119–120.

as object-lessons in justice. Castelvetro (1570),[1] however, who, in forming his critical opinions, always kept the actual theatre in mind, is closer to Horace, though mainly by implication, when he repeatedly insists that the "common people," who constitute the great body of theatre spectators are not fit to behold in undiluted form the violent actions of history. Many seventeenth-century critics, however, were strictly Horatian in their attitude. D'Aubignac,[2] for example, considered it "very reasonable" that "all those Storys full of *horrour* and *cruelty*, which made the pleasure of the *Roman* and *Athenian* Stages" should have been rejected by the French playwrights. And Boileau [3] does little more than paraphrase Horace:

> Ce qu'on ne doit point voir, qu'un récit nous l'expose;
> Les yeux en le voyant saisiroient mieux la chose,
> Mais il est des objets que l'art judicieux
> Doit offrir à l'oreille et reculer des yeux.

The closet tragedies of Seneca are, of course, full of sanguinary action, so that Elizabethan tragedy, which is based largely upon Senecan models, is bloody in the extreme; and the Senecan, or Elizabethan, tradition was continued uninterrupted — except for the Puritan interregnum — by the Restoration writers of tragedy.[4] The atmosphere of horror was so characteristic of English tragedy that Rapin [5] considered a love of "blood in their sports" an essential quality of the English temperament. "And, perhaps, it may be true," says Rymer,[6]

1. *Poetica d'Aristotle vulgarizzata et sposta* (Basel: 1576), pp. 22–23, 30.
2. *The Whole Art of the Stage* (1657), IV, 144.
3. *L'Art Poétique*, III, 51–54.
4. Compare Allardyce Nicoll, *A History of Restoration Drama, 1660–1700* (Cambridge, England: 1923), p. 159.   5. *Reflections* (1674), p. 111.
6. Rymer's Preface to Rapin's *Reflections*, sig. A5ᵛ; compare Rymer, *A Short View of Tragedy* (1693), p. 85.

that on our Stage are more Murders than on all the Theatres in *Europe*. And they who have not time to learn our Language, or be acquainted with our Conversation, may there in three hours time behold so much bloodshed as may affright them from the inhospitable shore, as from the Cyclops Den. Let our Tragedy-makers consider this, and examine whether it be the disposition of the People, or their own *Caprice* that brings this Censure on the best natur'd Nation under the Sun.

In *The Tragedies of the Last Age* (1678) Rymer [1] says, ingeniously but incorrectly, that the Greeks avoided violence upon the stage because they knew that violent characters could not easily arouse pity, and he implies that the English should avoid it for the same reason. Dryden,[2] who knew the actual theatre far better than Rymer, had considered the matter ten years earlier (1668), and had concluded that

if we are to be blamed for showing too much of the action, the French are as faulty for discovering too little of it: a mean betwixt both should be observed by every judicious writer, so as the audience may neither be left unsatisfied by not seeing what is beautiful, or shocked by beholding what is either incredible or undecent.

As usual, Rymer's is the strict, and Dryden's the liberal, view.

There was a similar divergence of opinion regarding the opposite kind of incident, the comic. In his definition of tragedy Aristotle, to be sure, says that tragedy should be "serious," but Greek tragedy is not altogether lacking in comic relief and comic character, and the Greeks apparently did not regard the effect of the so-called satyric

1. P. 28.
2. *An Essay of Dramatic Poesy*, in *Essays*, ed. Ker, I, 75.

drama as jarring with the effect of the preceding tragic trilogy. The Middle Ages, as in *The Killing of Abel*, were especially prone to mingle the comic and tragic. And Elizabethan tragedy, in Sidney's phrase, was a mixture of "funerals and hornpipes," in spite of the fact that Seneca, who had so great a share in teaching the Elizabethans their trade, "has not the slightest hint of comedy." [1] The neo-classic formalists, however, would have none of this mixture. For Rymer [2] a "merry Tragedy" was a "Monster," and he declared that "we want a law for Acting the *Rehearsal* once a week, to keep us in our senses, and secure us against the Noise and Nonsense, the Farce and Fustian which, in the name of Tragedy, have so long invaded, and usurp our Theater." D'Aubignac,[3] however, curiously enough, does not entirely condemn tragi-comedy. The liberals of the time, of course, did not condemn it either. Dryden [4] proudly claimed tragi-comedy as an English invention, and he defended it again and again,[5] although he too, at length, fell before the neo-classic onslaught.

The more philosophical elements of neo-classic tragic theory, just examined, were supplemented by the "mechanic rules" of the stage, the most important of which were

> The *Unites* [*sic*] of Action, Time, and Place,
> Which, if observed, give Plays so great a grace.[6]

1. J. W. Cunliffe, *The Influence of Seneca on Elizabethan Tragedy* (London and New York: 1893), p. 42 n.
2. *A Short View of Tragedy* (1693), pp. 157–158.
3. *The Whole Art of the Stage* (1657), IV, 139 ff.
4. *An Essay of Dramatic Poesy*, in *Essays*, ed. Ker, I, 70.
5. See, for example, the Dedication (1681) to *The Spanish Friar*, in *Essays*, ed. Ker, I, 249.
6. The Duke of Buckingham, *An Essay upon Poetry* (London: 1682), p. 12.

Saintsbury has called them "the Fatal Three, the Weird Sisters of dramatic criticism," but though in a derivative sense of the word they are weird, they are, or were, fated rather than fatal. To employ Aristotelian terminology, they were "final," not "primary," causes: they were the oak tree potentially present in the primal seed, which was imbedded in the soil of "reason," and influenced by that evil star, the theory of delusion. For the rules of the three unities, like almost all of the others, were designed to fool the audience into believing that it was "bodily present at the place and time of the supposed action."

The first of the three, the unity of action, was the only one backed by Aristotelian authority. Aristotle really did consider it a fundamental rule of art, and he was at considerable pains to make himself perfectly unmistakable about it. First of all, he says [1] that a poem cannot depend for its unity upon the fact that it is concerned with a single hero, "for infinitely various are the incidents in one man's life which cannot be reduced to unity." Nor, he says,[2] should the tragic poet "make an Epic structure into a Tragedy — by an Epic structure I mean one with a multiplicity of plots." In his definition of tragedy, as we have seen, he says that the action must be "complete," and his explanation of this word is his positive statement of the unity of action: [3]

A whole is that which has a beginning, a middle, and an end. A beginning is that which does not itself follow anything by causal necessity, but after which something naturally is or comes to be. An end, on the contrary, is that which itself naturally follows

1. *Poetics*, VIII, 1.
2. *Poetics*, XVIII, 4.
3. *Poetics*, VII, 2–3.

some other thing, either by necessity, or as a rule, but has nothing following it. A middle is that which follows something as some other thing follows it. A well constructed plot, therefore, must neither begin nor end at haphazard, but conform to these principles.

The action, in other words, should be an organism, the parts of which are vitally, and not simply mechanically or accidentally, related to one another.

The rule, thus stated, was adopted by the Renaissance, but sometimes with too little imagination, so that, in French classic drama especially, it was frequently interpreted as a prohibition against even relevant and harmonious episodes. But so interpreted the rule was too stringent for all but superlatively "regular" authors. Neander, that is, Dryden, in *An Essay of Dramatic Poesy*,[1] doubtless bearing Corneille particularly in mind, says, for example: "Eugenius has already shown us, from the confession of the French poets, that the Unity of Action is sufficiently preserved, if all the imperfect actions of the play are conducing to the main design." And in the *Heads*[2] Dryden restates his preference — which was that of the English generally — for the complex English over the simple Greek plot-structure. The tendency, indeed, to reduce the importance of the unity of action began as early as Castelvetro (1570),[3] who subordinated it to the unities of place and time.

These two latter unities, as has been said, were not Aristotelian. Aristotle,[4] of course, does state that "Tragedy endeavours, as far as possible, to confine itself to a

1. *Essays*, ed. Ker, I, 71. See also Ker, I, xxxix.
2. *Works*, ed. Scott and Saintsbury, XV, 387–388.
3. *Poetica d'Aristotele* (1576 ed.), p. 179.
4. *Poetics*, V, 4.

single revolution of the sun, or but slightly to exceed this limit." The statement, however, is merely one of historical fact, and is not meant as a universal law of the drama. It was Giraldi Cintio [1] who, sometime between 1540 and 1545, converted the statement of fact into a rule, the unity of time, which was reformulated by Castelvetro [2] in 1570 and by Jean de la Taille [3] in 1572.

Although the Renaissance had what looked like Aristotelian support for its unity of time, there is nothing in the *Poetics* that can possibly be interpreted as a statement of the unity of place. Nevertheless many believed that there was such a statement, and one at least, D'Aubignac,[4] explained away its absence by saying that this unity was "too well known" at the time of Aristotle to require mention. Castelvetro, however, it is now pretty well established, and not Aristotle or Scaliger, must be held responsible for adding this third member to the trinity.[5] Castelvetro it was, then, who at last got all three into shape [6] — in 1570. It is Boileau's [7] statement of them, however, that we remember:

> Qu'en un lieu, qu'en un jour, un seul fait accompli
> Tienne jusqu'à la fin le théâtre rempli.

We could easily forgive the Greeks had they formulated a rule requiring unity of time, because it would have been improbable in Greek tragedy for a chorus of old men or old women to have survived intact the passage of

1. *Discorso*, in *Scritti Estetici*, ed. Antimaco, in *Biblioteca Rara*, LIII, 10 f.
2. *Poetica* (1576 ed.), p. 534.
3. *Art de Tragédie*, in Robert, *Poétique de Racine*, p. 351.
4. *The Whole Art of the Stage* (1657), II, 98.
5. Compare Spingarn, *A History of Literary Criticism in the Renaissance* (2nd ed., 1908), pp. 97–98.
6. Compare H. B. Charlton, *Castelvetro's Theory of Poetry* (Manchester: 1913), p. 92.
7. *L'Art Poétique*, III, 45–46.

many years, or to have promptly reassembled at the
convenience of the dramatist. We cannot, however, so
easily forgive the Renaissance, for, the chorus having disappeared, the chief reason for the unity of time had vanished. Beginning with Giraldi Cintio, nevertheless, the
unity of time was staunchly defended — and on realistic
grounds. It was too improbable for belief, reasoned the
theorists, that a play requiring, let us say, three hours to
act should represent an action of three days, three months,
or three years. What happened, they asked, to the rest of
the time — to the difference in time, for example, between
three hours and three days? There was only one thing to
do, they thought, and that was to make the time of representation correspond exactly to the time of the action represented. Aristotle's phrase, "a single revolution of the
sun," was ambiguous, and everyone was free to interpret
it in his own way. D'Aubignac [1] wished to limit the time to
three hours, the actual time of representation. Scaliger,[2] at
least in the treatment of the story of Ceyx, was willing to
allow from six to eight hours. Castelvetro [3] said simply
that a play should not be so long as to interfere with "the
human necessity of eating, drinking, and sleeping," and
he [4] consequently set an extreme limit of twelve hours.
Dacier [5] is hesitant and indefinite. He believes that Aristotle did not mean a twenty-four-hour day, but rather a
"hemispherical day" of somewhat elastic limits. The time
of the action, he thinks, ought to correspond exactly with
the time of representation, but this means only that a four-

1. *The Whole Art of the Stage* (1657), II, 116–117.
2. *Poetices Libri Septem* (1561) (5th ed., 1617), III, 335. Compare also
D'Aubignac, II, 116.
3. *Poetica* (1576 ed.), p. 57.
4. P. 163.   5. *La Poétique* (1692), pp. 67–69.

hour action should not last ten hours, or a ten-hour action be squeezed into four, though it would be "better to sin on this side than on the other." Corneille [1] boldly allowed as many as thirty hours, and Dryden [2] concurred in this extension. But though there was considerable liberality of interpretation here, the fundamental absurdity of arguing for one limit rather than another seems to have struck only a few. Those alone who, like D'Aubignac, insisted upon an exact correspondence between representation and action had a leg to stand on, because a tenth of a second's discrepancy is logically as damaging as a discrepancy of ten years.

By simple induction from their own practise the Greeks might also have formulated legitimately a rule requiring unity of place, because their choruses would have rendered long leaps through space just as improbable as they rendered long flights through time. But here again the Renaissance, which had lost the chorus, had no valid reason for following the example of the Greeks. Castelvetro and his successors, however, were convinced that verisimilitude demanded unity of place. The stage, they argued, has a local habitation and a name, and the spectators sit before it, believing that they are bodily present at the place of the action represented upon it. The boards are not boards in a tangible theatre at Paris or London, but streets and the floors of dwellings in Athens or Rome. "The Stage," says D'Aubignac,[3]

is but a Representation of things; and yet we are not to imagine, that there is anything of what we really see, but we must think

1. *Des Trois Unités*, in *Oeuvres*, ed. Marty-Laveaux, I, 111–112.
2. Dedication (1697) to *The Aeneis*, in *Essays*, ed. Ker, II, 157.
3. *The Whole Art of the Stage* (1657), II, 99–100.

the things themselves are there of which the Images are before us. . . . This Truth, well understood, makes us to know that the place cannot change in the rest of the Play, since it cannot change in the Representation, for one and the same Image remaining in the same state, cannot represent two different things.

The spectators, moreover, are not at Paris or London, but at Athens or Rome. If, then, the action shifts from Athens, say, to Sparta, what becomes of the poor spectator? Must he "fly like a witch through the air?" Or imagine himself to be in two places at the same time? Common sense tells us that he cannot do either; so that if a play shifts its place of action, the spectator's illusion, or delusion, is destroyed. And, besides, observes the quick-witted Voltaire,[1] "no one action can go on in several places at once." "But surely," comments Butcher,[2] "a single action can go on in several places *successively*." Just as surely I can imagine my typewriter to be a machine-gun at one moment and a birthday cake at the next. And I can imagine myself in Chicago at midnight and in Heaven two seconds later.

Certainly the imagination of the Renaissance was in some respects strangely feeble. The modern imagination, however, is just as weak in its own way. We sympathize with D'Aubignac,[3] for example, when he writes:

As for the Extent which the Poet may allow to the Scene he chuses, when it is not in a House but open, I believe it may be as far as a man can see another Walk, and yet not know perfectly that 'tis he; for to take a larger space would be ridiculous, it being improbable that two people being each of them at one end of the Stage, without any Object between, should look at one another, and yet not see one another.

1. *Oeuvres Complètes de Voltaire* (Paris: 1784–1789), I, 68.
2. P. 297 n.
3. *The Whole Art of the Stage* (1657), II, 103.

This sort of limitation of space seems to us reasonable enough, but it got the seventeenth century into serious difficulties, because it was impossible to reconcile with the other sort of limitation, which forbade a shift in place. For the moderns, Corneille [1] observed, were limited by peculiar conventions. The conversation of their kings could be held only in the privacy of the royal apartments, as regal dignity required. Probability, indeed, imposed the necessity of having all private intercourse take place, as its nature demands, in private. In the days of the Hotel de Bourgogne the dramatist's task had been easy, for various places — Paris, Rome, Athens; or a street, a bed-chamber, a throne room — had been represented by various parts of the same stage. But when the neo-classic unity of place overthrew this convention, the playwrights were in a quandary. The French, in their attempt to extricate themselves from it, invented a *lieu théâtral*, that is to say, a space that was no place in particular, but might, Corneille asserted, represent several places so long as they were all in a single town, and so long as the action did not shift from one to another in the same act. For once the French imagination was livelier than that of Dryden,[2] who says that in the regular French play "the street, the window, the houses, and the closet, are made to walk about, and the persons to stand still." For the most part, however, the English, as well as the French, adhered in principle to the unity of place, which in practise was frequently violated.

A natural corollary of the unities was the rule requiring the *liaison des scènes*, which was almost always supported by the critics. Dryden, it is true, makes some fun of it in

1. *Des Trois Unités*, in *Oeuvres*, ed. Marty-Laveaux, I, 119.
2. *An Essay of Dramatic Poesy* (1668), in *Essays*, ed. Ker, I, 77.

An Essay of Dramatic Poesy, but even he was generally in favor of "scenes unbroken." In the same essay he makes the statement that in "the regular French play" the stage is "never empty all the while," but he exaggerates. D'Aubignac, in *La Pratique du Théâtre*,[1] notes that in practice the French classical dramatists made use of "four ways of uniting the Scenes together." Of these only the "Union of *Presence*," as the name indicates, required that an actor in one scene remain as a link between that scene and the following. A scene, according to D'Aubignac's observation, was considered sufficiently united with the preceding if it was opened by an actor who came "seeking" another who had just gone off, who had been attracted by a "noise" at the end of the preceding scene, or who came on "in such a nick of time, that he could not reasonably be suppos'd to do it sooner or later" — whatever that may mean. The passage makes it clear that only continuous action was absolutely necessary. The object was to preserve the illusion of unity. As Corneille [2] puts it, the *liaison des scènes* was "an ornament and not a rule."

The Renaissance thought that it had good reason for adopting the unities. Not all of the theorists, as we have seen, believed them to be of Aristotelian origin. But some did — even as late as Frederick the Great.[3] He objects to the plays of Shakespeare, he says, "because they offend against all the rules of the theatre; rules not in themselves arbitrary; rules that you will find in the Poetics of Aristotle, in which the unities of time, place, and action, are prescribed, as the only means of rendering tragedies affect-

---

1. That is, *The Whole Art of the Stage* (1657), III, 88–90.
2. *Des Trois Unités*, in *Oeuvres*, ed. Marty-Laveaux, I, 101.
3. *On German Literature*, in *Posthumous Works of Frederic II, King of Prussia* London: 1789), XIII, 431.

ing." Others, who had a more accurate knowledge of Aristotle, were in favor of the unities because, in their opinion, they were "the soul of *Poesie*"; for, says Rapin,[1] "unless there be the *unity* of *place*, of *time*, and of the *action* in the great Poems, there can be no *verisimility*." They added, thought Dennis,[2] "grace and clearness and comeliness to the representation."

The unities, however, in common with the other rules, had their enemies. In France, even before Chapelain had had time to reformulate them, they had been assailed by such men as Pierre de Laudun (1598)[3] and François Ogier (1628);[4] and Englishmen generally regarded them with something less than religious reverence, though, to be sure, important figures like Jonson, Milton, and Dryden occasionally came to their assistance with both precept and example. It is of especial significance, so far as the English attitude is concerned, that Rymer—according to Mr. G. B. Dutton,[5] who has made the most thorough study of this usually "regular" critic — "although [he] does not flout the unities . . . seems to regard them as of minor importance." And in 1698 a particularly violent but uncritical assault was made upon the unities by an anonymous writer,[6] who looked upon them as essentially foreign to the spirit of English drama: "The strict Observation of these *Corneillean* Rules," he says, "are [*sic*] as Dissonant to the

1. *Reflections* (1674), p. 17.
2. Quoted by Ker, *Essays of John Dryden*, I, li.
3. *L'Art Poétique François*, ed. Joseph Dedieu (Paris: 1909), pp. 165–167.
4. "Préface au Lecteur," prefixed to Jean de Schélandre's *Tyr et Sidon*, in *European Theories of the Drama*, ed. Clark, pp. 118–123.
5. "The French Aristotelian Formalists and Thomas Rymer," *P. M. L. A.*, XXIX (1914), 160. But see Rymer, *The Tragedies of the Last Age* (1678), p. 24.
6. *A Defence of Dramatic Poetry* (London: 1698), II, 28. This essay has been attributed to Edward Filmer.

English Constitution of the Stage, as the *French* Slavery to our *English* Liberty." They had taken so deep a root, however, that they could not easily be blighted: they lived vigorously on into the eighteenth century.

So far as the really live issues of neo-classic tragic theory are concerned, this account might well end here, but a few minor considerations deserve a word or two. The first of these is the chorus. In early Greek tragedy, as we know, the chorus was all-important, and it retained a prominent position down to the time of Sophocles. Aristotle,[1] who was old-fashioned in this respect, believed that "the Chorus . . . should be regarded as one of the actors; it should be an integral part of the whole, and share in the action." Three hundred years later Horace[2] said the same thing. And more than sixteen hundred years after Horace there were men — Dacier[3] and Rymer,[4] for instance — who still considered the chorus a useful ornament of tragedy. But even as early as Aeschylus, who, Aristotle says,[5] "diminished the importance of the Chorus," it had begun to fade into the background. The choral songs were still relevant in Sophocles, but in Euripides they ceased to be so, and, beginning with Agathon, they were "sung as mere interludes."[6] After Horace, in the words of Mr. Lucas,[7] "it is only the bare dishevelled ghost of the chorus that wails between the acts of the tragedies of Seneca." And in the seventeenth century D'Aubignac[8] is able to record the fact "that now adays *Tragedy* has quite lost its

1. *Poetics*, XVIII, 7. 2. *Ars Poetica*, ll. 193–195.
3. *La Poétique* (1692), p. 330.
4. *A Short View of Tragedy* (1693), p. 1.
5. *Poetics*, IV, 13. 6. *Poetics*, XVIII, 7.
7. *Tragedy*, p. 68.
8. *The Whole Art of the Stage* (1657), IV, 118.

Choruses." Dacier and Rymer, then, were supporting a cause that had been lost for centuries.

In Greek tragedy the choric odes had served to divide the action into parts, which were not sufficiently distinct, however, to be regarded as acts in the modern sense. The only remark that Aristotle [1] makes about the length of a play is that it should be long enough to "admit of a change from bad fortune to good, or from good fortune to bad." It was Horace [2] who laid down the five-act rule:

> To five acts lengthened be the piece, not more,
> That asks the long applause and loud encore,

and it was Seneca who gave it vogue in later European tragedy. The division, it appears, had no structural significance. D'Aubignac [3] does not know "whether it be that that is a Proportion that just hits the Weakness of the Audience, or that by Custom we are made Friends to it." He is only "certain, that we do not naturally like a Play that has more or less than Five Acts, which divide the Time of so many Hours as we can well spare to a Diversion, without making it a Toil." But in spite of the fact that the division was perfectly arbitrary it became a fixed convention, in neo-classic drama especially, but also, to a large extent, in the romantic drama of Elizabethan England.

Another convention — which seems not to have found much favor, however — was that of the fourth speaker. For some reason, which is not very clear today, the Greeks suddenly stopped when they had added the third speaking actor, but it was Horace [4] again who formulated the rule:

1. *Poetics*, VII, 7.
2. *Ars Poetica*, ll. 189–190, Francis Howes' translation.
3. *The Whole Art of the Stage* (1657), III, 67.
4. *Ars Poetica*, l. 192.

> Nor in distracting dialogue engage
> At once four speakers on the crowded stage.

This rule, it seems, was too Spartan for most neo-classicists, though there may have been others besides Dr. Edward Filmer [1] who prided themselves, in the face of failure in the theatre, upon their observance of it. Considering the almost complete silence on the subject, most theorists of the seventeenth century at least seem to have been of D'Aubignac's [2] opinion, "that the Poet may bring on as many as he pleases, provided neither their number, nor their discourses do confound the Spectators Attention."

The only other thing that requires mention is the matter of style. Aristotle [3] says that tragedy should be written "in language embellished with each kind of artistic ornament," and, Professor Butcher points out,[4] he is sufficiently clear about what he means not to have been misunderstood by his many followers. Everyone, even in the mistaking Renaissance, was able to distinguish between "verse of tragic texture" and "the sock's light chit-chat and colloquial strains."[5] Verse, in spite of an exception made by Horace,[6] was considered essential to tragedy during the Renaissance, and the language of which it was composed, according to Rapin's [7] typical prescriptions, had to be *"apt," "clear," "natural," "lofty* and *splendid,"* and *"numerous."*

1. See Nicoll, *Restoration Drama*, p. 132.
2. *The Whole Art of the Stage* (1657), III, 4.
3. *Poetics*, VI, 2.   4. Pp. 242–243.
5. Horace, *Ars Poetica*, ll. 89–91.
6. *Ars Poetica*, ll. 95–98:
> "Et tragicus plerumque dolet sermone pedestri
> Telephus et Peleus, cum pauper et exsul uterque
> Proicit ampullas et sesquipedalia verba,
> Si curat cor spectantis tetigisse querela."
7. *Reflections* (1674), pp. 41–44.

In England, between 1664 and 1677 especially — the "heroic" period — the question of style was somewhat complicated by the use of rime in tragedy. Rime had been in use in France since the beginning of the classic period. In England it had been employed occasionally by the Elizabethan and Jacobean writers of tragedy, and Dryden is right when he says in his dedication of *The Rival Ladies* (1664) [1] that the use of heroic couplets in tragedy is "not so much a new way amongst us, as an old way new revived." Under the influence of the French dramatists, of Waller and Denham in English non-dramatic verse, and of D'Avenant and Orrery in English drama, the couplet became first fashionable and then obligatory in tragedy. But the popularity of rime quickly passed. Even Dryden, who at one time was its enthusiastic champion, finally "grew tired" of his "long lov'd Mistress." According to Professor Nicoll,[2] about forty-seven rimed tragedies appeared in England between 1660 and 1700, and about six after the turn of the century. That rime was not considered a necessity by the English formalists Rymer [3] makes perfectly clear. "Our Ear," he writes, "shou'd not be hankering after the Ryme, when the business should wholly take us up, and fill our Head. The words must be all free, independant, and disengag'd, no entanglement of Ryme to be in our way. We must clear the Decks, and down with the Ornaments and Trappings in the day of Ac-

---

1. *Essays*, ed. Ker, I, 5.
2. *Restoration Drama*, p. 90.
3. *A Short View of Tragedy* (1693), p. 63. Compare Lord Roscommon's couplet in *An Essay on Translated Verse* (London: 1684), p. 23:

> "Of many faults, *Rhyme* is (perhaps) the *Cause*,
> Too *strict* to *Rhyme* We slight more *useful* Laws."

Roscommon's remark, however, is on rimed verse in general.

tion, and Engagement." To all intents and purposes rime as a tragic medium died with the seventeenth century, and blank verse and prose took its place.

From this review of neo-classic tragic theory three conclusions are obvious. The first is that the theory was not purely Aristotelian. Aristotle does, indeed, outline the doctrine of decorum, but his outline is primarily rhetorical, and was therefore improperly applied to esthetic matters by the Renaissance. He also formulates the unity of action, which was taken over fairly intact by the neo-classicists, though it was considerably narrowed in the process. The second conclusion is that there was wide disagreement among the theorists themselves. They fell roughly into two groups, the Aristotelian formalists and the liberals; but it must be kept in mind that there was as much war within each of these two camps as there was between the camps. The third conclusion, a corollary of the second, is that the phrase "neo-classic theory of tragedy" is in the highest degree ambiguous, since there was no one theory to which all theorists alike tendered their allegiance. When, therefore, in summing up this chapter I speak of "the neo-classic theory of tragedy," it must be understood that I am merely using a convenient label. It must be further understood that I am deliberately neglecting the exceptions and objections that were made to almost every clause of the theory; and that nearly everything I attribute to the "neo-classicists" would have brought a blush of mingled indignation and shame to some neo-classic cheek.

The two fundamental philosophical tenets of neo-classic tragic theory are the following. First, tragedy, in common with the other imitative arts, is a rational imitation of nature; that is to say, it is a representation of that part of crude nature that "participates" in the principle of order, rule, and harmony — namely, reason; and since it is thus eclectic it must be, not a representation of truth, but of things like truth; for true things are likely to be improbable and therefore incredible. Secondly, the function of tragedy is, not merely the esthetic purging of the emotions of pity and fear, but rather "delightful teaching," or the judicious combining of instruction with pleasure.

It logically follows, then, as a third tenet that in tragedy the good should be rewarded and the bad punished, because to observe the working of poetic justice is both instructive and pleasurable. Besides instructing and delighting us, however, tragedy should also move us to admiration of the hero, for unless we admire him the efforts of the poet are wasted; not mere terror at the misfortunes of the hero is to be moved, but terror mingled with admiration. Nor is pity, one of the "black ideas" of the Greeks, to be moved by the ancient means. The poet is not to make us "pity others where in like circumstances we should fear for ourselves." On the contrary, he is to introduce the "soft" and "frequent passion" of love, which, owing to near kinship, easily arouses the emotion of pity, or rather "love-pity." The poet is justified in doing so, for love is heroic and admirable. The heroic, the admirable, and the good, moreover, are the exclusive qualities of persons of high rank, so that the characters of tragedy, and especially the tragic hero, must be drawn from the upper reaches of society; and their manners, as a consequence, must be those of the court. The manners of the personages must conform also, not only to the usages of their class, but to the types that they represent: a king should behave like a king, a soldier like a soldier, a lady like a lady, and so for the rest. It is also inconsistent with the nature of tragedy that murders should be enacted upon the stage. In the first place, violence is undignified, especially when it is performed upon a raised platform, and is therefore out of keeping with the dignity of the characters. In the second place, it is likely to transgress the laws of etiquette, as when, for example, a king kills a subject, or the reverse. In the third place, if the hero commits murder before the eyes of the spectators, he becomes less admirable and consequently less effective as a tragic figure. Because it jars upon the tragic mood, the comic scene, of course, should also be excluded from tragedy.

The principal "mechanic rules" of the stage consist of the three unities and the *liaison des scènes*. The unity of action requires that not more than one thread of plot should be admitted into a play, that all episodes not strictly necessary to the design should be rigorously excluded; the unity of time, that the time of the action should correspond exactly to the time of the representation; and the unity of place, that the place of the action should not change during the course of the play. The unity of action is necessitated by the fact that a work of art should be a whole; the unity of time, by the fact that credibility demands that every moment of the time during which the action takes place should be accounted for; and the unity of place, by the fact that the spectator cannot imagine himself to be in two different places at the same time, or, indeed, at successive times. The *liaison des scènes*, stated in its most general form, is simply the requirement that each scene be naturally and inevitably linked with its successor; otherwise the impression of unity will be destroyed.

This, then, was the general state of tragic theory[1] in the year 1699. The following chapters trace the disintegration of the theory in eighteenth-century England.

1. For a study of the influence that the theory had upon the Restoration writers of tragedy see G. B. Dutton, "Theory and Practice in English Tragedy, 1650–1700," *Englische Studien*, XLIX (1916), 190–219. Concerning the tragedy of the last twenty-five years of the century, it may here be briefly noted, Mr. Dutton writes as follows (pp. 215–216): "In regard to the spirit of the serious drama neo-classical principles won ground in this period. And in regard to form, neo-classicism may be regarded as having won the day, though not in full possession of the field. Breaches of the neo-classical rules there were, here and there, but the rules in general prevailed."

PART II

THE NEO–CLASSIC THEORY
OF TRAGEDY

CHAPTER I

An Age of Criticism

THE eighteenth century thought of itself as an age of criticism, but not everyone was pleased at the thought. Many writers considered critics and criticism the destroyers of genius and poetry, — especially ignorant critics and stupid criticism, of which, it was thought, the country had more than enough. "Among the many Disadvantages attending Poetry," writes Farquhar (1702),[1] "none seems to bear a greater Weight, than that so many set up for Judges, when so very few understand a tittle of the matter." "*Poetry* alone, and chiefly the *Dramma*, lies open to the Insults of all Pretenders."[2] These pretenders, or "half-learn'd witlings," as Pope (1711)[3] calls them, were so numerous that

> To tell 'em, would a hundred tongues require,
> Or one vain wit's, that might a hundred tire.

Their number had not diminished by the middle of the century. "By a Record in the Censors Office," reports Fielding[4] on January 11, 1752, "and now in my Custody, it appears, that at a censorial Inquisition, taken *Tricesimo qto. Eliz.* by one of my illustrious Predecessors, no more

1. *A Discourse upon Comedy, in Reference to the English Stage*, in *Critical Essays of the Eighteenth Century, 1700–1725*, ed. W. H. Durham (New Haven, London, and Oxford: 1915), p. 257. Hereafter this collection of essays will be referred to as Durham.
2. Durham, p. 258.
3. *An Essay on Criticism*, ed. Ward, ll. 44–45.
4. *The Covent-Garden Journal*, ed. G. E. Jensen (New Haven, London, and Oxford: 1915), No. 3.

than 19 Critics were enrolled in the Cities of London and Westminster; whereas at the last Inquisition taken by myself, 25°. *Geo*. 2*di*. the Number of Persons claiming a Right to that Order, appears to amount to 276302." Pessimistically impressed by this figure, he is led, three days later, to include the following definition in his "Modern Glossary": "CRITIC. Like *Homo*, a Name common to all human [*sic*] Race." [1]

Fielding

In 1753 one public-spirited journalist [2] warns his public that criticism is a disease that "has infected all ranks and orders of men. . . . The persons most liable to the contagion . . . are young masters of arts, students in the temple, attorneys clerks, haberdashers prentices, and fine gentlemen." Four years later another journalist,[3] who finds critics swarming "in every coffee-house," adds to the list of those subject to infection "idle physicians, damned poets, broken tradesmen, [and] discarded footmen." And in 1761 Goldsmith [4] adds "the puny beau" to the unfortunate band. "At present," complains George Colman (1775),[5] with whose word it is just as well to end, "the press swarms with Criticks. A louse, say the naturalists, is a very lousy animal; and there is not a lousy author in town, especially a Dramatick Author, that has not fifty lousy Criticks on his back."

In *The Guardian* [6] for March 25, 1713, Steele attempted to account for the epidemic, or pest:

1. No. 4.
2. *The World*, ed. "Adam Fitz-Adam," No. 32 (August 9, 1753).
3. *The Literary Magazine: or, Universal Review*, II (1757), 426.
4. *Upon Taste*, in *The Works of Oliver Goldsmith*, ed. J. W. M. Gibbs (London: 1884–1886), I, 324.
5. *The Gentleman*, No. 6, in *Prose on Several Occasions* (London: 1787), I, 206.
6. No. 12.

When a Poem makes its first Appearance in the World, I have always observed, that it gives Employment to a greater number of Criticks, than any other kind of Writing. Whether it be that most Men, at some time of their Lives, have try'd their Talent that way, and thereby think they have a right to judge; or whether they imagine, that their making shrewd Observations upon the Polite Arts, gives them a pretty figure; or whether there may not be some Jealousie and Caution in bestowing Applause upon those who write chiefly for Fame. Whatever the Reasons be, we find few discouraged by the Delicacy and Danger of such an Undertaking.

Fielding (1749),[1] however, writes as one having authority:

The critic, rightly considered, is no more than the clerk, whose office it is to transcribe the rules and laws laid down by those great judges whose vast strength of genius hath placed them in the light of legislators, in the several sciences over which they presided. This office was all which the critics of old aspired to; nor did they ever dare to advance a sentence, without supporting it by the authority of the judge from whence it was borrowed.

But in process of time, and in ages of ignorance, the clerk began to invade the power and assume the dignity of his master. The laws of writing were no longer founded on the practice of the author, but on the dictates of the critic. The clerk became the legislator, and those very peremptorily gave laws whose business it was, at first, only to transcribe them.

The training that the contemporary critic received is described by James Ralph (1731):[2]

These Gentlemen, at the Expence of much Labour and Birch, are whipp'd at School into bad Translations, false *Latin* and dull

1. *The History of Tom Jones, a Foundling* (Everyman's Library, London, Toronto, and New York: 1925), V, i.
2. *The Taste of the Town: or, a guide to all publick diversions* (London: 1731), p. 161. Compare Addison, *The Tatler*, ed. G. A. Aitken (London: 1898–1899), No. 165 (April 29, 1710), and *The Spectator*, No. 592 (September 10, 1714).

Themes; from thence they run the Gantlope through all the pedantick Forms of an University-Education: There they grow familiar with the Title-Pages of antient and modern Authors, and will talk of *Aristotle*, *Longinus*, *Horace*, *Scaliger*, *Rapin*, *Bossu*, *Dacier*, as freely, as if bosom Acquaintance: Their Mouths are fill'd with the Fable, the Moral, Catastrophe, Unity, Probability, Poetick, Justice [*sic*], true Sublime, Bombast, Simplicity, Magnificence, and all the critical Jargon, which is learn'd in a quarter of an Hour, and serves to talk of one's whole Life after.

Ralph [1] was not alone in thinking that "the profess'd Criticks of this Age have brought upon us, from Time to Time, those Showers of bad PLAYS, which have almost wash'd the Shadow of *Dramatick Poetry* from off the Earth." Francis Gentleman [2] asserts, in 1770, that for "twenty years," owing to "the enervating false delicacy of criticism," English tragedies have been only "elaborate escapes from genius." Wilkie,[3] dreaming that he is talking with Homer, who accuses him of having in his poems "few circumstances mix'd of various grain," replies:

> "Certes," quoth I, "the critics are the cause
> Of this, and many other mischiefs more. . . .
> Each bard now fears the rod, and trembles while he sings."

Sterne's exclamation (1761) [4] expresses the feeling of at least half of the literary men of the century: "Of all the cants which are canted in this canting world — though the cant of hypocrites may be the worst — the cant of criticism is the most tormenting."

1. P. 165.
2. *The Dramatic Censor; or, Critical Companion* (London: 1770), I, 216.
3. *A Dream, in the Manner of Spenser*, added to the second edition of *The Epigoniad* (London: 1759), p. 222.
4. *The Life & Opinions of Tristram Shandy, Gentleman*, ed. George Saintsbury (Everyman's Library, London, Toronto, New York: 1922), III, xii.

Most men who felt in this way were inclined to blame contemporary critics and criticism for the poor quality of contemporary poetry, rather than to look upon all three as different results of the same cause. More judicial than his fellows, Joseph Warton (1756) [1] asks tentatively "whether, that philosophical, that geometrical, and sys- tematical spirit so much in vogue, which has spread itself from the sciences even into polite literature, by consulting only REASON, has not diminished and destroyed SENTI- MENT; and made our poets write from and to the HEAD rather than the HEART." He is satisfied with stating the "remarkable fact" that in periods "after criticism has been much studied" creative literature has never reached a high level of achievement. [2]

But though attacks upon criticism were perennial, they were not universal: some there were to defend it. Early in the century Shaftesbury (1711) was its champion: [3]

In every science, every art, the real masters or proficients rejoice in nothing more than in the thorough search and examina- tion of their performances, by all the rules of art and nicest criti- cism. Why therefore (in the Muses 'name!) is it not the same with our pretenders to the writing art, our poets, and prose authors in every kind? Why in this profession are we found such critic- haters, and indulged in this unlearned aversion, unless it be taken for granted that as wit and learning stand at present in our nation, we are still upon the foot of empirics and mountebanks?

From these considerations I take upon me absolutely to condemn the fashionable and prevailing custom of inveighing against critics as the common enemies, the pests and incendiaries of the commonwealth of Wit and Letters. I assert, on the con-

1. *An Essay on the Writings and Genius of Pope* (London: 1756), I, 204.
2. I, 203.
3. *Characteristics of Men, Manners, Opinions, Times, etc.*, ed. J. M. Robertson (London: 1900), I, 153; and see II, 257.

shaftesbury 1711

trary, that they are the props and pillars of this building; and that without the encouragement and propagation of such a race, we should remain as Gothic architects as ever.

In 1724 Leonard Welsted [1] declared that "true Criticism is the truest Friend of Poetry." In *The Critical Review* [2] for 1789 a writer defended the "infant science" of criticism by pointing out the absurdity of "decrying" it "because it has not the strength and the perfection of maturity." These are only three representative samples of what can be found scattered up and down the literature of the century, for, after all, the eighteenth century was an age of criticism, and it would be strange indeed if criticism had had no defenders.

As in the seventeenth century, Aristotle and the *Poetics* were a storm-center. Aristotle-haters were continually mistaking their wish for its fulfilment, — Farquhar,[3] for example: "The vast Tomes of *Aristotle* and his Commentatore are all taken to pieces, and their Infallibility is lost with all Persons of a free and unprejudic'd Reason." Fielding's definition [4] of "nonsense," in "A Modern Glossary," sums up a large body of eighteenth-century opinion, though, we may be sure, it does not sum up Fielding's own opinion: "NONSENSE. Philosophy, especially the Philosophical Writings of the Antients, and more especially of Aristotle." A writer for *The World* [5] says in the middle of the century, by way of compliment to his own age, that "the distinguishing characteristic of the last

---

1. *A Dissertation Concerning the Perfection of the English Language, The State of Poetry, &c.*, in Durham, p. 376.
2. LXVIII, 464.
3. *A Discourse upon Comedy* (1702), in Durham, p. 264; see also pp. 271–272.
4. *The Covent-Garden Journal*, ed. Jensen, No. 4 (January 14, 1752).
5. No. 93 (October 10, 1754).

age" — he probably means the age of Anne — "was
PEDANTRY"; and by "pedantry" he means talking about
Plato and Aristotle. Such folly in the dark age of Queen
Anne was understandable, even forgivable — but not in
the enlightenment of the second George. "After learning
has been not only revived but improved," says another
writer,[1] in 1752, who is not specifically slandering the age of
Queen Anne, "after genius has again formed the taste, and
criticism regulated the judgment, the same fondness for
antiquity is ridiculous; nor is it more absurd to prefer the
philosophy of *Aristotle* to that of *Newton*, than to prefer his
rudiments to the more perfect plan of the modern drama."
Aristotle had nothing to teach, so that the young poet,
according to William Hayley [2] in 1782, was

> To deem infallible no Critic's word;
> Not e'en the dictates of thy Attic HURD:
> No! not the Stagyrite's unquestion'd page,
> The Sire of Critics, sanctified by age!

Just as with critics and criticism in general, however,
Aristotle and the *Poetics* were not friendless, and it is significant that their friends were, upon the whole, the most
competent men of the century. Charles Gildon (1718),[3]
whose competency, to be sure, there may be some reason
to doubt, calls Aristotle "the Father and best of *Criticks*,"
who, he says in another place,[4] "gives not his *Rules* as
Legislators do their *Laws*, without any other *Reason* than

1. *The Gentleman's Magazine*, XXII, 224. Compare Dr. John Brown, *A Dissertation on the Rise, Union, and Power . . . of Poetry and Music* (London: 1763),
p. 110.
2. *An Essay on Epic Poetry; in Five Epistles to the Revd. Mr. Mason* (London:
1782), I, 301–304.
3. *The Complete Art of Poetry*, etc. (London: 1718), I, 84.
4. I, 134.

his Will; all that he advances is confirm'd by Reasons drawn from the common Sentiments of Mankind, so that Men themselves become the *Rule* and Measure of what he lays down." Joseph Warton (1756) [1] calls him "the first and best of critics," and says of the *Poetics* that "to attempt to understand poetry without having diligently digested this treatise, would be as absurd and impossible, as to pretend to a skill in geometry, without having studied Euclid." [2] Samuel Johnson (1751) [3] speaks of the "Laws of *Aristotelian* Criticism" as "indispensable."

Later in the century the encomiums are less unmeasured, but they carry more weight, since they are based on a more accurate scholarship. The coolness of the following passage from Thomas Twining (1789) [4] does not render it the less impressive:

What *would* have been the present state of poetical criticism, had Aristotle never written, it is impossible to say: two facts, however, are certain; that he was the first who carried philosophical investigation into these regions of imagination and fiction, and that the ablest of his successors have not disdained to pursue the path which he had opened to them, and even, in many instances, to tread in his very footsteps. It may therefore, *possibly*, be true, that modern critics are, in some measure, indebted to Aristotle himself for their very pretensions to despise him. At least, the more we admire the skill of those, who have raised and finished the structure, the more reason we have to respect the Architect, who not only gave the plan, but, with it, many specimens of masterly execution.

1. *An Essay on the Writings and Genius of Pope*, I, 168.
2. I, 170. Compare *The Works of Alexander Pope, Esq.*, ed. J. Warton (London: 1797), I, 252–253, where it is clear that forty-one years later Warton had not changed his mind.
3. *The Rambler*, No. 139 (July 16, 1751).
4. *Aristotle's Treatise on Poetry*, pp. xvi–xvii. Compare *The Critical Review*, LXVIII (1789), 358–359, which heartily seconds Twining.

Henry James Pye (1792),[1] another commentator at the end of the century, though he concedes that "the age of blind veneration is now over, and Aristotle, like other writers, can only be estimated by his merit," states with the assurance that a close study of his subject has given him "that Aristotle is not so great a blockhead as some take him to be who have never read him."

On the whole, the impression that one gets of the century is that it loved rather than hated criticism. Even those whose outcries are the loudest seem to be enjoying the exercise. The criticism of criticism, after all, is a kind of criticism.

1. *A Commentary illustrating the Poetic of Aristotle*, etc. (London: 1792), p. xiii. See *The Monthly Review*, XVII (1795), 323, where, in a review of Thomas Tyrwhitt's *Aristotelis de Poetica Liber Graece et Latine* (London: 1794), the reviewer gives it as his opinion that the more the precepts of the *Poetics* "are illustrated, the more will they contribute to a general accuracy of thinking, and to the advancement of philosophical criticism."

CHAPTER II

Rules in General — The Defense

> First follow Nature, and your judgment frame
> By her just standard, which is still the same:
> Unerring NATURE, still divinely bright,
> One clear, unchang'd, and universal light,
> Life, force, and beauty, must to all impart,
> At once the source, and end, and test of Art.
>
> .   .   .   .
>
> Learn hence for ancient rules a just esteem;
> To copy nature is to copy them.

THESE lines embody Pope's (1711) [1] advice to his generation. It looked simple and clear, but was not — at least, Dennis (1711) [2] thought so. Nature may be "unerring," but what is Nature?

Now here wou'd I fain ask one or two Questions? Is he giving Rules here for Judging or for Writing? And is he prescribing those Rules to the Knowing or the Ignorant? If he says to the Knowing, what is it that he tells them here? That they must judge according to Nature, or write according to Nature. Now does he tell them any thing in this that they did not know before? Well, but he says, he is laying down these Rules for the Ignorant; why then I humbly conceive that he ought to have told them what he means by Nature, and what it is to write or to judge according to Nature. For by expressing himself at the rate that he does, he neither says any thing to the Learned which they did not know before, nor any thing to the Ignorant which they can possibly understand.

1. *An Essay on Criticism*, ed. Ward, ll. 68–73, 139–140.
2. *Reflections Critical and Satyrical, Upon a Late Rhapsody, Call'd, An Essay Upon Criticism*, in Durham, p. 226.

Dennis [1] himself, however, was not above equivocation in his use of the word. In defending Shakespeare against the charge of learning, he asks:

For whether is it more honourable for this Island to have pro-duc'd a Man who, without having any Acquaintance with the Ancients, or any but a slender and a superficial one, appears to be their Equal or their Superiour by the Force of Genius and Nature, or to have bred one who, knowing the Ancients, falls infinitely short of them in Art, and consequently in Nature it self?

The "Nature" that he equates with "Genius" surely can-not be the same "Nature" that he equates with "Art." And neither one seems very closely related to the "Nature" mentioned, but not defined, in the following sentence of Dr. Johnson's (September 7, 1751): [2] "No Fame can spread wide or endure long that is not rooted in Nature, and ma-nured by Art."   Bishop Hurd (1762), [3] who observes that "the source of bad criticism, as universally of bad phi-losophy, is the abuse of terms," and who objects to the restriction of the meaning of the word "nature" to "the known and experienced course of affairs in this world," introduces further confusion by extending its meaning so as to include "human nature," and by insisting that the poet's "supernatural world" is "yet not *unnatural* in one sense." Nature meant whatever you wanted it to mean. "*Nature, Nature* is the great Cry against the Rules," complains Gildon (1709). [4] It was also the great cry for the rules, as

1. *On the Genius and Writings of Shakespear* (1711), in *Eighteenth Century Essays on Shakespeare*, ed. D. N. Smith (Glasgow: 1903), pp. 41-42. Hereafter this collection of essays will be referred to as Smith.

2. *The Rambler*, No. 154.

3. *Letters on Chivalry and Romance*, ed. Edith J. Morley (London: 1911), pp. 138-139.

4. *An Essay on the Art, Rise, and Progress of the Stage in Greece, Rome, and England*, in *The Works of Mr. William Shakespear*, ed. Nicholas Rowe (2nd ed., London: 1714), IX, vi.

Pope's lines prove. It could be what makes art art, or that raw material, "unimproved by human art," [1] which art must improve.

It is safe to say, nevertheless, that the neo-classicist, in his most characteristic moments, equated "nature" with "order" and "reason." [2] But when he used "nature" in this sense, of course, he was not thinking of the nature that was "methodiz'd" in the rules; he was thinking rather of the nature that did the methodizing, in spite of the fact that in the later echoes of Pope's phrase nature is always the patient, never the agent.[3] George Colman (1778),[4] the elder, explicitly equates "Nature and right reason." Shaftesbury (1711) [5] does so implicitly when he says that "a painter, if he has any genius, understands the truth and unity of design; and knows he is even then unnatural when he follows Nature too close, and strictly copies Life." Nature, as reason or order, was a touchstone by means of which the excellence of a new work of art could be esti-

1. William Richardson, *On the Faults of Shakespeare*, in *Essays on Shake-speare's Dramatic Characters* (London: 1784), p. 139.

2. See, for example, Dennis, *The Advancement and Reformation of Modern Poetry* (1701), sigs. A8^v–a1.

3. Compare Gildon, *The Complete Art of Poetry* (1718), I, 94: "*Art* entirely includes *Nature*, that being no more, than *Nature reduc'd to Form*"; Edward Taylor, *Cursory Remarks on Tragedy* (London: 1774), p. 28: "Nor are we to suppose that rules are an unnecessary prescription, or that they reduce nature into method more than is convenient or fit"; the Rev. Henry Boyd, "An Essay on French Tragedy," *Anthologia Hibernica*, I (1793), 286: "Those who are most sanguine on the side of untutored genius, and most averse to the tyranny of poetic laws, ought at least, before they pronounce, to consider that art is only nature methodized."

4. *Preface to the Works of Beaumont and Fletcher*, in *Prose on Several Occasions*, II, 152.

5. *Characteristics*, ed. Robertson, I, 94. Compare Goldsmith, *Upon Taste* (1765), in *Works*, ed. Gibbs, I, 338: "It is the business of art to imitate nature, but not with a servile pencil; and to choose those attitudes and dispositions only, which are beautiful and engaging."

mated. "The same comparison of the imitation with nature which enables us to determine that some performances excel others, will enable us to determine the absolute merit of any new performance, without referring it to what has been before approved, or considering whether it is better or worse," says *The Monthly Review* [1] in 1769. This is what Pope means when he says that nature is the "test of Art."

Nature as a rule, or standard, is consequently of general, or universal, not merely of particular, validity; and so likewise is the instance of this universal standard that one finds in a particular work of art. "The Poet," writes Gildon (1709),[2] "is not oblig'd to relate things just as they happen, but as they might, or ought to have happen'd: that is, the Action ought to be general and allegorical, not particular; for particular Actions can have no general Influence." Nature, in this aspect, is identical with truth, as Bishop Hurd (1749) [3] rigorously demonstrates:

Truth, in poetry, means such an expression, as conforms to the general nature of things; *falshood* [*sic*], that, which, however suitable to the particular instance in view, doth yet not correspond to such *general nature*. To attain to this *truth* of expression in dramatic poetry two things are prescribed: 1. A diligent study of the Socratic philosophy; and 2. A masterly knowledge and comprehension of human life. The *first*, because it is the peculiar distinction of this school *ad veritatem vitae propius accedere*. [Cic. de Or. i. 51.] And the *latter*, as rendering the imitation more universally striking. This will be understood by reflecting that *truth* may be followed too closely in works of imitation, as is evident in two respects. For, 1. the artist, when he would give a Copy of

1. XLI, 133.
2. *An Essay on the Art*, etc., in Rowe's Shakespeare (2nd ed., 1714), IX, xxxii. Compare Gildon, *The Complete Art of Poetry* (1718), I, 136.
3. Note on l. 317 of Horace's *Art of Poetry*, ed. Hurd, in *The Works of Richard Hurd, D.D., Lord Bishop of Worcester* (London: 1811), I, 255–257.

nature, may confine himself too scrupulously to the exhibition of *particulars*, and so fail of representing the general idea of the *kind*. Or, 2. in applying himself to give the *general* idea, he may collect it from an enlarged view of *real* life, whereas it were still better taken from the nobler conception of it as subsisting only in the *mind*. . . .

We see then that in deviating from particular and partial, the poet more faithfully imitates *universal*, truth. And thus an answer occurs to that refined argument, which Plato invented and urged, with much seeming complacency, against poetry. It is, that *poetical imitation is at a great distance from truth.* "Poetical expression, says the Philosopher, is the copy of the poet's own conceptions; the poet's conception, of things, and things, of the standing archetype, as existing in the divine mind. Thus the poet's expression, is a copy at third hand, from the primary, original truth." [Plat. De rep. l. x.] Now the diligent study of this rule of the poet obviates this reasoning at once. For, by abstracting from existences all that peculiarly respects and discriminates the *individual*, the poet's conception, as it were neglecting the intermediate particular objects, catches, as far as may be, and reflects the divine archetypal idea, and so becomes itself the copy or image of truth.

These words are perhaps the most adequate exposition of one phase of neo-classic doctrine, which, of course, was not peculiar to Hurd. Johnson [1] held the same view, though he never gave it careful utterance. It motivates, too, the frequent expressions of the following bit of advice, which is here couched in the words of George Colman (1775): [2] "Let the admirer and imitator of Nature also be on his guard, not to fall into insipidity, or to indulge the minute touches of a Dutch pencil." Sweeping, unbroken line, generalized action, constitute truth and nature.

1. *Preface to Shakespeare* (1765), in *Johnson on Shakespeare*, ed. Walter Raleigh (Oxford: 1929), p. 11.
2. *The Gentleman*, No. 6, in *Prose on Several Occasions*, I, 210.

The necessity of rules followed as a matter of strict logic. They were *generalizations* that were based upon the observation of the method in nature, or the method in the imitation of nature known as art, whichever way you chose to regard them. "They are eternal and irrevocable," says Dennis (1711),[1] "and never to be dispens'd with but by Nature that made them; and the only Rule for that Dispensation is this, that a less Law may be violated to avoid the infringing of a greater." More intelligent, as well as less intelligent, men than Dennis were in agreement with him. "Though poetry," writes Hume (1742),[2] "can never submit to exact truth, it must be confined by rules of art, discovered to the author either by genius or observation." And for the thousandth time a Grub-Street reviewer (1769)[3] lays it down that "rules are nothing more than nature at second hand."

Rules are simply a means, which every wise man will use to attain an end. "Poetry is either an Art, or Whimsy and Fanaticism. If it is an Art, it follows that it must propose an End to it self, and afterwards lay down proper Means for the attaining that End: For this is undeniable, that there are proper Means for the attaining of every End, and those proper Means in Poetry we call the Rules."[4] The words are Dennis's (1704) again, but they would have come as appropriately from dozens of other men. Gildon's words (1709)[5] look like a paraphrase of Dennis's — and

---

1. *Reflections Critical and Satyrical*, etc., in Durham, p. 231.

2. *Of the Standard of Taste*, in *Essays Moral, Political, and Literary*, ed. T. H. Green and T. H. Grose (London: 1898), I, 270.

3. *The Monthly Review*, XLI, 135.

4. Dennis, *The Grounds of Criticism in Poetry* (1704), in Durham, p. 145.

5. *An Essay on the Art*, etc., in Rowe's Shakespeare (2nd ed., 1714), IX, xvi; see also p. xv.

indeed they may be: "Poesy is an Art, because we see from its Rise it has propos'd a certain End, and must necessarily have certain Means to be conducted to that End. For where there is a *Right* and a *Wrong*, there must be some Art or Rules to avoid the one, and arrive at the other." Theory and science are as necessary to the writer, says Shaftesbury (1711),[1] as to the horseman, wrestler, or dancer. "The skill and grace of writing is founded, as our wise poet tells us, in knowledge and good sense; and not barely in that knowledge which is to be learnt from common authors, or the general conversation of the world; but from those particular rules of art which philosophy alone exhibits."

But although "philosophy exhibits" the rules, they are not, according to their defenders, mere deductive principles on the same plane as scholastic logic. They are, on the contrary, inductive principles. "Thus dramatic poetry stands upon the same footing with our noble system of Newtonian philosophy. It is not derived from any hypothesis which experiments are tortured to serve, but the result of repeated effects from certain causes." So William Guthrie [2] wrote in 1747, and the same defense was made again and again before the end of the century. Bishop Hurd's account (1751) [3] of the critical process reads like a text-book on scientific methodology, though "the *art*" of criticism, he admits, "is, as yet, far short of perfection." Dr. Johnson (September 21, 1751) [4] says that "to proceed from one Truth to another, and connect distant Propositions by

---

1. *Characteristics*, ed. Robertson, I, 127.
2. *An Essay upon English Tragedy* (London: *ca.* 1747), p. 6.
3. Note on l. 210 of Horace's *Epistola ad Augustum*, ed. Hurd, in *Works* (1811), I, 391.
4. *The Rambler*, No. 158.

regular Consequences is the great Prerogative of Man,"
and the proper function, he implies, of criticism and literary art. "Incapable professors" of the art, or science, of
criticism, writes Alexander Gerard (1759),[1]

have attempted to prescribe rules, formed by their own imaginations. . . . Genuine criticism is evidently very different; and is
justly esteemed a faithful transcript of nature. For it investi-
gates those qualities in it's objects, which, from the invariable
principles of human nature, must always please or displease; de-
scribes and distinguishes the sentiments, which they in fact produce; and impartially regulates it's most general conclusions
according to real phaenomena.

In 1792 Pye[2] combats the notion that the principles of
criticism are like "the authority of imperial rescripts."
"The true principles of just criticism," such as those of
Aristotle, he asserts, are founded rather "on reason and
justice, enforced by universal consent, and sanctioned by
the wisdom of ages."

Since the rules were inductive generalizations based
upon the observation of nature, which was synonymous
with reason and order, it followed that they were not inconsistent with taste. It was true, of course, that the word
"taste" was used at least as loosely as the word "nature"
itself. On March 22, 1753, a writer who subscribes himself

1. *An Essay on Taste* (London: 1759), pp. 185–186. Compare *The Universal Magazine*, LXXXI (1787), 3: "True criticism is the application of taste and good sense to the several fine arts. Its object is to distinguish the beautiful and faulty in every performance; to ascend from particular instances to general principles; and thus to form rules or conclusions concerning the several kinds of beauty in works of genius. — The rules of criticism are not formed by a train of abstract reasoning, independent of facts and observations. It is an art founded wholly on experience; on the observation of such beauties as have approached nearest to the standard of taste; that is, of such beauties as have been found to please man- kind most generally."

2. *A Commentary Illustrating the Poetic of Aristotle*, p. xiv.

"H. S." [1] instances "the poor monosyllable TASTE" as one of the "words to which we have no ideas at all." "I would not be thought," he goes on, "to require, like an ill-bred logician, that every pretty woman, or even every pretty man, who makes use of the word TASTE, should define what they mean by it; that would be too cruel; but I should rather chuse, when they are really conscious to themselves that they are going to utter it without any idea annexed, that they would be so good as to change it for the word WHIM." But all good things are abused, and the word "taste," or more properly the thing for which it stood, was good despite the abuse to which it was subject. How, then, could it be inconsistent with the rules considered as the formulations of reason and nature? Inconsistent with arbitrary rules it was, no doubt, which only went to prove that "a petulant rejection, and an implicit veneration, of the rules of the ancient critics, are equally destructive of true taste." [2]

No, true taste, like the rules themselves, was the off-spring of judgment. Shaftesbury,[3] indeed, speaks of "taste or judgment," as if they were the same thing. The commoner view, however, was that it consisted, as Fielding [4] says, in "a nice Harmony between the Imagination and the Judgment." Such was the view of Hume,[5] Alexander

---

1. *The World*, No. 12.

2. J. Warton, *An Essay on Pope* (1756), I, 124.

3. *Characteristics* (1711), ed. Robertson, II, 257. See Aisso Bosker (*Literary Criticism in the Age of Johnson* [Groningen and The Hague: 1930], p. 18, *et passim*) for an interesting discussion of the rationalization of taste in the eighteenth century.

4. *The Covent-Garden Journal*, ed. Jensen, No. 10 (February 4, 1752). A writer in *The Connoisseur*, ed. George Colman and Bonnell Thornton, No. 120 (May 13, 1756), quotes this observation of Fielding's with approval.

5. *Of the Standard of Taste* (1742), in *Essays*, ed. Green and Grose, I, 278–279: "Strong sense, united to delicate sentiment, improved by practice, per-

Gerard,[1] James Beattie,[2] William Richardson,[3] and many others. "TASTE, in my opinion," says "H. S." again,[4] ought to be applied to nothing but what has as strict rules annexed to it, though perhaps imperceptible by the vulgar, as Aristotle, among the critics, would require, or Domenichino, among the painters, practice. People may have whims, freaks, caprices, persuasions, and even second sights if they please, but they can have no TASTE which has not its foundation in nature, and which, consequently, may be accounted for.

"J. T.," another writer for *The World*,[5] shows how far beyond mere *je ne sais quoi* his group was capable of going: "Were we to erect a temple to TASTE, every SCIENCE should furnish a pillar, every VIRTUE should there have an altar, and the three GRACES should hold the high-priesthood in commission."

The simon-pure neo-classicist was never guilty of light-hearted dilettantism. He never said, "I don't know anything about art, but I know what I like." For him, to possess taste meant having passed through a discipline. "Taste," writes Goldsmith,[6] "cannot be brought to per-

---

fected by comparison, and cleared of all prejudice, can alone entitle critics to this valuable character; and the joint verdict of such, wherever they are to be found, is the true standard of taste and beauty."

1. *An Essay on Taste* (1759), p. 104: Taste "consists in certain *excellences* of our original powers of judgment and imagination combined."

2. *Dissertations Moral and Critical* (Dublin: 1783), I, 202: "To be a person of taste, it seems necessary, that one have, first, a lively and correct imagination; secondly, the power of distinct apprehension; thirdly, the capacity of being easily, strongly, and agreeably affected, with sublimity, beauty, harmony, exact imitation, &c.; fourthly, Sympathy, or Sensibility of heart; and, fifthly, Judgment, or Good Sense, which is the principal thing, and may not very improperly be said to comprehend all the rest." Beattie is avowedly a disciple of Gerard.

3. *On the Faults of Shakespeare*, in *Shakespeare's Dramatic Characters* (1784), p. 144: "Taste is perfect, when sensibility, discernment, and knowledge, are united." 4. No. 12 (March 22, 1753).

5. No. 67 (April 11, 1754).

6. *Upon Taste* (1761), in *Works*, ed. Gibbs, I, 324.

fection without proper cultivation." Goldsmith, of course, was not in many respects a neo-classicist of the purest ray, but when he insists [1] that trained reason and judgment are necessary to curb "the luxuriancy of the young imagination, which is apt to run riot," he is as pure as the purest could have wished. Lord Kames,[2] on the contrary, *was* a neo-classicist, and his view of the education requisite for the development of taste may safely be taken as standard: "There must be a good natural taste . . . this taste must be improved by education, reflection, and experience: it must be preserved alive, by a regular course of life, by using the goods of fortune with moderation, and by following the dictates of improved nature, which gives welcome to every rational pleasure without deviating into excess." If there is something of the judge and the Scotch moralist in this, it merely helps to explain why men like Kames found themselves so much at home in the neo-classic fold. Essentially neo-classicism was judicial and moral. Taste, therefore, was not a capacity for enjoying delicious and mindless shudders, but was "allowed to be the result of knowledge"[3] and intellectual training. For this reason the study of criticism was considered salutary exercise. "It is . . . necessary," writes Addison,[4] "for a Man who would form to himself a finished Taste of good Writing, to be well

1. I, 336.
2. *Elements of Criticism* (2nd ed., London: 1763), III, 422–423. The first edition, inaccessible to me, appeared in 1762. Compare "The Enquirer," No. 12, *The Monthly Magazine*, III (1797), 273: "That we are often pleased with things which ought not to please us, is as true in matters of taste, as in morals; and, in both cases, it is only by bringing our feelings to the standard of reason, that we can determine whether they ought to be indulged."
3. John Penn, Notes to Ranieri di Calsabigi's *Letter to Count Alfieri, on Tragedy*, in Penn, *Critical and Poetical Works* (London: 1797), p. 97.
4. *The Spectator*, No. 409 (June 19, 1712). Compare Shaftesbury, *Characteristics* (1711), ed. Robertson, II, 257.

versed in the Works of the best *Criticks* both Ancient and Modern." The circle, to be sure, is a bit vicious: to be a good critic one must have a true taste, and to have a true taste one must read the good critics; but the neo-classicist thought it no more vicious than the circle of the dilettante: to be a good critic one need only have taste, and to have taste one need only criticize.

Shakespeare, enjoyable as he was, would have been still more enjoyable if he had followed the rules. This truth was rationally demonstrable. Both the rules and taste are grounded in reason; taste is the faculty of esthetic enjoyment; the rules are the measure of artistic excellence; Shakespeare violated the rules; therefore he would have been more enjoyable if he had not. "*Shakespear*," writes Gildon (1718),[1] "is great in nothing, but what is *according to the Rules of Art*." He was "a Miracle, for the Age he liv'd in," says Gildon (1709)[2] again, but if he had only had correctness as well as genius "it would have given him the only Perfection he wanted."[3] Dennis (1711),[4] as usual, is with Gildon: "what would he not have been, if he had join'd to so happy a Genius Learning and the Poetical Art?" This question was asked repeatedly. William Mason (1751)[5] regretted Shakespeare's ignorance, not so much for Shakespeare's sake as for the sake of the lesser men who followed his pernicious example. Dr. Johnson (1765)[6] obviously wished away the "incrustations" that "clouded" the "diamonds" of Shakespeare's "mine," and

1. *The Complete Art of Poetry*, I, 99.
2. *An Essay on the Art*, etc., in Rowe's Shakespeare (2nd ed., 1714), IX, ii.
3. IX, v.
4. *On the Genius and Writings of Shakespear*, in Smith, p. 26.
5. "Letters Concerning the Following Drama," prefixed to *Elfrida, a Dramatic Poem* (2nd ed., 1752), pp. iv-v.
6. *Preface to Shakespeare*, in *Johnson on Shakespeare*, ed. Raleigh, p. 34.

the "impurities" that "debased" his "gold." Shakespeare "will be condemned indeed not for neglecting a positive institution, but for omissions, commissions, or deviations, which would have been faults if they had by no law been forbidden," said *The Monthly Review* in 1769,[1] and the clear implication is that they had been forbidden by a law. As late as 1780 William Hodson[2] believed that "Shakespeare himself would doubtless" have soared "to greater heights" if he had observed the rules. "They do no more, than save Genius from Error," wrote James Harris[3] a year later, "by shewing it, that *a Right to err* is *no Privilege at all*." Shakespeare had no more right than another. "We venture to add," he says,[4] ". . . that if there be any things in *Shakspeare* OBJECTIONABLE (and who is hardy enough to deny it?) THE VERY OBJECTIONS, as well as THE BEAUTIES, *are to be tried* BY THE SAME RULES, as the same Plummet alike shews, both what is *out of* the Perpendicular, and *in* it; the same Ruler alike proves, both what is *crooked*, and what is *strait*."

Defense of the rules could go no further than an attack upon Shakespeare for their violation, because even as far back as the dark age of Queen Anne his magic had ravished his severest critics. "In spite of his known and visible Errors," Gildon (1709)[5] is forced to admit,

when I read *Shakespear*, even in some of his most irregular Plays, I am surpriz'd into a Pleasure so great, that my Judgment is no longer free to see the Faults, tho they are ever so gross and evident. There is such a Witchery in him, that all the Rules of Art,

1. XLI, 132.
2. "Observations on Tragedy," bound with his play, *Zoraida*, p. 75 n.
3. *Philological Inquiries*, p. 217.
4. P. 230.
5. *An Essay on the Art*, etc., in Rowe's Shakespeare (2nd ed., 1714), IX, iii.

which he does not observe, tho built on an equally solid and infallible Reason, as intirely vanish away in the Transports of
those that he does observe, as if I had never known any thing of
the matter.

By 1776, the date of Voltaire's *Letter to the French Academy*,
which was part of his war against the English, and especially against Shakespeare, "an attack upon Shakespeare,"
says Lounsbury,[1]

was either received with absolute indifference or produced the
same amused wonderment with which one would now regard an
attack upon the Copernican system. An attitude, not controver-
sial but contemptuous, was taken towards those, whether natives or foreigners, who continued still to cherish the rapidly dis-
appearing belief of a vanished age that Shakespeare was simply
an inspired barbarian.

It is all the more significant, in the light of this fact, that
Hodson and Harris, in 1780 and 1781, could have written
as they did about Shakespeare. It gives one "a just
esteem" of at least the longevity of the "ancient rules."

1. *Shakespeare and Voltaire* (New York: 1902), p. 404.

CHAPTER III

Rules in General — The Attack

THE tone that the eighteenth-century defender of the rules usually adopted was that of the justifier. He felt that they were of God, or at least of Nature, and therefore justifiable to men, but he was also painfully aware that his was a stiff-necked generation which demanded, somewhat obtusely, that their justice be demonstrated. "There has been a sudden and sensible change in the opinions of men within these last fifty years," Hume [1] wrote in 1742, "by the progress of learning and of liberty. Most people, in this island, have divested themselves of all superstitious reverence to names and authority." The words have reference to religion and kingship, but they would have applied equally well to the authority of Aristotle and the ancient rules. "Lettered critics are of two sorts, one of which may be said to judge *according* to rule, and the other *by* rule," wrote John Penn [2] a half a century later.

The first when they form their judgment of a work, have already qualified their minds for the task by knowledge of the rule, but now dismiss all thoughts of it, and are influenced solely by feeling; the latter, being destitute of feeling, have nothing to direct them but the rule, from which they cannot depart.

1. *Whether the British Government inclines more to Absolute Monarchy, or to a Republic,* in *Essays, Moral, Political, and Literary,* ed. Green and Grose (1898), I, 125.
2. *Letters on the Drama* (London: 1796), p. 51.

The defense insisted that it was merely asking artists to create, and critics to judge, according to rule, not by rule. The prosecution, often but by no means always, considered this a distinction without a difference, and incontinently rejected all rule and authority.

This phase of the assault was almost purely emotional, but those who participated in it sometimes claimed to be fighting under the egis of reason. There is just as good ground for submitting to the practise of Shakespeare, who was a poet and must have had some judgment in his art, as to submit to the precepts of Aristotle, thought Farquhar (1702).[1] "But to stoop to the Authority of either, without consulting the Reason of the Consequence, is an Abuse to a Man's Understanding; and neither the Precept of the Philosopher, nor Example of the Poet, shou'd go down with me, without examining the Weight of their Assertions." In the heat of the conflict a man sometimes mistook a friend for an enemy, and savagely ran him through. The pot, to alter the figure, sometimes called the kettle black. Thus Dennis (1711)[2] calls Pope "a pedantick Slave to Authority and Opinion," and speaks of "the servile Deference which he pays to the Ancients."[3] Those who breathed "the classic vein," said Robert Lloyd (1760),[4] were

> Delighted with the pomp of rules,
> The specious pedantry of schools,
> (Which rules, like crutches, ne'er became
> Of any use but to the lame).

---

1. *A Discourse upon Comedy*, in Durham, pp. 284–285.
2. *Reflections Critical and Satyrical*, in Durham, p. 216.
3. P. 218.
4. "Shakespeare: an Epistle to Mr. Garrick," in *The Poetical Works of Robert Lloyd* (London: 1774), I, 80. Compare *The Monthly Review*, XXIII (1760), 373, which approves of Lloyd's lines on the rules.

Why, then, to the devil with the rules, said Sterne in *Tristram Shandy* (1761),[1] or would have said to the devil with them if he could have found a Latin parallel for the curse. He solicits Apollo instead: "Great Apollo! If thou art in a giving humour — give me — I ask no more, but one stroke of native humour, with a single spark of thy own fire along with it — and send Mercury, with the *rules and compasses*, if he can be spared, with my compliments to — no matter."

The more serious and the more judicial rule-haters, however, had a method in their hatred. They made distinctions, too, and, indeed, cannot be classified simply as opponents to rules in general, but only to rules in particular. "Off with their heads," or to the devil "with the *rules and compasses*," was not their cry. "When I speak of *Rules* in Poetry as useless," writes Leonard Welsted (1724),[2]

I do not mean that Experience, Knowledge, Application, and every Method, by which Excellency is attain'd in other Things, are not necessary for the aiding a good Genius: What I contend against is, the common traditionary Rules; such as, for Example, "*Poetry is an Imitation; It has Nature for its Object; As an Art, it has some End, and consequently Means or Rules to attain that End; An English Verse contains five Feet; A Play ought to consist of neither more nor less than Five Acts,*" etc.

Dr. Johnson (September 14, 1751)[3] makes a distinction between "the accidental Prescriptions of Authority" and "the Laws of Nature." Some laws, he goes on,

1. III, xii.
2. *A Dissertation Concerning the Perfection of the English Language*, etc., Durham, p. 370.
3. *The Rambler*, No. 156. Warton (*An Essay on Pope* [1756], I, 127–128) quotes these words of Johnson's and comments upon them as follows: "This

are indeed to be considered as fundamental and indispensable, others only as useful and convenient; some as dictated by Reason and Necessity, others as enacted by despotick Antiquity; some as invincibly supported by their Conformity to the Order of Nature, and Operations of the Intellect, others as formed by Accident, or instituted by Example, and therefore always liable to Dispute and Alteration. . . . It ought to be the first Endeavour of a Writer to distinguish Nature from Custom, or that which is established because it is right, from that which is right only because it is established.

James Beattie (1783),[1] who seems to have had these very passages in mind, makes a similar distinction between "two sorts of rules . . . the Essential, and the Ornamental." It is a virtue, he says, to observe essential rules, and may be an equal virtue to break ornamental ones.

That there was something radically wrong with the

---

liberal and manly censure of critical bigotry, extends not to those fundamental and indispensable rules, which nature and necessity dictate, and demand to be observed; such, for instance . . . in the drama, that no more events be crowded together, than can be ju:tly supposed to happen during the time of representation, or to be transacted on one individual spot, and the like. But the absurdity here animadverted on,i ; the scrupulous nicety of those, who bind themselves to obey frivolous and unimportant laws; such as . . . that in a tragedy, only three personages should appear at once upon the stage; and that a tragedy must consist of five acts; by the rigid observation of which last unnecessary precept, the poet is deprived of using many a moving story, that would furnish matter enough for three perhaps, but not five acts; with others of like nature." Compare *The Works of Alexander Pope*, ed. Warton (1797), I, 188–189, where these words are reprinted with no substantial change.

1. *Dissertations Moral and Critical*, I, 221. In support he quotes (I, 222) the following well-known lines of Pope (*An Essay on Criticism*, ed. Ward, ll. 159–160, 152–153):

> "Great wits sometimes may gloriously offend,
> And rise to faults true Critics dare not mend.
>
> .   .   .   .
>
> From vulgar bounds with brave disorder part,
> And snatch a grace beyond the reach of art."

Some further remarks on this phase of the attack have been reserved for Chapter IV.

merely ornamental or mechanical rules seemed obvious from the fact that the plays that were written in accordance with them were often failures on the stage. "The Town," wrote Farquhar (1702),[1]

has been often disappointed in those Critical Plays, and some Gentlemen that have been admir'd in their speculative Remarks, have been ridicul'd in the practick. All the Authorities, all the Rules of Antiquity have prov'd too weak to support the Theatre, whilst others who have dispenc'd with the Criticks, and taken a Latitude in the *OEconomy* of their Plays, have been the chief Supporters of the Stage, and the Ornament of the *Drama*; this is so visibly true, that I need bring in no instances to enforce it.

The French theatre in particular was "hag-ridden" by the rules, and Englishmen satisfied many an ancient grudge by never letting the world forget it. Freeborn Englishmen, it was true, submitted too frequently to the slavery of the rules, a submission that came naturally to Frenchmen; but when they did, their submission was really French, not English, a sort of bastard Norman inheritance. Even Frenchmen, "enslaved as they are to rules, and modes," were believed subconsciously to have felt their own depravity, which was the bane of their stage; "still I do not doubt," says Walpole,[2] "that many, both of their tragic and comic authors, would be glad they dared to use the liberties which are secured to our stage. They are so cramped by the rigorous forms of composition, that they would think themselves greatly indemnified by an ampler latitude of thought."

1. *A Discourse upon Comedy*, in Durham, p. 263.
2. "The Author's Postscript" to *The Mysterious Mother* (Dublin: 1791), p. 101. According to Mr. R. W. Babcock (*The Genesis of Shakespeare Idolatry, 1766–1799* [Chapel Hill: 1931], p. 48 n.), the "Postscript" "first appeared in J. Dodsley's Edition, 1781," but the copy of this edition in the Boston Public Library does not contain the "Postscript."

The failure in practise of merely "regular" plays proved that something else besides the observation of rules was necessary. The proof held not only in the drama, but in all poetry. "So many are the Qualifications, as well natural as acquir'd," said Edward Bysshe (1702),[1] "that are essentially requisite to the making of a good Poet, that 'tis in vain for any Man to aim at a great Reputation on account of his Poetical Performances, by barely following the Rules of others, and reducing their Speculations into Practice." If the "mechanic" rules are "infallible," and alone sufficient, says Steele (April 16, 1709),[2] "it is wonderful there should be so few writers." He means good writers, of course, for there was a plentiful crop of "regular" writers. The question was, would their regularity alone make them pleasing? Gray's [3] experience had taught him to answer emphatically no. The "regularity . . . established" by "*The Rules of the Drama*," says Thomas Whately,[4] "though highly proper, is by no means the first requisite in a dramatic composition." More important are "imagination or sensibility" and the "preservation of *Character*." And everyone knew that the imagination, which men whose brains were as yet unaddled by German philosophy could not distinguish from the fancy, was a sore disrupter of your regularity. "Imagination," says Dr. Johnson (May 28, 1751),[5] "a licentious and vagrant Faculty, im-

---

1. *The Art of English Poetry* (4th ed., London: 1710), sig. *1.

2. *The Tatler*, ed. Aitken, No. 3.

3. "Mr. Gray's Remarks on the Letters prefixed to Mason's Elfrida," in *The Works of Thomas Gray*, ed. J. Mitford (London: 1858), IV, 3. Mitford does not give the date of the "Remarks," but C. S. Northup (*Essays and Criticisms by Thomas Gray* [Boston and London: 1911], p. 165) gives 1751.

4. *Remarks on Some of the Characters of Shakespeare* (London: 1785), pp. 1–2. According to the editor, these remarks were written before 1770.

5. *The Rambler*, No. 125.

patient of Limitations, and unsusceptible of Restraint, has always endeavoured to baffle the Logician, to perplex the Confines of Distinction, and burst the Inclosures of Regularity. . . . Every new Genius produces some Innovation, which, when invented and approved, subverts the Rules which the Practice of foregoing Authors had established." Yet imagination, genius, and certain other nameless and mercurial quiddities could not be dispensed with.

> Where nature warmth and genius has deny'd,
> In vain are art's stiff languid powers apply'd.[1]

Where they have affirmed, the rules of art are equally inapropos:

> Great wits sometimes may gloriously offend,
> And rise to faults true Critics dare not mend.[2]

The greatest wit of all, naturally, was Shakespeare. He was the constant excuse for irregularity. The conservatives seem at times to have wished that he had never lived, so sore a thorn was he in their sides. The radicals quoted his example with an unholy glee. But there were always some who were simply in doubt about him. Perhaps a knowledge of the rules, which everyone was sure he had not had, would have done him good, — perhaps not; they did not know. "Whether his ignorance of the Antients were a disadvantage to him or no, may admit of a dispute: For tho' the knowledge of 'em might have made him more correct, yet it is not improbable but that the regularity and deference for them, which would have attended that

---

1. Mrs. Judith (Cowper) Madan, *The Progress of Poetry*, in *The Flower-Piece: A Collection of Miscellany Poems. By Several Hands* (London: 1731), p. 130.
2. Pope, *An Essay on Criticism*, ed. Ward, ll. 159–160.

correctness, might have restrain'd some of that fire, impetuosity, and even beautiful extravagance which we admire in *Shakespear*."[1] Thus Rowe had thought in 1709, but in 1795 the same, or a worse, doubt was yet alive. In his remarks on Pye's *Commentary* a reviewer says:[2] "The question of altering Shakspeare is here gently touched; and Mr. Garrick's labours in this line are approved. The nation is not yet ripe for the attempt: it still talks of Shakspeare with bigotry; secretly fearing lest his merits be insufficient to protect him against much just blame from the French critics."

But Rowe and that part of "the nation" to which our reviewer alludes were distinctly in the minority — at least by the middle of the century. In 1769 Mrs. Montagu,[3] agreeing with Pope, says that Shakespeare, "even when he deviates most from rules, *can rise to faults true critics dare not mend*." Twenty years before, William Warburton (1747)[4] had said what amounted to the same thing: "Tho' it be very true, as Mr. *Pope* hath observed, that *Shakespear is the fairest and fullest subject for criticism*, yet it is not such a sort of criticism as may be raised mechanically on the Rules which *Dacier*, *Rapin*, and *Bossu* have collected from Antiquity; and of which such kind of Writers as *Rymer*, *Gildon*, *Dennis*, and *Oldmixon*, have only gathered and chewed the Husks." To critics like Mrs. Montagu and

---

1. Nicholas Rowe, *Some Account of the Life &c. of Mr. William Shakespear* (1709), in Smith, p. 2.
2. *The Monthly Review*, second series, XVIII (1795), 128. Is it, then, true, as Mr. Nichol Smith says (*Eighteenth Century Essays on Shakespeare* [Glasgow: 1903], p. xxxii), that "the dramatic rules had been finally deposed"? or (p. xxxiii) that "the rules are forgotten, — we cease to hear even that they are useless"? Both remarks refer to the third quarter of the century.
3. *An Essay on the Writings and Genius of Shakespear* (London: 1769), p. 20.
4. *Preface to Shakespeare*, in Smith, p. 105.

Warburton, Shakespeare was above and beyond the mechanical rules; he "was a man to whom Aristotle would have fallen down and worshipped, as the author [1] of the Essay on Falstaff has pleasantly said." [2]

The rules, said their defenders, were only a means to the end of all art, esthetic enjoyment; but if this was true, Shakespeare cast suspicion upon the means, for his plays, which were admittedly incorrect, were more enjoyable than the most correct productions. "Our inimitable *Shakespear* is a Stumbling-block to the whole Tribe of those rigid Criticks. Who would not rather read one of his Plays, where there is not a single Rule of the Stage observed, than any Production of a modern Critick, where there is not one of them violated"? [3] The question is Addison's, whose *Cato* (1713), though it was diligently praised by the very sort of critics alluded to by its author, achieved a lasting and deserved reputation for coldness. The "feelings" of men's "hearts" told them that, even if Shakespeare had been "without recourse to Grecian art," [4] he was superior to those who were not without it. They may need drawbridges and paved ways, but "Shakespeare proceeds by storm. He knows nothing of regular approaches to the fort of the human heart. He effects his

---

1. That is, Maurice Morgann, *An Essay on the Dramatic Character of Sir John Falstaff*, in Smith, p. 251. Speaking of the lapse of time, change of place, and metamorphoses of character in *Macbeth*, he says: "On such an occasion, a fellow, like *Rymer*, waking from his trance, shall lift up his Constable's staff, and charge this great Magician, this daring *practicer of arts inhibited*, in the name of *Aristotle*, to surrender; whilst *Aristotle* himself, disowning his wretched Officer, would fall prostrate at his feet and acknowledge his supremacy. — O supreme of Dramatic excellence! (*might he say*) not to me be imputed the insolence of fools."

2. Thomas Davies, *Dramatic Micellanies (sic)*, etc. (London: 1784), III, 130.

3. Addison, *The Spectator*, No. 592 (September 10, 1714).

4. Robert Lloyd, "Shakespeare" (1760), in *The Poetical Works* (1774), I, 82–83.

breach by the weight of his metal, and makes his lodgment, though the enemy's artillery is thundering round him from every battery of criticism, learning, and even probability." [1] Paradoxical as it may seem, in view of his faults, his manifold improprieties and wanton violations of rule, his very faults, says Belsham (1789),[2] "afford the most decisive proofs of his excellence. It is an acknowledged fact, that to his works all classes of men, the young and the old, the learned and the ignorant, the clown and the courtier, are indebted for the most exquisite entertainment and delight." Pope's explanation [3] of the paradox was perhaps the best that the century succeeded in making: "Most of our Author's faults are less to be ascribed to his wrong judgment as a Poet, than to his right judgment as a Player"; which was a neat, if unconscious, slander of the poetic laws.

The more usual but less precise explanation was that "art had so little, and nature so large a share in what he did." The words are Rowe's (1709),[4] but the sentiment was that of all but the most art-bound of conservatives. Pope, who, in *An Essay on Criticism* (1711), had done his not inconsiderable best to make the rules obligatory, and had prescribed the imitation of nature as a nostrum for all poetic ills, admitted [5] in 1725 that Shakespeare "is not so much an Imitator, as an Instrument, of Nature; and 'tis

1. *The Critical Review*, XX (1765), 322.

2. *Essays Philosophical and Moral, Historical and Literary* (2nd ed., London: 1799), II, 464. Volume II of the *Essays* was first published in 1789, volume I in 1791.

3. *Preface to Shakespeare* (1725), in Smith, p. 51.

4. *Some Account of the Life &c. of Mr. William Shakespear*, in Smith, p. 4.

5. *Preface to Shakespeare*, in Smith, p. 48. Compare William Guthrie, *An Essay upon English Tragedy* (*ca.* 1747), p. 11: "It is not Shakespear who speaks the language of nature, but nature rather speaks the language of Shakespear."

not so just to say that he speaks from her, as that she speaks thro' him." By 1761 it was quite clear to many, George Colman,[1] for example, that "irregularity" and "unnaturalness," in spite of the canonized definitions, were not synonymous. "The mind," he says, in speaking of Shakespeare's "Inconsistencies," "is soon familiarized to Irregularities, which do not sin against the Truth of Nature, but are merely Violations of that strict Decorum of late so earnestly insisted on." Shakespeare's indecorum might fan "the Flames of critic Rage," but Shakespeare, cased in heaven-sent asbestos, remained unscorched.

> Our SHAKESPEARE yet shall all his Rights maintain,
> And crown the Triumphs of ELIZA's Reign.
> Above Controul, above each classic Rule,
> His Tutress Nature, and the World his School.[2]

Most of those who praised his "naturalness" were able to keep their heads while doing it. Not so the Reverend Martin Sherlock (1786),[3] whose prose glitters and rocks a little madly as it traces Shakespeare's natural-supernatural lineage:

It is she [Nature] who was thy book, O Shakspeare; it is she who was thy study day and night; it is she from whom thou hast drawn those beauties which are at once the glory and delight of thy nation. Thou wert the eldest son, the darling child, of Na-

1. *Critical Reflections on the Old English Dramatick Writers,* in *Prose on Several Occasions* (1787), II, 112–113.

2. George Keate, *Ferney: an Epistle to Monsr de Voltaire* (London: 1768), p. 13.

3. *A Fragment on Shakspeare, Extracted from Advice to a Young Poet . . . Translated from the French* (London: 1786), pp. 13–14. According to the "Preface" of the French translator of the *Fragment,* Sherlock's *Advice* was first written in Italian. The *Fragment,* he says, was translated into French, and from French into English. The date of the Italian original is not clear; 1786 is the date of the publication of the *Fragment* in English.

ture; and, like thy mother, enchanting, astonishing, sublime, graceful, thy variety is inexhaustible. Always original, always new, thou art the only prodigy which Nature has produced. Homer was the first of men, but thou art more than man. The reader who thinks this elogium [*sic*] extravagant is a stranger to my subject. To say that Shakspeare had the imagination of Dantè, and the depth of Machiavel, would be a weak encomium: he had them, and more. To say that he possessed the terrible graces of Michael Angelo, and the amiable graces of Correggio, would be a weak encomium: he had them, and more. To the brilliancy of Voltaire he added the strength of Demosthenes; and to the simplicity of La Fontaine, the majesty of Virgil.— But, say you, we have never seen such "a being." You are in the right; Nature made it, and broke the mould.

The practical failure of classical plays was, as has been seen, a suspicious circumstance, but it became scandalous and devastatingly illuminating when it was compared with the practical success of Shakespeare's plays. The illumination enabled, or should have enabled, it was thought, everyone unblinded by prejudice to see the superiority of "nature" to "art." The Earl of Orrery (1759) [1] could see it plainly enough: "He [Shakespeare] is . . . become a strong instance how far superior nature is to art, since our best, our most correct, our most applauded dramatic writers appear stiff, constrained, and void of force, when compared with his native fire and exuberance of imagination." The comparison was not merely one between eighteenth-century playwrights and the greatest Elizabethan; it was also, if not chiefly, a comparison between intellectual and emotional art, or, rather, between the intellectual and the emotional, for the word "art" was contaminate; so

1. "Preface" to *The Greek Theatre of Father Brumoy*, translated by Mrs. Charlotte Lennox and others (London: 1759), I, x.

that, in the opinion of Samuel Rogers (1763),[1] Ben Jonson fared as ill by the comparison as the puniest contemporary:

> Great Shakespeare, with genius disdaining all rules,
> Above the cold phlegm or the fripp'ry of schools,
> Appeal'd to the heart for success of his plays,
> And trusted to nature alone for the bays.
>
> Despairing of glory but what rose from art,
> Old Johnson applied to the head, not the heart.
> On the niceness of rules he founded his cause,
> And ravish'd from regular method applause.
>
> May we judge from the favours each poet has shar'd,
> Insipid is ART when with NATURE compar'd.

No period could furnish a "regular" poet equal to Shakespeare. Colman (1763) [2] considered Fletcher worthy to be mentioned in the same breath with Shakespeare, but "in pedant schools" he had apparently looked in vain for his equal. Even Shakespeare, thought Hurd (1762),[3] "is greater when he uses Gothic manners and machinery, than when he employs classical"; then he is more "*sublime*." Belsham (1789) [4] admitted that "the observation of certain long established rules of composition pleases in a certain degree," and named some regular plays — "Cato, Irene, and Phaedra and Hypolitus" — that were not alto-

---

1. "An ars naturâ sit perfectior," in *St. James's Magazine*, II, 63.

2. "Prologue" to *Philaster*, in *The Dramatick Works of George Colman* (London: 1777), III, sigs. B6ᵛ–B7. Compare Mrs. Elizabeth Montagu (*An Essay on the Writings and Genius of Shakespear* [1769], p. 79), who, daring anything to refute Voltaire and defend Shakespeare, maintains that the English, as well as the French, have "a pedant school": "The French critic apologizes for our persisting in the representation of Shakespear's plays, by saying we have none of a more regular form. In this he is extreamly mistaken; we have many plays written according to the rules of art; but nature, which speaks in Shakespear, prevails over them all."

3. *Letters on Chivalry and Romance*, ed. Morley, p. 117.

4. *Essays Philosophical and Moral*, etc. (2nd ed., 1799), II, 465–467.

gether without merit; but it was obvious, when they were compared with "Lear, Macbeth, or Othello," that something was lacking. He concluded that they were "defective in *genius* — a term easy to comprehend, impossible to define." The inescapable moral was that mere obedience to the rules did not guarantee an enjoyable play. Genius like that of Shakespeare was the *sine qua non* of successful play-writing.

Nothing was more characteristic of his genius, thought the eighteenth century, than his mastery over character. He might violate the unities of time and place, but he never violated the "unity of character." Lounsbury [1] has said that this unity "was devised to offset the very ancient and respectable ones which he [Shakespeare] confessedly disregarded," but the validity of his assertion is open to question, as Lounsbury's own work on Shakespeare's reputation during the eighteenth century makes clear.[2] Such an hypothesis fails to explain the universality of the interest in Shakespeare's characters during the period, especially during the latter half of it, or the continuance of the interest into the nineteenth century, when, except for a few belated classical survivals, there was no need for a device to offset the unities.

An extended discussion of this interest and of its bearing upon the conflict over the rules would be gratuitous. It may be said, however, that it was coeval with the study of Shakespeare, and was not confined strictly to the latter half of the century. It was bound up with the belief in his naturalness. Indeed Pope (1725) [3] said that "his *Charac-*

---

1. *Shakespeare and Voltaire*, p. 158.

2. See the book just cited, but particularly *Shakespeare as a Dramatic Artist* (New York and London: 1902).

3. *Preface to Shakespeare*, in Smith, p. 48.

ters are so much Nature her self, that 'tis a sort of injury to call them by so distant a name as Copies of her." Shakespeare's supremacy over other writers, thought Arthur Murphy (December 15, 1753),[1] was chiefly due to his power of characterization, and this became a standard opinion. He granted that Shakespeare violated the rules. He even granted that the rules were "agreeable to Nature." "I as freely assent . . . that inferior Genius's may avail themselves by a skilful Conformity to them . . . . But Fable is but a secondary Beauty; the Exhibition of Character, and the Excitement of the Passions, justly claiming the Precedence in dramatic Poetry." No more damaging form of attack could have been invented. To be ignored on the ground that one is unimportant, though one may be a "likeable chap," in the opinion of the ignorer, is many degrees worse than being openly, or even secretly, attacked.

Everything went to prove that Shakespeare was "the greatest genius that any nation ever produced."[2] He was "one of those prodigies that heaven vouchsafes some times to produce to give an idea of the *possible* powers of the human mind, and to moderate the vanity of those who are disposed to assume to themselves a superiority above others."[3] The "thermometer" of his "glory," it was said, in an eighteenth-century variation of Jonson's words, "is graduated to the end of time."[4] James Plumptre (1797)[5] was not alone in doubting "whether it is fair to judge

1. *The Gray's Inn Journal*, No. 12.
2. *The Monthly Review*, XIII (1755), 495.
3. "Critical Remarks on Some Celebrated Authors," *The Bee*, ed. James Anderson, XVI (Edinburgh: 1793), 273.
4. *The Monthly Mirror*, III (1797), 147.
5. *An Appendix to Observations on Hamlet* (Cambridge, England: 1797), p. 64.

Shakspeare by the rigid laws of learned criticism." But if it was not fair to judge him by those laws, the only drawable inference was that it was not fair to judge anyone by them. At least, it was not fair to expect mere mortals to obey those laws. If they cramped Shakespeare, what would they do to the village Shakespeare?

Another reason why it was unfair to judge Shakespeare by the laws that Plumptre mentions was that they had originated with a Greek philosopher of remote times and different climate and circumstances, whose notions about the drama, as a consequence, were utterly different from those of the ignorant Elizabethan genius, William Shakespeare. The historical point of view, which had been taken in the seventeenth century, came strongly, if not fully, into its own in the eighteenth, and the defenders of Shakespeare were largely responsible. The rules of Aristotle were the rules of the Greek stage, said Rowe (1709),[1] "but as *Shakespear* liv'd under a kind of mere light of nature, and had never been made acquainted with the regularity

---

1. *Some Account of the Life &c. of Mr. William Shakespear*, in Smith, p. 15. "It is absurd," Thomas Warton wrote (*Observations on the Fairy Queen of Spenser* [2nd ed., London: 1762], I, 15), "to think of judging either Ariosto or Spenser by precepts which they did not attend to. We who live in the days of writing by rule, are apt to try every composition by those laws which we have been taught to think the sole criterion of excellence. Critical taste is universally diffused, and we require the same order and design which every modern performance is expected to have, in poems where they never were regarded or intended." Mr. Aisso Bosker (*Literary Criticism in the Age of Johnson*, p. 195) says that "this passage has been termed the first clear enunciation of the new way of approach, and the *Observations* have for that reason been said to mark the beginning of a new era in criticism. This is of course not quite true." The new era began in the sixteenth century, and in the eighteenth several writers, besides Rowe, enunciated "the new way of approach" before Warton. "Many previous truths," wrote Shaftesbury in 1711 (*Characteristics*, ed. Robertson, I, 97), "are to be examined and understood in order to judge rightly of historical truth, and of the past actions and circumstances of mankind, as delivered to us by ancient authors of different nations, ages, times, and different in their characters and interests."

of those written precepts, so it would be hard to judge him by a law he knew nothing of." Rowe should have received the credit and the blame for this statement, but it went to Pope instead, presumably because of his greater promi-

---

In the same year (1711) Pope (*An Essay on Criticism*, ed. Ward, ll. 118–123, 233–234) wrote as follows:

> "You then whose judgment the right course would steer,
> Know well each ANCIENT's proper character;
> His fable, subject, scope in ev'ry page;
> Religion, Country, genius of his Age:
> Without all these at once before your eyes,
> Cavil you may, but never criticize.
>
> .   .   .   .
>
> A perfect Judge will read each work of Wit
> With the same spirit that its author writ."

Gildon, in 1718 (*The Complete Art of Poetry*, I, 135), with characteristic refractoriness, so far as the rules were concerned, shut his eyes to the new way, but the deliberation with which he did it showed that he knew the way existed. In 1725 Pope (*Preface to Shakespeare*, in Smith, p. 50) once again pointed out the way. In 1742 Hume (*Of the Standard of Taste*, in *Essays*, ed. Green and Grose, I, 282) wrote that "the poet's *monument more durable than brass*, must fall to the ground like common brick or clay, were men to make no allowance for the continual revolutions of manners and customs, and would admit of nothing but what was suitable to the prevailing fashion." Thomas Warton anticipated himself in his first edition (*Observations on the Faerie Queene of Spenser* [London: 1754], p. 217): "In reading the works of an author who lived in a remote age, it is necessary, that we should look back upon the customs and manners which prevailed in his age; that we should place ourselves in his situation, and circumstances; that so we may be the better enabled to judge and discern how his turn of thinking, and manner of composing were biass'd, influenc'd, and, as it were, tinctur'd, by very familiar and reigning appearances, which are utterly different from those with which we are at present surrounded." Though he changed the phrasing he left the idea unaltered in the second edition (*Observations* [1762], II, 87). The passage with which this note opened, however, did not appear in the first edition. His brother, Joseph Warton (*An Essay on Pope*, I, 5), expressed the idea also, in 1756: "We can never completely relish, or adequately understand any author, especially any Ancient, except we constantly keep in our eye his climate, his country, and his age." The historical point of view, says Mr. G. M. Miller (*The Historical Point of View in English Literary Criticism from 1570–1770* [Heidelberg: 1913], p. 151), "reached a fairly complete development in English criticism by 1770," though he admits (p. 16) that "there were no complete formulations or applications . . . before the middle of the eighteenth century."

nence, although Pope (1725) [1] simply rephrased the sentiment: "To judge therefore of *Shakespear* by *Aristotle*'s
rules, is like trying a man by the Laws of one Country, who
acted under those of another." Later on in the century,
when the interest in the "Gothic" origins of poetry had
begun to spring up, the idea assumed primary critical importance, as, for example, with Bishop Percy (1765): [2]

If it be the first canon of sound criticism to examine any
work by those rules the author prescribed for his observance,
then we ought not to try Shakespear's HISTORIES by the general

1. *Preface to Shakespeare*, in Smith, p. 50. Compare the previous note. In
1769 Mrs. Montagu (*An Essay on the Writings and Genius of Shakespear*, p. 7)
approves of Pope's remark. She says (pp. 13–14) further of Shakespeare's plays:
"We may securely applaud what the ancients have crowned; therefore should not
withhold our approbation wherever we find our countryman has equalled the
most admired passages in the Greek tragedians: but we shall not do justice to his
native talents, when they are the object of consideration, if we do not remember
the different circumstances under which these writers [*sic*] were composed."
Edward Taylor (*Cursory Remarks on Tragedy* [1774], p. 35) denies the truth of
Pope's statement: "Yet surely there are laws of general society," he then goes
on, "as well as of particular communities, laws that bind each individual as a
citizen of the world; the infringment of which would justly excite the universal
indignation and resentment of mankind." Very curiously, however, he himself
uses the relative argument in a defense of Ruccellai's *Rosmunda* (pp. 146–147):
"I am well aware that the English critic will be apt to pronounce the tragedy before us, as well as the theatrical compositions in general of all southern nations,
insipid, uninteresting, and unaffecting: but he would do well to consider the different characters of nations, various as the climates they inhabit, warm and genial
as the sun that makes all nature smile around them, or cold and barren, like the
snow-capt mountains that environ them. What at Naples or at Rome would
appal the heart with terror and dismay, or convulse it with all the agonizing
throbs of pity and compassion, would, in the more impenetrable northern bosom,
scarce excite the transitory shudder, or the feeble half-formed sigh."
2. "An Essay on the Origin of the English Stage," in *Reliques of Ancient English Poetry* (London: 1765), I, 127. Compare Richard Hurd, *Letters on Chivalry
and Romance* (1762), ed. Morley, p. 80: "Would we know, from what causes the
institution of *Chivalry* was derived? The time of its birth, the situation of the
barbarians, amongst whom it arose, must be considered: their wants, designs, and
policies must be explored: We must inquire when, and where, and how it came to
pass that the western world became familiarized to this *Prodigy*, which we now
start at." Compare also pp. 115, 118.

laws of Tragedy or Comedy. Whether the rule itself be vicious or not, is another inquiry: but certainly we ought to examine a work only by those principles according to which it was composed. This would save a deal of impertinent criticism.

In 1745 Dr. Johnson,[1] in a note on *Macbeth*, implies that taking into consideration the circumstances that determine the rules that an author prescribes for his own observance is a standard maxim of criticism, which it is not necessary to stress: "In order to make a true estimate of the abilities and merit of a writer, it is always necessary to examine the genius of his age, and the opinions of his contemporaries." The word "always" is equivalent to "of course." Voltaire, who could be counted upon for an almost annual fling at the English "barbarian," was particularly prone to violate the maxim, and he was repeatedly rebuked for his weakness by the English. "But he [Voltaire]," Mrs. Elizabeth Griffith [2] wrote in 1775, "unfairly tries him [Shakespeare] by Pedant laws, which our Author either did not know, or regarded not. His compositions are a distinct species of the Drama; and not being an imitation of the Greek one, cannot be justly said to have infringed its rules." Voltaire, or "a fellow, like *Rymer*," to use Maurice Morgann's [3] example (1777), might "lift up his Constable's staff, and charge this great Magician, this daring *practicer of arts inhibited*, in the name of *Aristotle*, to surrender; whilst *Aristotle* himself, disowning his wretched

1. *Johnson on Shakespeare*, ed. Raleigh, p. 167. Compare Arthur Murphy, *The Gray's Inn Journal*, No. 8 (November 17, 1753): "In order to calculate the Merit and Abilities of an Author with any Degree of Exactness, it is highly necessary to consider the Genius of his Age, and to examine the Opinions of his Cotemporaries."

2. *The Morality of Shakespeare's Drama* (London: 1775), p. vi.

3. *An Essay on the Dramatic Character of Sir John Falstaff*, in Smith, p. 251.

Officer, would fall prostrate at his feet and acknowledge his supremacy. — O supreme of Dramatic excellence! (*might he say*) not to me be imputed the insolence of fools."

Once again the unavoidable inference from Shakespeare's exemption was that all were exempt if he was. If Aristotle and his rules and compasses were too remote to have bearing on the sixteenth century they were obviously too remote to have any on the eighteenth. The rules were altogether in a bad way, at least the merely ornamental rules, for they, it was obvious, did not work out well in practise. People thought they liked regular plays, but they were mistaken, or so one of Mrs. Catharine Clive's [1] characters believed:

Mrs. Hazard. — . . . The Town has been so overwhelmed with Tragedies lately, that they are in one entire Fit of the Vapours. — They think they love 'em, but it's no such thing. I was there one Night this Season at a Tragedy, and there was such an universal Yawn in the House, that, if it had not been for a great Quantity of Drums and Trumpets, that most judiciously every now and then came in to their Relief, the whole Audience would have fallen asleep.

If Shakespeare observed the essential rules, the further inference from his example was that the essential rules were good, because his plays were not soporific; but the difficulty was that nobody seemed to know precisely what they were. Perhaps, after all, the explanation of the difference between Shakespeare and the practisers of white magic was that Shakespeare had genius, and they had not. Or was it really true that Shakespeare was divine?

1. *The Rehearsal: or, Bays in Petticoats* (London: 1753; acted 1750), Act I, pp. 15–16.

CHAPTER IV

Rationalism and Revolt

NEO-CLASSICISM we are apt to regard as a purely rationalistic movement. Nevertheless, it is dangerous and misleading to say without qualification that neo-classicism was grounded in reason, or that the neo-classicist followed the dictates of reason. Neo-classicists were as complex and "impure" as other men. One lobe of a neo-classicist's brain might be, and generally was, rationalistic, while the other lobe might be, and generally was, something very different. The naive reader would almost certainly get the impression that John Dennis, for example, was as pure a rationalist as one could wish for; but "to his age," writes Mr. H. G. Paul,[1] "Dennis stood as the champion of emotion as the basis of poetry, as an advocate of the exaltation and inspiration of the poet that so ill accorded with the prevailing spirit of the times that he was derisively dubbed 'Sir Longinus.'" It is the purpose of this chapter to analyze and set in opposition some of the conflicting and confused tendencies of the eighteenth century, which was almost equally "classic" and "romantic," or rationalistic and emotional. The rationalistic elements naturally call for attention first, since in one sense they were fundamental: they were the generally prevailing older order of things, which at length gave way before a new order.

1. *John Dennis, His Life and Criticism* (New York: 1911), p. 134.

The eighteenth century, in its rationalistic phase, or mood, worried a good deal over the scarcity of men of judgment, or the paucity of judgment in most men. In 1702 Dennis [1] lamented the fact that "tho a fine Imagination is to be met with in few, Judgment is to be found in fewer"; and in 1711 he speaks [2] disapprovingly of "those who are guided more by Imagination than they are by Judgment, which is the Case of three parts of the World, and three parts of the other Part." Damning "imagination" in its lower manifestations was just a part of the game of damning "enthusiasm." The game was traditional. Religious enthusiasm, Hobbes had said in his *Leviathan* (1651),[3] was a disease of madmen. Locke, in his *Essay Concerning Human Understanding* (1689),[4] had condemned the "internal light" of revelation, which was only another name for "enthusiasm," because it could not bear the test of reason, "the last judge and guide in every thing." In his essay, "Of Superstition and Enthusiasm" (1742), Hume [5] helped to perpetuate the tradition: "Hope, pride, presumption, a warm imagination, together with ignorance, are, therefore, the true sources of ENTHUSIASM." Here the close relationship between imagination and enthusiasm is made explicit. In his commendation of Congreve for having cured poetry of "Pindarick madness," Dr. Johnson (1780) [6] implies an equally close relationship between them. Congreve, he says, "has shewn us that en-

---

1. *A Large Account of the Taste in Poetry*, in Durham, p. 118.
2. *Reflections Critical and Satyrical*, etc., in Durham, p. 240.
3. *The English Works of Thomas Hobbes*, ed. Sir William Molesworth (London: 1839–1845), III, 102.
4. (London: Routledge, 1905), IV, xix, 595.
5. *Essays*, ed. Green and Grose (1898), I, 145.
6. *Life of Congreve*, in *Lives of the English Poets*, ed. G. B. Hill (Oxford: 1905), II, 234.

thusiasm has its rules, and that in mere confusion there is neither grace nor greatness." The word "enthusiasm" has disappeared, but a writer in *The Monthly Magazine* [1] for 1797 is apparently still talking about it when he asserts that "it is only by bringing our feelings to the standard of reason, that we can determine whether they ought to be indulged."

Judgment and wit, fancy and imagination — these are the two pairs of twins that caused so much mischief. Locke (1689) had furnished the philosophical and literary worlds with a useful and accurate description of "judgment": it "lies," he said,[2] "in separating carefully one from another ideas wherein can be found the least difference, thereby to avoid being misled by similitude and by affinity to take one thing for another." Addison (May 11, 1711) [3] accepted this view, and Alexander Gerard (1759) [4] was apparently remembering it when he said that judgment is "the faculty which distinguishes things different, separates truth from falsehood, and compares together objects and their qualities." Gerard's definition conveyed the common acceptation of the word.

There was more difficulty with the word "wit." Like "nature," it was used by everyone, and often with equal vagueness. Dennis wondered what Pope meant by it in these lines of *An Essay on Criticism* (1711): [5]

> What is this Wit, which must our cares employ?
> The owner's wife, that other men enjoy;
> Then most our trouble still when most admir'd,
> And still the more we give, the more requir'd.

---

1. III, 273 ("The Enquirer," No. 12).
2. *An Essay Concerning Human Understanding*, II, xi, 102.
3. *The Spectator*, No. 62.   4. *An Essay on Taste*, p. 90.
5. Ed. Ward, ll. 500–503.

"What," asked Dennis (1711),[1] "does he mean by acquir'd Wit? Does he mean Genius by the word Wit, or
Conceit and Point?" and concluded that he should not mean
either of these things. Again it was Locke (1689) who had
supplied a meaning that could be relied upon. "Wit," as
he had used the word, had a clear and definite meaning,
which was logically distinguishable from "judgment." He[2]
had found wit to be "lying most in the assemblage of
ideas, and putting those together with quickness and
variety wherein can be found any resemblance or congruity, thereby to make up pleasant pictures and agreeable visions in the fancy." This explanation occurs in the
same place as the explanation of judgment, and Addison
(May 11, 1711)[3] accepted both. Lewis Theobald (1733)[4]
found Locke's explanation of wit so agreeable that he
simply lifted it bodily, with the change of only three words,
and set it down as his own. The fact that Theobald, like a
monarch, could invade Locke with impunity indicates that
those who read prefaces to Shakespeare did not read philosophy, and probably did not care about rigorous definition. It may also help to explain why "wit" was used so
cavalierly by the literary.

But though "wit" was loosely used it had a strict sense
that anyone who knew enough or cared enough might
employ. The words "fancy" and "imagination" were
in worse case. Addison may not have been the dilettante

1. *Reflections Critical and Satyrical*, etc., in Durham, p. 239.
2. *An Essay Concerning Human Understanding*, II, xi, 102.
3. *The Spectator*, No. 62.
4. *Preface to Shakespeare*, in Smith, pp. 84–85: "Besides, *Wit* lying mostly in
the Assemblage of *Ideas*, and in the putting Those together with Quickness and
Variety, wherein can be found any Resemblance, or Congruity, to make up
pleasant Pictures, and agreeable Visions in the Fancy; the Writer, who aims at
Wit, must of course range far and wide for Materials."

that Mr. T. S. Eliot[1] considers him to have been, but it must be confessed that he did not display great perspicacity in the following remarks on the two words. What he says,[2] though it is not highly illuminating, is of some historical interest, and is given at length.

By the Pleasures of the Imagination or Fancy (which I shall use promiscuously) I here mean such as arise from visible Objects, either when we have them actually in our View, or when we call up their Ideas into our Minds by Paintings, Statues, Descriptions, or any the like Occasion. We cannot indeed have a single Image in the Fancy that did not make its first Entrance through the Sight: but we have the Power of retaining, altering and compounding those Images, which we have once received, into all the Varieties of Picture and Vision that are most agreeable to the Imagination; for by this Faculty a Man in a Dungeon is capable of entertaining himself with Scenes and Landskips more beautiful than any that can be found in the whole Compass of Nature.

There are few Words in the *English* Language which are employed in a more loose and uncircumscribed Sense than those of the *Fancy* and the *Imagination*. I therefore thought it necessary to fix and determine the Notion of these two Words, as I intend to make use of them in the Thread of my following Speculations. ... I must therefore desire [the reader] to remember, that by the Pleasures of the Imagination, I mean only such Pleasures as arise originally from Sight, and that I divide these Pleasures into two Kinds: My Design being first of all to discourse of those Primary Pleasures of the Imagination, which entirely proceed from such Objects as are before our Eyes; and in the next place to speak of those Secondary Pleasures of the Imagination which flow from the Ideas of visible Objects, when the Objects are not actually before the Eye, but are called up into our Memories, or formed

1. See *The Use of Poetry and the Use of Criticism* (Cambridge, Massachusetts: 1933), pp. 51–54.
2. *The Spectator*, No. 411 (June 20, 1712).

into agreeable Visions of Things that are either Absent or
Fictitious.

The Pleasures of the Imagination, taken in the full Extent,
are not so gross as those of Sense, nor so refined as those of the
Understanding. The last are, indeed, more preferable, because
they are founded on some new Knowledge or Improvement in
the Mind of Man; yet it must be confest, that those of the Imagination are as great and as transporting as the other.

James Beattie (1783),[1] although he admits that the two
words "are not perfectly synonymous" as commonly used,
decides not to distinguish them, because they "are often,
and by the best writers, used indiscriminately." He *does*,
however, make a feeble effort to distinguish them, but
none to define them: "They are, indeed, names for the
same faculty; but the former seems to be applied to the
more solemn, and the latter to the more trivial, exertions
of it. A witty author is a man of lively Fancy; but a sublime poet is said to possess a vast Imagination."

Beattie here throws as much light on the eighteenth-
century meaning of the words as anyone seemed capable of
throwing. It is dim, but not so dim as Addison's. What it
reveals is that the "fancy" — and the "imagination" also
by indiscrimination — is "trivial" and closely related to
"wit." Both faculties were often looked upon as the gift
of the Evil One to mankind, and, as Milton had taught
long before, in opposition to reason, or judgment. "The
question is," wrote Shaftesbury (1711),[2] "whether they
[the fancies] shall have it wholly to themselves, or whether
they shall acknowledge some controller or manager. If

1. *Dissertations Moral and Critical*, I, 87.
2. *Characteristics*, ed. Robertson (1900), I, 208. Compare Dennis, *A Large
Account of the Taste in Poetry* (1702), in Durham, p. 130: "It is not Wit, but
Reason and Judgment, which distinguish a man of Sense from a Fool."

none, 'tis this, I fear, which leads to madness. 'Tis this, and nothing else, which can be called madness or loss of reason. For if Fancy be left judge of anything, she must be judge of all. . . . 'Tis by means therefore of a controller and corrector of fancy that I am saved from being mad."

Much the same thing was true of wit,

> For wit and judgment often are at strife,
> Tho' meant each other's aid, like man and wife.[1]

It was "false wit," not "true wit," of course, that was thus at strife with judgment. True wit consisted in the "assemblage" of proper ideas, false wit of improper ideas, — "in the Resemblance and Congruity sometimes of single Letters, as in Anagrams, Chronograms, Lipograms, and Acrosticks: Sometimes of Syllables, as in Ecchos and Doggerel Rhymes: Sometimes of Words, as in Punns and Quibbles." [2] The eighteenth century was never more satisfied with itself for having made an improvement over past ages than it was for having improved punning out of existence. It "delighted our ancestors," said Shaftesbury (1711),[3] ". . . but 'tis now banished the town, and all good company," and it remained in banishment throughout the century. Shakespeare's "descending beneath himself" in this respect "may have proceeded from a Deference paid to the then *reigning Barbarism*," Theobald (1733) [4] magnanimously allowed. The century agreed to rest its case here, but it did not agree to avoid iteration. A five-foot shelf would not contain the excuses that were made for

1. Pope, *An Essay on Criticism*, ed. Ward, ll. 82–83.
2. Addison, *The Spectator*, No. 62 (May 11, 1711).
3. *Characteristics*, ed. Robertson, I, 46.
4. *Preface to Shakespeare*, in Smith, p. 73.

his "miserable Punns" [1] — at the expense of "the vicious taste of [his] age." [2]

In the preceding chapter [3] it was pointed out that some critics attacked the rules on the ground that many of them were merely "ornamental" and "convenient," and insisted that only the "essential" and "fundamental" rules were worthy of observance. The attitude of these men was rationalistic. The ornamental rules, they were apt to maintain, like the fancy and false wit, were the enemies of reason. Farquhar (1702), dogmatically as was usual with him, flatly denied that the rules of Aristotle were "the pure effect of his immense Reason." "If his Rules of Poetry," he said,[4] "were drawn from certain and immutable Principles, and fix'd on the Basis of Nature; why shou'd not his *Ars Poetica* be as efficacious now, as it was two Thousand Years ago? And why shou'd not a single Plot, with perfect Unity of Time and Place, do as well at *Lincolns-Inn-Fields*, as at the Play-house in *Athens*. No, no, Sir, I am apt to believe that the Philosopher took no such Pains in Poetry as you imagine." About some rules Dr. Johnson was in agreement with Farquhar. Fancy, indeed, the exact opposite of reason, was responsible for them. "Criticism," he asserts,[5] "has sometimes permitted fancy to dictate the laws by which fancy ought to be restrained, and fallacy to perplex the principles by which fallacy is to be detected." Such laws, to use Fielding's (1749)

1. Sir Thomas Hanmer (?), *Some Remarks on the Tragedy of Hamlet Prince of Denmark, written by Mr. William Shakespeare* (London: 1736), p. 50.

2. Hanmer, *Preface to Shakespeare* (1744), in Smith, p. 94.

3. See pp. 84–85.

4. *A Discourse upon Comedy*, in Durham, p. 269.

5. *The Rambler*, No. 156. The phrasing of the sentence is not that of the first collected edition of 1751–1752, but represents Johnson's revision. The sense is that of the original version (September 14, 1751).

words,[1] "have not the least foundation in truth or nature," that is to say, in reason. They are arbitrary [2] and capricious, both of which attributes are proper, not to reason, but to fancy.

Oddly enough, however, these very laws, capricious and fanciful though they might be, were bad also because they restrained the fancy. The hard-headed Dr. Johnson (September 21, 1751),[3] again, was of this opinion. He is worth quoting in full.

CRITICISM, though dignified from the earliest Ages by the Labours of Men eminent for Knowledge and Sagacity, and since the Revival of polite Literature, the favourite Study of *European* Scholars, has not yet attained the Certainty and Stability of Science. The Rules, that have been hitherto received, are seldom drawn from any settled Principle or self-evident Postulate, nor are adapted to the natural and invariable Constitution of Things; but will be found upon Examination to be the arbitrary Edicts of Dictators exalted by their own Authority, who out of many Means by which the same End may be attained, selected those which happened to occur to their own Reflection, and then by an Edict, which Idleness and Timidity were willing to obey, prohibited any new Experiments of Wit, restrained Fancy from the Indulgence of her innate Inclination to hazard and adventure, and condemned all future Flights of Genius to pursue the Path of the *Meonian* Eagle.

After this glimpse at the Protean eighteenth-century mind, nothing should surprise us.

1. *Tom Jones*, V, i.
2. Compare Hanmer (?), *Some Remarks on the Tragedy of Hamlet* (1736), pp. 1–2: "I am going to do what to some may appear extravagant, but by those of a true Taste in Works of Genius will be approv'd of. I intend to examine one of the Pieces of the greatest Tragick Writers [*sic*] that ever liv'd, (except *Sophocles* and *Euripides*,) according to the Rules of Reason and Nature, without having any regard to those Rules established by Arbitrary Dogmatising Criticks, only as they can be brought to bear that Test."   3. *The Rambler*, No. 158.

It is not surprising, for example, that true wit, which consisted in the "Resemblance and Congruity of Ideas," [1] was not opposed to judgment. Wit was, on the contrary, Nature herself — in Sunday clothes.

> True Wit is Nature to advantage dress'd,
> What oft was thought, but ne'er so well express'd.[2]

Dennis (1711) [3] could not "conceive how any one can have store of Wit without Judgment," which seems to mean that they are the concave and convex surfaces of the curve of the human mind. Gildon (1718),[4] a rationalist if ever there was one, believed that "Judgment without Wit, is cold and heavy," so that for him wit was a kind of necessary yeast.

The same kind of nice harmony marked the relations of fancy, or imagination, and judgment. Imagination lent a grace to truth, Bishop Berkeley (June 9, 1713),[5] the idealist, appropriately believed:

Those Parts of Learning which relate to the Imagination, as Eloquence and Poetry, produce an immediate Pleasure in the Mind. And sublime and useful Truths, when they are conveyed in apt Allegories or beautiful Images, make more distinct and lasting Impressions; by which means the Fancy becomes subservient to the Understanding, and the Mind is at the same time delighted and instructed.

1. Addison, *The Spectator*, No. 62 (May 11, 1711).
2. Pope, *An Essay on Criticism* (1711), ed. Ward, ll. 297–298.
3. *Reflections Critical and Satyrical*, etc., in Durham, p. 229. He is commenting on the following lines in Pope's *Essay on Criticism* (ll. 80–81):

> "There are whom Heav'n has blest with store of wit,
> Yet want as much again to manage it."

Ward (*The Poetical Works of Alexander Pope* [1924], p. 51 n.) prints these lines as a variation of the following lines:

> "Some, to whom Heav'n in wit has been profuse,
> Want as much more, to turn it to its use."

4. *The Complete Art of Poetry*, I, 71.   5. *The Guardian*, No. 77.

Pope did not outdo Gildon (1718), for whereas the one said that wit was nature dressed to advantage, the other [1] said as much for fancy: "Fancy is what we generally call *Nature*, or a *Genius*; *Judgment* is what we mean by Art, the Union of which in one Man makes a complete Poet." Each was absolutely dependent on the other. Dr. Johnson did not go so far as Gildon; but in his *Life of Milton* (1780) [2] he defined poetry as "the art of uniting pleasure with truth, by calling imagination to the help of reason"; and in his *Life of Roscommon* (1779) [3] he declared it "ridiculous to oppose judgement to imagination; for it does not appear that men have necessarily less of one as they have more of the other."

But though judgment, or reason, functioned best and most gracefully when it was aided by wit and fancy, there was no doubt in the mind of the rationalist, or of the neo-classicist in his rationalistic phases, that reason was superior to wit and fancy. It was the "controller and corrector," the guarantor of sanity, and detector of truth; and "truth," Shaftesbury (1711) [4] wrote, "is the most powerful thing in the world, since even fiction itself must be governed by it, and can only please by its resemblance." This generalization about fiction held particularly for dramatic fiction; because, said an anonymous writer in 1760,[5] "since a Drama is a representation, there can be no truth or reality in it; but some method must be contrived to supply the

1. Gildon, *The Complete Art of Poetry*, I, 125; see also I, 97.
2. *Lives of the English Poets*, ed. Hill, I, 170.   3. I, 235.
4. *Characteristics*, ed Robertson, I, 6. Compare John Upton, *Critical Observations on Shakespeare* (London: 1746), p. 96: "But 'tis truth, or it's resemblance, that gives the pleasure."
5. *An Essay upon the Present State of the Theatre in France, England and Italy*, etc. (London: 1760), p. 81.

place of truth, for men require truth, or something that has a resemblance to it." These are reaffirmations of the hoary doctrine of verisimilitude, which had a vigorous old age. The verisimilar was still considered good in the eighteenth century because it was probable.

The question was how much like truth fiction ought to be in order to be accepted as probable by reason. You could say, as did Alexander Gerard (1759),[1] that "improbability, which is a want of resemblance to natural things, always renders a fable or story less entertaining; and if the improbability be very great, or extend to the material parts, it often makes it wholly nauseous"; but you would not be very helpful if you did not define "natural." Or you could say with James Beattie (1783)[2] that "in works of fiction, a like regard is to be had to probability; and no events are to be introduced, but such as, according to the general opinion of the people to whom they are addressed, may be supposed to happen"; but again you would not be very helpful if you did not know whether, in the opinion of the people to whom works of fiction are addressed, probable impossibilities are preferred to improbable possibilities, — if you did not know what your audience supposed capable of happening. Aristotle[3] limits us to a choice between universal events ("what may happen,— what is possible according to the law of probability or necessity") and particular events ("what has happened"), and throws the weight of his authority in favor of the first. But if you were looking for a definition of probable events you would find no help in Aristotle, for if you

1. *An Essay on Taste,* p. 51.
2. *Dissertations Moral and Critical,* I, 223.
3. *Poetics,* IX, 1–4.

defined them as universal events your definition was tautological. Gildon (1718),[1] nevertheless, preferred tautology to heterodoxy, "*Generals*" to "*Particulars*." He merely paraphrased Aristotle. Like Aristotle also he admitted [2] that the poet "has the same Right to this Name, when he presents us with true *Incidents*, provided that these true *Incidents* have the Poetic Qualities of Verisimilitude, and that Possibility which is requir'd by the Art, which indeed are very rare; and therefore a Fable wholly fictitious will generally be more Poetic, as well as more easily adapted to Nature and Art, than any that History does afford." Joseph Warton (1756) decided in favor of "particulars," being convinced, no doubt, that "what has happened is manifestly possible" [3] and therefore probable. "Events that have actually happened," he thought,[4] "are, after all, the properest subjects for poetry. . . . In the best-conducted fiction, some mark of improbability and incoherence will still appear." Because ancient romancers had recounted events that had never happened, though not, of course, as a result of Aristotle's teaching, their fictions were utterly improbable, and because modern romancers had confined themselves to events that *had happened*, or at least *could happen*, their fictions were utterly dull. In *The Castle of Otranto* [5] Horace Walpole (1765) tried "to reconcile the two kinds." "It was an attempt to blend the two kinds of Romance, the ancient and the modern. In the former, all was imagination and improbability: in the latter, nature is always intended to be, and sometimes has

1. *The Complete Art of Poetry*, I, 234–235.
2. I, 236.
3. Aristotle, *Poetics*, IX, 6.
4. Warton, *An Essay on Pope* (1756), I, 253–254.
5. See the "Preface" to the second edition (London: 1765), p. vi.

been, copied with success. Invention has not been want-ing; but the great resources of fancy have been dammed up, by a strict adherence to common life. But if in the latter species Nature has cramped imagination, she did but take her revenge, having been totally excluded from old Ro-mances." There were three possibilities, then. You could be Aristotelian with Gildon, largely anti-Aristotelian with Warton, or a modern hybrid with Walpole.

What you could not afford to be was incredible, for if you were you destroyed the possibility of illusion, or delusion,[1] which it is one of the chief functions of art to induce. Of course there were some tough-minded critics who were con-vinced that fiction, especially dramatic fiction, never in-duces belief in its reality. "The Poet," Farquhar (1702) wrote,[2] "expects no more that you should believe the Plot of his Play, than old *Æsop* design'd the World shou'd think his *Eagle* and *Lyon* talk'd like you and I." Hurd (1749) agreed that in a tragedy "the representation, how-ever distressful, is still seen to be a representation." [3] Pye (1792) said [4] that the source of "the false reasoning of the French critics" lay in "the mistaken notion that dramatic imitation ever was, or ever could be a real deception." This extreme skeptical view is rationalism *par excellence*,

1. For a further discussion of delusion see below, pp. 205–216.
2. *A Discourse upon Comedy*, in Durham, p. 281.
3. Note on l. 103 of Horace's *Art of Poetry*, ed. Hurd, in *Works* (1811), I, 119. In non-dramatic poetry, however, Hurd (*Letters on Chivalry and Romance* [1762], ed. Morley, p. 144) was willing to be deceived: "Critics may talk what they will of *Truth and Nature*, and abuse the Italian poets, as they will, for transgressing both in their incredible fictions. But believe it, my friend, these fictions with which they have studied to delude the world, are of that kind of creditable de-ceits, of which a wise antient pronounces with assurance, '*That they, who deceive, are honester than they who do not deceive; and they, who are deceived, wiser than they who are not deceived.*'"
4. *A Commentary Illustrating the Poetic of Aristotle*, p. 136.

and comes near to a confession that the probable is never probable enough.

Rationalism begins to shade off when the possibility of belief is granted. Hurd, who, in 1749, had seemed to doubt the possibility, insisted [1] upon belief in 1762: "We must first *believe*, before we can be *affected*." But before we can believe in a dramatic action, he said,[2] "that, which passes in *representation* and challenges, as it were, the scrutiny of the eye, must be truth itself, or something very nearly approaching to it." Because it is true that "to feel we must first believe," wrote Edward Taylor (1774),[3] who seems to have written with Hurd at his elbow, it is essential that "the tragic poet . . . adhere strictly to veresimilitude, not only in the subject of the drama, but in the conduct of it." The same, also, was William Cooke's opinion (1775), "for," he said,[4] "though we know we are to be deceived, and we desire to be so, no reasonable man was ever yet deceived, but with a probability of truth." This was still pure rationalism, and it was still a faith in verisimilitude. Those with eyes to see, however, might have seen something to shake their faith. For if you *insist* upon belief you may find yourself irrationally believing in the improbable.

It is true that as late as 1780 William Hodson [5] was of the opinion "that all the powers of Shakespeare cannot now preserve the witches in Macbeth," and that he gave "the

1. *Letters on Chivalry and Romance*, ed. Morley, p. 139.
2. P. 140. Compare Thomas Blackwell, *An Enquiry into the Life and Writings of Homer* (London: 1735), p. 286: "'Tis the Traces of *Truth* that are only irresistible." And p. 290: "The Fiction every now and then discovers its cloven foot, betrays its Dissimilitude to Truth, and tho' never so willing, we *cannot* believe."
3. *Cursory Remarks on Tragedy*, p. 2.
4. *The Elements of Dramatic Criticism* (London: 1775), p. 81.
5. "Observations on Tragedy," bound with *Zoraida*, p. 87 n.

ghost in Hamlet, and those in Richard" only a limited time to live. It is true that in 1781 James Harris [1] praised the *Oedipus Tyrannus* and Lillo's *Fatal Curiosity* for getting along "without the help of Machines, Deities, Prodigies, Spectres, or any thing else, incomprehensible, or incredible." But it is also true that as early as 1709 Nicholas Rowe [2] had shown a dangerous and hair-brained capacity for believing in the marvels of *The Tempest*: "I am very sensible that he do's, in this play, depart too much from that likeness to truth which ought to be observ'd in these sort of writings; yet he do's it so very finely, that one is easily drawn in to have more faith for his sake, than reason does well allow of." By 1749 the critics' fear of the supernatural had become the butt of Fielding's laughter,[3] which was both Homeric and satiric.

The only supernatural agents which can in any manner be allowed to us moderns, are ghosts; but of these I would advise an author to be extremely sparing. These are indeed, like arsenic, and other dangerous drugs in physic, to be used with the utmost caution; nor would I advise the introduction of them at all in those works, or by those authors, to which, or to whom, a horse-laugh in the reader would be any great prejudice or mortification.

As for elves and fairies, and other such mummery, I purposely omit the mention of them, as I should be very unwilling to confine within any bounds those surprising imaginations, for whose vast capacity the limits of human nature are too narrow; whose works are to be considered as a new creation; and who have consequently just right to do what they will with their own.

These two paragraphs, in isolation, may, by the perverse, be interpreted at their face value as indictments of supernatural machinery, but in their context, where Fielding

---

1. *Philological Inquiries*, p. 157.
2. *Some Account of the Life &c. of Mr. William Shakespear*, in Smith, p. 14.
3. *Tom Jones*, VIII, i.

completely boxes the compass of opinion concerning the probable and improbable, they are clearly satirical. His conclusion clinches the matter: "As a genius of the highest rank observes in his fifth chapter of the Bathos, 'The great art of all poetry is to mix truth with fiction, in order to join the credible with the surprizing.'" Gray,[1] in 1751, thought it perfectly possible "by good management" to render "*verisimile*" even "such absurd stories as the Tempest, the Witches in Macbeth, or the Fairies in the Midsummer Night's Dream." George Colman,[2] in 1761, said that "dramatick Nature is of a more large and liberal quality than they [modern critics] are willing to allow," and considered it the poet's proper business "to body forth, by the Powers of Imagination, the forms of things unknown, and to give to airy Nothing a local Habitation and a Name." By 1769 even the reviewers had caught up with the times, and *The Monthly Review*[3] asserted that Shakespeare "never carried his preternatural beings beyond the limits of popular tradition, but ghosts, fairies, goblins, and elves, gave as much of the sublime and marvellous to his fictions, as nymphs, satyrs, and fawns to the works of antiquity." From this time on to the end of the century, despite Hodsons and Harrises, the ability to believe in the improbabilities of Shakespeare grew rapidly. The older rationalism faded visibly.

Aside from the fact that there continued to be an obstinate few who refused to be taken in by the absurdities of Shakespeare, and that some, notably Dr. Johnson,[4]

1. "Mr. Gray's Remarks on the Letters prefixed to Mason's Elfrida," in *The Works of Thomas Gray*, ed. Mitford (1858), IV, 3.
2. *Critical Reflections on the Old English Dramatick Writers*, in *Prose on Several Occasions*, II, 116–117.   3. XLI, 140.
4. See below, pp. 209–211.

steadfastly denied any degree of deception in the drama, however probable it might be made by the studious observance of verisimilitude, the belief that deception took place and was eminently desirable consistently gained ground. This belief was shared by men who otherwise disagreed about almost everything, and who disagreed especially about what constituted the probable and the verisimilar. Dennis,[1] as far back as 1693, had granted "that there is an occasion for us to give way to a wholsome delusion, if we design to receive either delight or profit from the *Drama*." By mid-century, critics were giving way on every hand. Lord Chesterfield (1752)[2] was "very willing" to see tragedy "with a degree of self-deception." Ten years later the judicious Lord Kames (1762)[3] asserted briefly that "it is of importance to employ every means that may promote the delusion." William Hodson (1780), who refused his countenance to Shakespeare's witches and ghosts, "willingly" submitted[4] "to the deceit" of supposing the dramatic scene "some place which it is not." James Harris, who disliked "machines" and "prodigies," easily confessed[5] that his incredulity vanished before the magic of Garrick's acting. And, finally, Twining (1789),[6] whose edition of the *Poetics* was generally admired, gave a kind of official sanction to poetic deceit by writing of the master as follows:

1. *The Impartial Critic*, in Spingarn, *Critical Essays of the Seventeenth Century*, III, 189.
2. *The Letters of Philip Dormer Stanhope, 4th Earl of Chesterfield*, ed. Bonamy Dobrée (London: 1932), V, 1821.
3. *The Elements of Criticism* (2nd ed., London: 1763), III, 260.
4. "Observations on Tragedy," bound with *Zoraida*, p. 85.
5. *Philological Inquiries*, p. 108.
6. *Aristotle's Treatise on Poetry*, pp. xv–xvi.

He never loses sight of the *end* of Poetry, which, in conformity to common sense, he held to be *pleasure*. He is ready to excuse, not only impossibilities, but even absurdities, where that *end* appears to be better answered with them, than it would have been without them. In a word, he asserts the privileges of Poetry, and gives her free range to employ her *whole* power, and to do all she *can* do — that is, to impose upon the imagination, by whatever means, as far as imagination, for the sake of its own pleasure, will consent to be imposed upon. Poetry can do no more than this, and, from its very nature and end, ought not to be required to do less. If it is our interest to be cheated, it is her duty to cheat us. The critic, who suffers his philosophy to reason away his pleasure, is not much wiser than the child, who cuts open his drum, to see what it is within that caused the sound.

After this, nothing more needed to be said. If to accept the improbable was more reasonable than to reject it, he who was pleased only with the probable was mad. The gates through which fancy, imagination, and emotion might enter had swung wide open, and through them the sunny and irregular groves of another country could be seen by anyone who cared to look.

They had begun to open, it should be evident by now, long before Twining gave them their final push in 1789. Pope, though his neo-classic fingers may have itched to get at them, had caught a glimpse of the "natural" groves by 1715. His words [1] should be quoted in full:

It is the Invention that in different degrees distinguishes all great Genius's: The utmost Stretch of human Study, Learning, and Industry, which masters every thing besides, can never attain to this. It furnishes Art with all her Materials, and without it Judgment itself can at best but *steal wisely*: For Art is only like a prudent Steward that lives on managing the Riches of Nature. Whatever Praises may be given to Works of Judgment,

1. Preface to *The Iliad*, in Durham, pp. 323–324.

there is not even a single Beauty in them but is owing to the Invention: As in the most regular Gardens, however Art may carry the greatest Appearance, there is not a Plant or Flower but is the Gift of Nature. The first can only reduce the Beauties of the latter into a more obvious Figure, which the common Eye may better take in, and is therefore more entertain'd with. And perhaps the reason why most Criticks are inclin'd to prefer a judicious and methodical Genius to a great and fruitful one, is, because they find it easier for themselves to pursue their Observations through an uniform and bounded Walk of Art, than to comprehend the vast and various Extent of Nature.

Here, as in 1711, art is "Nature methodiz'd," but the significant fact is that the emphasis has shifted from the methodizing to nature, which is aligned with invention in opposition to judgment. On May 28, 1751, Dr. Johnson [1] observed, not as one who wished to reprove, but as one who was stating a known and natural fact that should not be neglected, that "Imagination, a licentious and vagrant Faculty, impatient of Limitations and unsusceptible of Restraint, has always endeavoured to baffle the Logician, to perplex the Confines of Distinction, and burst the Inclosures of Regularity." Such conduct, he said, is the prerogative of the imagination of "every new Genius." Hurd,[2] in 1762, was more outspoken. He condemned unequivocally the rationalistic revolution that had driven the fanciful "tales of faery" into exile. "What we have gotten by this revolution, you will say, is a great deal of good sense. What we have lost, is a world of fine fabling."

In 1711 Dennis [3] expressed his disapproval of the dominance of imagination over judgment, but he was talking

1. *The Rambler*, No. 125.
2. *Letters on Chivalry and Romance*, ed. Morley, p. 154.
3. See above, p. 103.

then of the kind of imagination that manifests itself in such diseases as religious enthusiasm. He was far from disapproving of the active poetic imagination that inspires, or the passive imagination that is capable of experiencing, "Enthusiastick Passion, or Enthusiasm"; for "the greater Poetry," he asserted (1704),[1] "is an Art by which a Poet justly and reasonably excites great Passion." Poetry, said Thomas Blackwell (1735)[2] also, raises a "Commotion in the Soul," which it is not the part of reason to still: "It would be like prying into the Author of *Fairy-Favours*, which deprives the curious Enquirer of his present Enjoyment." The emotions so raised are often so subtle that "they cannot bear to be stared at, and far less to be criticized, and taken to pieces." Joseph Warton (1756)[3] wondered "whether, that philosophical, that geometrical, and systematical spirit so much in vogue, which has spread itself from the sciences even into polite literature, by consulting only REASON, has not diminished and destroyed SENTIMENT; and made our poets write from and to the HEAD rather than the HEART." The prestige of imagination and emotion grew rapidly during the second half of the century, largely as a result of Shakespeare's increasing fame. Such phrases as "unrestrained Warmth of Imagination," "daring flights of imagination," and "divine fire" were on other tongues besides those of John Brown,[4] James Plumptre,[5] and Mrs. Montagu.[6]

---

1. *The Grounds of Criticism in Poetry*, in Durham, pp. 150, 151.
2. *An Enquiry into the Life and Writings of Homer*, pp. 154, 155.
3. *An Essay on Pope*, I, 204.
4. *Essays on the Characteristics of the Earl of Shaftesbury* (2nd ed., London: 1751), p. 34.
5. *An Appendix to Observations on Hamlet* (1797), p. 64.
6. *An Essay on the Writings and Genius of Shakespear* (1769), p. 7.

The enjoyment of "sentiment," however, and of "daring flights of imagination" was the special privilege of the advocates of taste; not the taste of the more liberal rationalists, which has already been discussed,[1] but that of the men of "feeling" and instinctive insight. The more exaggerated types of this kind of esthete were the objects of constant ridicule. They "are generally Talkers," wrote Steele in *The Englishman* (October 20, 1713),[2] "of glittering Fancies, and hurried Imaginations; who despise Art and Method, who admire what was never said before, and affect the Character of *Wits*." The word "taste" as these men used it, thought Fielding (January 14, 1752),[3] could be defined as "the present Whim of the Town, whatever it be." An anonymous writer for *The Connoisseur* (August 26, 1756) [4] ironically felicitated the age for possessing such people and such a faculty:

> BLEST age! when all men may procure
> The title of a Connoisseur;
> When noble and ignoble herd
> Are govern'd by a single word;
>
> Tho', like the royal *German* dames,
> It bears an hundred Christian names;
> As Genius, Fancy, Judgment, *Goût*,
> Whim, Caprice, *Je ne sçai quoi*, *Virtù*:
> Which appellations all describe
> TASTE, and the modern tasteful tribe.

Serious descriptions of taste came from the very citadel of reason itself. Pope (1711) [5] celebrates the "nameless graces which no methods teach." Addison (June 19,

---

1. See above, pp. 110–112.
2. No. 7.
3. *The Covent-Garden Journal*, ed. Jensen, No. 4.
4. Ed. Colman and Thornton, No. 135.
5. *An Essay on Criticism*, ed. Ward, l. 144.

1712),[1] who, of course, did not consider taste irrational, defines it as "*that Faculty of the Soul, which discerns the Beauties of an Author with Pleasure, and the Imperfections with Dislike.*" Addison [2] believed that it was possible to train the taste. Tamworth Reresby (1721),[3] who writes as if he ought to believe the same thing, really denies that it can be trained. His is the attitude of the anti-rational school:

> When we have a *fine Taste* by *Nature*, Instructions, or Comments . . . seem superfluous. What we dignify with this Title, is a *natural Sentiment, inherent in the Soul,* and altogether independent of the *Sciences. A good Taste is a certain Relation betwixt the Mind and the Object*: Or, in other Terms, *a Sort of Instinct of right Reason, which directs us better than all Rules and Arguments whatsoever.*

Similar to Reresby's view was that of Leonard Welsted (1724).[4] He did not rule out reason altogether, but he maintained that there was a difference between "poetical" and "mathematical" reason. Taste, moreover, could not be trained. Men either are or are not born "with the Talent of judging . . . and to go about to pedagogue a Man into this sort of Knowledge, who has not the Seeds of it in himself, is the same thing, as if one should endeavour to teach an Art of seeing without Eyes."

It is sometimes said [5] that the non-rationalistic, if not anti-rationalistic, meaning of the word "taste," such as

1. *The Spectator*, No. 409.
2. See above, pp. 78–79.
3. *A Miscellany of Ingenious Thoughts and Reflections, in Verse and Prose* (London: 1721), p. 371.
4. *A Dissertation Concerning the Perfection of the English Language*, etc., in Durham, pp. 366, 367.
5. See, for example, Bosker, *Literary Criticism in the Age of Johnson* (1930), p. 138.

that of Reresby and Welsted, was supplanted during the second half of the century by the rationalistic meaning. This view appears to be mistaken, as one might suspect *a priori* after watching the revolt against reason gain momentum. It is true that many men, up to the end of the century, continued to believe that taste was subservient to reason; but it is equally true that many denied this subservience and maintained, not only the separate, but the antagonistic, status of taste. To demonstrate the truth of this statement it will be excusable to quote two late critics at some length. The first is Vicesimus Knox (1777): [1]

I cannot help thinking, that the effect which a literary work is found to produce is the best criterion of its merit; and that sentiment or feeling, after all that has been urged by theoretical critics, is the ultimate and infallible touchstone to appreciate with precision the works of taste and genius. Theoretical criticism constitutes, indeed, a very ingenious species of writing; but before I can be really pleased with a poem or a piece of oratory, I must feel its excellence. . . .

Some men are distinguished by a superior sensibility and a delicacy of taste, others for an acute and logical understanding: those are formed to excel in criticism, and these in philosophy. The provinces are separate; and it must be allowed, that philosophy has oftener invaded the province of criticism, than criticism of philosophy. Philosophy may, indeed, derive much and valuable matter from philology; but she will assimilate it to herself, and the whole will yet be philosophy. She must allow criticism to judge by a test the least fallible, when applied to works of imagination and sentiment, — the genuine feelings of improved and cultivated nature.

A little later [2] he expresses his admiration for "the philosophical criticism" of Aristotle, the Scottish critics, and

1. *Essays, Moral and Literary* (London: 1808), I, 164, 165.
2. I, 167.

of Hurd and Harris; but it is, after all, in his opinion, philosophy, not criticism, and consequently inferior, as criticism, to "the works of Longinus, Bouhours, and Addison." The second of these late critics is Belsham (1789): [1]

The end of poetry is to please; and it is by an appeal to taste, and not to reason, that the question must be decided whether that end be actually attained. To decry all rules of poetical composition as impertinent or useless, would nevertheless be running into a very absurd extreme. As there is a certain degree of uniformity in our mental feelings and perceptions, there is a real foundation for that uniformity; and it is both entertaining and instructive, by any fair process of induction, to point out the immediate, though we cannot trace the ultimate causes of those uniform emotions of disgust or admiration; which is in effect to point out the means of avoiding or exciting them. Or, in other words, it is to establish certain fixed rules of composition upon the authority of experience; but the pedantry of appealing to speculative principles in opposition to the decisions of taste, and the vanity of attempting to demonstrate by argument, in defiance of feeling, that men ought or ought not to admire, are equally to be avoided.

Knox and Belsham, to be sure, are not in favor of wallowing in pure emotion or in following "uncultivated" instinct, but neither are they willing to submit everything to the test of reason. They represent the prevailing mood of the late eighteenth century better than Kames or Johnson represent it. It is easier to see the coming romanticism

---

1. *Essays Philosophical and Moral*, etc. (2nd ed., 1799), II, 494. He condemns Kames on this ground. *The Critical Review* (LXVIII [1789], 464) approved of Belsham's position: "We are persuaded that there is no rule the correctest taste can suggest, which may not be explained: but we will not put philosophy on so despotic a throne, as to reject what she cannot explain. In subjects of taste, the ultimate decision should belong to taste alone; and we shall regret only that the philosophy is so little cultivated, as to be unequal to the explanation."

in them than it is to see it in *The Elements of Criticism* or the *Preface to Shakespeare*.[1]

With this summary account of the revolt against the early emphasis upon reason and judgment the preliminaries close. The remaining chapters will trace the effect of this general upheaval on one branch of neo-classic theory, the theory of tragedy.

1. *The Critical Review* (XX [1765], 321–322) took the same attitude toward taste in its review of Johnson's *Preface* as it later assumed in its review of Belsham's *Essays* (see the previous note): "We cannot help thinking that Mr. Johnson has run into the vulgar practice, by estimating the merits of Shakespeare according to the rules of the French academy, and the *little* English writers who adopted them, as the criterions of *taste*. We have often been surprized how that word happens to be applied in Great-Britain to poetry, and can account for it only by the servility we shew towards every thing which is French. Of all our sensations, *taste* is the most variable and uncertain: Shakespeare is to be tried by a more sure criterion, that of *feeling*, which is the same in all ages and all climates. To talk of trying Shakespeare by the rules of *taste*, is speaking like the spindle-shanked beau who *languished* to thresh a brawny coachman." It is strange that a writer in 1765 should have associated taste only with the rules; but what he says about "feeling" harmonizes with the anti-rationalistic meaning of the word.

CHAPTER V

The Function of Tragedy

IN ITS widest sense the function of tragedy, as well as of the other arts, was, for the neo-classicist, to imitate nature. In a narrower sense the function of dramatic art, both tragic and comic, was, in the opinion of a large body of neo-classicists and in their own phrase, to delude the audience into a belief in the reality of the action represented upon the stage. The peculiar function of tragedy, according to Aristotle, whom nearly everyone would have been glad to follow if it had been possible, was to effect the proper purgation of the emotions of pity and fear. The eighteenth century, however, which in this respect did not differ from the centuries that preceded or from the two that have so far followed, considered the pronouncement "somewhat obscure," [1] and preferred a clearer-sounding formula — a formula that had received expression by Sir Philip Sidney. It preferred to say with Gildon (1718) [2] that poetry, as a genus, is "directed to *teach*, and, at the same time, to *delight*"; or with Dennis (1704) [3] that tragedy, as a species, "must necessarily both

---

1. Hugh Blair, *Lectures on Rhetoric and Belles Lettres* (London: 1783), II, 479. A discussion of the late eighteenth-century attempt to determine precisely what Aristotle meant would be outside the scope of this study, since the attempt had no intimate connection with neo-classic theory.

2. *The Complete Art of Poetry*, I, 51.

3. *The Grounds of Criticism in Poetry*, in Durham, p. 152. In *A Large Account of the Taste in Poetry* (1702) (Durham, pp. 123, 134) Dennis had said the same thing about comedy, agreeing with Farquhar (*A Discourse upon Comedy* [1702], in Durham, pp. 273, 274, 276–277).

please and instruct." The very few who denied the formula will receive honorable mention later. The many who accepted it, who actually repeated it, are — the phrase is unavoidable — too numerous to mention.

Moral England was just the place for this doctrine to flourish. An Englishman found no difficulty in accepting the definition of playwright as a lecturer on morals, or of "Dramatick Poem" as "a philosophical and moral Lecture, in which the Poet is Teacher, and the Spectators are his Disciples." The latter definition (1726) is John Dennis's,[1] but Francis Gentleman (1770),[2] more than forty years later, did no more than echo Dennis's thought when he "laid down as an irrefragable maxim, that moral tendency is the first great and indispensible merit of any piece written for the stage." Tragedy merely obeys the law of its genus, poetry; for, wrote Beattie (1783),[3] stating the general rule, "every composition ought to have a moral tendency, or at least to be innocent. That mind is perverted, which can either produce an immoral book, or be pleased with one. Virtue and good taste are so nearly allied, that what offends the former can never gratify the latter." William Richardson (1774),[4] therefore, appealed, not to esthetes, but to the "moralists of all ages" to support him in saying that "Poetry as an art [is] no less instructive than amusing; tending at once to improve the heart, and entertain the fancy." The Reverend Henry Boyd (1793),

---

1. *The Stage Defended, from Scripture, Reason, Experience, and the Common Sense of Mankind, for Two Thousand Years. Occasion'd by Mr. Law's Late Pamphlet against Stage-Entertainments* (London: 1726), p. 7.
2. *The Dramatic Censor*, I, 104.
3. *Dissertations Moral and Critical*, I, 224.
4. *Philosophical Analysis and Illustration of Some of Shakespeare's Remarkable Characters* (London: 1774), p. 1.

then, was not being merely clerical when he recommended [1]
"an accurate study of morality as a science" to "poets in
general, and dramatic writers in particular." Defenders of
Shakespeare, finding that their idol pleased, jumped too
recklessly at times to the conclusion that he also instructed.
A pathetic example of the outcome of this logic by association is Mrs. Griffith's book, *The Morality of Shakespeare's
Drama* (1775). She begins with the bold intention of
pointing out the moral of the "fable" of each of the plays
in turn, but finding some difficulty in doing so with *The
Tempest, A Midsummer-Night's Dream, The Two Gentlemen of Verona,* and *Measure for Measure,* the first four on
her list, she gives over this plan at the beginning of her discussion of the fifth play, *The Merchant of Venice.* "I shall
take no further notice of the want of a moral fable, in the
rest of these Plays," she writes, [2] "but shall proceed to observe upon the characters and dialogue, without interrup-
tion, for the future." When she reaches *Romeo and Juliet* she nearly calls a halt. She will say little about it,
because its moral tone is vicious. With a faith known
only to the highly moral she nevertheless tries [3] to find a
sermon even in this stone — for the benefit of the tender
minds that she is addressing: "As my young Readers might
not forgive my passing over this Play unnoticed, I shall
just observe, that the catastrophe of the unhappy lovers
seems intended as a kind of moral, as well as poetical justice, for their having ventured upon an unweighed engagement together, without the concurrence and consent of
their parents." Mrs. Griffith's way was that of the neo-
classic moralist at his amusing worst.

1. "An Essay on French Tragedy," *Anthologia Hibernica*, I, 286.
2. P. 51.   3. P. 497.

Many years before, Shaftesbury (1711) had found less difficulty than Mrs. Griffith in discovering a moral in Shakespeare, for, besides the aptness of the great poet's descriptions and the naturalness of his characterizations, he said,[1] "the justness of his moral . . . pleases his audience, and often gains their ear without a single bribe from Luxury or Vice." The observation is interesting, not because Shaftesbury succeeded where Mrs. Griffith failed, but because it states a relationship between the instruction and the pleasure, the relationship of cause and effect. In one place Gildon (1718) wrote as if he saw the same relationship. From a work of literary art, he said,[2] "the Pleasure, that we have, proceeds from its Goodness, unless our deluded Eyes, and corrupt Imaginations, mislead us." In another place,[3] however, he said (1709) that poetry aims "at the Instruction of Men by Pleasure," and thus reversed the positions. They were reversed also by Leonard Welsted (1724).[4] "Does not Poetry instruct too, while it pleases?" he asked. "Does it not instruct much more powerfully, thro' its superior Charm of pleasing?" Dr. Johnson (1765)[5] answered yes: "the end of poetry is to instruct by pleasing." The truth was that the two were at once effects and causes, as the philosopher Bishop Berkeley (June 9, 1713)[6] had seen in the early part of the century:

Those Parts of Learning which relate to the Imagination, as Eloquence and Poetry, produce an immediate Pleasure in the

1. *Characteristics*, ed. Robertson, I, 180.
2. *The Complete Art of Poetry*, I, 136.
3. *An Essay on the Art*, etc., in Rowe's Shakespeare (2nd ed., 1714), IX, xv.
4. *A Dissertation Concerning the Perfection of the English Language*, etc., in Durham, p. 382.
5. *Preface to Shakespeare*, in *Johnson on Shakespeare*, ed. Raleigh, p. 16.
6. *The Guardian*, No. 77.

Mind. And sublime and useful Truths, when they are conveyed in apt Allegories or beautiful Images, make more distinct and lasting Impressions; by which means the Fancy becomes sub-servient to the Understanding, and the Mind is at the same time delighted and instructed. The Exercise of the Understanding, in the discovery of Truth, is likewise attended with great Pleasure, as well as immediate Profit. It not only strengthens our Facul-ties, purifies the Soul, subdues the Passions; but besides these Advantages there is also a secret Joy that flows from intellectual Operations, proportioned to the Nobleness of the Faculty, and not the less affecting because inward and unseen.

These words of Bishop Berkeley's, besides asserting the reciprocal relation between instruction and pleasure, give part of the answer to the question, *How* does poetry, and therefore tragedy, instruct? The answer is that poetry, being an expression of truth, as Aristotle himself had said, involves "the Exercise of the Understanding," an exercise that "strengthens our Faculties, purifies the Soul, subdues the Passions." The fact that tragedy subdued the passions was generally accepted, as was the fact that the passions so subdued had first to be raised. Both the raising and the subduing of them were good. "*I find by experience*," said Dennis (1701),[1] "*that I am no further pleas'd nor in-structed by any Tragedy, than as it excites Passion in me.*" The excitation of passion was pleasing in itself, but even more important was the fact that the subduing of passion — "reducing the Passions to a just mediocrity from their violence and irregularity"[2] — led to instruction. For pas-sion is a form of disorder and unreason, and to subdue it is

1. *The Advancement and Reformation of Modern Poetry*, sig. A6. See also Dennis, *The Grounds of Criticism in Poetry* (1704), in Durham, p. 150; and his *Reflections Critical and Satyrical*, etc. (1711), in Durham, p. 231.

2. Dennis, *The Impartial Critic* (1693), in *Critical Essays of the Seventeenth Century*, ed. Spingarn, III, 187.

to restore order and set reason once more upon her throne.
"The great Design of Arts," again wrote Dennis (1704),[1]
"is to restore the Decays that happen'd to human Nature
by the Fall, by restoring Order." The object in "purging"
pity and terror, said Gildon through the mouth of Laudon
in *The Complete Art of Poetry* (1718),[2] is to "reduce them
to such a Degree of Temperance, as that they may not
have a Power of carrying us from, or contrary to the Rules
and Dictates of right Reason." In this devious way even
passion, for Dennis and Gildon, ministered to its enemy,
reason.

For the same two the theatre was "the School of Virtue,"
because, as Dennis (1693) said,[3] "it teaches some Moral
Doctrine by the Fable, which must always be allegorical
and universal." To show that he had the courage of his
convictions Dennis altered *Coriolanus* so that it accorded
with this principle, and congratulated himself upon the result. "The *Coriolanus*, as I have alter'd it," he wrote [4] to
Sir Richard Steele on March 26, 1719, "having a just
Moral, and by Consequence at the Bottom a general and
allegorical Action, and universal and allegorical Characters, and for that very reason a Fable, is therefore a true
Tragedy." The source of the emphasis upon allegorical
action was the belief that the theatre should teach by
"moral lesson and example," a belief that was asserted and
reasserted throughout the century. In 1711 Shaftesbury,[5]
apropos of tragedy, wrote as follows:

1. *The Grounds of Criticism in Poetry*, in Durham, p. 146; see also p. 145.
2. I, 197.
3. *The Impartial Critic*, in *Critical Essays of the Seventeenth Century*, ed.
Spingarn, III, 187. Compare Gildon, *The Complete Art of Poetry* (1718), I, 136.
4. *Original Letters, Familiar, Moral and Critical* (London: 1721), I, 108.
5. *Characteristics*, ed. Robertson, I, 143. Compare Gildon, *The Complete Art*

The genius of this poetry consists in the lively representation of the disorders and misery of the great; to the end that the people and those of a lower condition may be taught the better to content themselves with privacy, enjoy their safer state, and prize the equality and justice of their guardian laws.

Tragedy, in this view, was a sort of propaganda to maintain the *status quo*. As the belief was usually stated, however, it revealed no ulterior motive, and the form that it took in J. P. Kemble's *Macbeth Reconsidered* (1786) [1] is typical: "Plays are designed, by the joint powers of precept and example, to have a good influence on the lives of men." Those that had most of this good influence were necessarily best. *The Universal Magazine* (1753) [2] commended Edward Moore's *Gamester* for inculcating "an abhorrence of gaming." Horace Walpole [3] thought well of his own play, *The Mysterious Mother*, because it pointed "the moral resulting from the calamities attendant on unbounded passion." Lillo's *George Barnwell* was a great favorite with the moralists. Vicesimus Knox (1777), [4] another who specifically called the theatre "the School of Virtue," estimates that "it [*George Barnwell*] has, perhaps, saved as many from an ignominious end as the Beggar's

---

of Poetry (1718), I, 63: "*Tragedy* opens the greatest Wounds, and discovers the Ulcers that are hidden by Tishue. That makes Kings fear to be Tyrants, and Tyrants discover openly their Tyrannical Inclinations. That by stirring up *Fear* and *Compassion*, teaches the Uncertainty of this World, and on what weak Foundation the gilded Palaces of Princes are built." For a few other statements to the effect that the theatre should teach by moral lesson and example, see Addison, *The Spectator*, No. 418 (June 30, 1712); William Guthrie, *An Essay upon English Tragedy* (ca. 1747), p. 32; anonymous, *An Essay upon the Present State of the Theatre* (1760), pp. 67–68.

1. P. 3.   2. XII, 86.
3. "The Author's Postscript" to *The Mysterious Mother* (Dublin: 1791) p. 94.
4. *Essays, Moral and Literary* (London: 1808), III, 22.

Opera has hastened to it." "Timothy Touchstone" re-
told in *The Trifler* [1] for August 23, 1788, the story about
the renegade apprentice upon whom it had had so benefi-
cent an influence.

In the year 1752, Mr. Ross and Mrs. Pritchard performed the
characters of George Barnwell and Millwood, where a young
apprentice was so forcibly struck with the similarity of his own
conduct, that the depression of his spirits confined him to his
room. His physician suspecting that something lay heavy upon
his mind which he dreaded to divulge, attempted to discover the
secret; after long solicitations he confessed, that having formed
an improper acquaintance, like George Barnwell, he had made
free with some draughts entrusted to his care, and therefore
wished to die, to avoid the consequent shame.

The Doctor instantly wrote to his father, who remitted the
deficiency, and this converted prodigal lived to be an eminent
merchant. The Stage therefore *may* be directed to good purposes, if properly regulated.

Timothy's way was also that of the neo-classic moralist at
his worst. Here, however, he was melodramatic, and his
words put us in mind, not of the parables, but of the
mourners' bench.

Modern instances like that of the errant apprentice,
nevertheless, were of no general value. *George Barnwell*
was a home-thrust to the few only. Tragedy, if it was to
benefit the many, had to teach "some moral truth" [2] of
universal application. It had not only to instill in men a
hatred of peculation and an abhorrence of gaming but generally to improve their "virtuous sensibility." [3] Good
tragedy taught men, not to love this virtue, or abhor that

---

1. No. 13.
2. Lord Kames, *The Elements of Criticism* (1762) (2nd ed., 1763), III, 250.
3. Hugh Blair, *Lectures on Rhetoric and Belles Lettres* (1783), II, 479.

vice, but "to love virtue, and abhor vice." [1] If a play was "ill calculated to promote virtue," as was Cumberland's *Mysterious Husband* in the opinion of *The Critical Review* (1783),[2] then it was not good tragedy. But there were some specific truths of wide application that tragedy could and should stoop to, such as the wisdom of being content with one's lot, however humble, and, indeed, because of its humbleness.[3] "The secret Comparison which we make between our selves and the Person who suffers . . . ," said Addison (June 30, 1712),[4] plainly teaches us to "prize our good Fortune, which exempts us from the like Calamities." According to Addison (April 14, 1711) [5] also, tragedies have an opposite effect to this, but equally good, for "they soften Insolence, sooth Affliction, and subdue the Mind to the Dispensations of Providence." The anonymous author of *An Essay upon the Present State of the Theatre* (1760) held the same opinion: tragedies, he said,[6] "should confirm the heart, and give lessons of courage." Above all, thought Addison (August 1, 1712),[7] the stage — and in this respect, he said, the English stage would do well to imitate the Athenian — ought to recommend "the Religion, the Government, and Publick Worship of its Country." Dennis (1704) [8] had said the same thing about poetry in general. The overwhelming impression given by the century as a whole, indeed, is that it expected tragedy to teach moral truth, and thereby give solid pleasure, and that the *utile* took precedence over the *dulce*. That it sometimes too narrowly insisted upon the reformation of

1. J. P. Kemble, *Macbeth Reconsidered* (1786), p. 3.
2. LV, 151.
3. See Shaftesbury, above, pp. 133–134; and Gildon, above, pp. 133 n.–134 n.
4. *The Spectator*, No. 418.   5. *The Spectator*, No. 39.
6. P. 68.   7. *The Spectator*, No. 446.
8. *The Grounds of Criticism in Poetry*, in Durham, p. 147.

sinful apprentices and gamblers, of strayed revelers, and faithless husbands and wives should not be allowed to count too heavily against it. Now, as then, not even the love of pleasure is more subject to abuse than the love of preventing pleasure-seekers from seeking it in the wrong part of town.

A few bold spirits, however, if they did not rule out instruction altogether as a function of poetry, definitely subordinated it to pleasure. In 1742 Hume [1] allotted to history the instructive function, and said that it was "the object . . . of poetry to please by means of the passions and the imagination." In 1749 Bishop Hurd [2] lamented "the unnatural separation of the DULCE ET UTILE," but in 1757, when, by the passage of eight years, he had presumably learned wisdom, although he granted [3] that instruction might be the "best *use*" of tragedy and comedy, he was certain that it "is by no means their primary *intention*. Their proper and immediate *end*," he said, "is, to PLEASE." John Berkenhout,[4] in 1777, was also convinced that "amusement" is "the principal design of the theatre." The most vigorous and authoritative expression of this point of view was that of Thomas Twining (1789),[5] who apparently agreed with what he was sure Aristotle had meant — that pleasure was the end of poetry:

For, that this, in Aristotle's view, was the great end of the art, and of all its branches, appears, if I mistake not, evidently, from

1. *Of the Standard of Taste*, in *Essays*, ed. Green and Grose (1898), I, 277.
2. Note on l. 343 of Horace's *Art of Poetry*, ed. Hurd, in *Works* (1811), I, 267.
3. *A Dissertation on the Provinces of the Drama*, in *Works* (1811), II, 98. *The Monthly Review* (XXXIII [1765], 291–292) severely criticized Dr. Johnson's *Preface* for its moralistic tone.
4. See *The Monthly Review*, LVII (1777), 194, which quotes from Berkenhout's *Biographia Literaria*. I have not seen Berkenhout's book.
5. *Aristotle's Treatise on Poetry*, pp. 561–562.

many other passages of this treatise, as well as from that now
before us.[1] Nor does he, any where, appear to me to give any
countenance to an idea, which rational criticism has, now, pretty
well exploded — that *utility* and *instruction* are the end of
Poetry. That it may indeed be rendered, in some degree, useful
and improving, few will deny; none, that it *ought* to be made so,
if it can. But, that the *chief end* and *purpose* of Poetry is to *instruct* — that Homer wrote his *Iliad* on purpose to teach mankind the mischiefs of discord among chiefs, and his *Odyssey*, to
prove to them the advantages of staying at home and taking
care of their families — this is so manifestly absurd, that one is
really astonished to see so many writers, one after the other, dis-
coursing gravely in defence of it.

It is true indeed, that Aristotle, in his account of Tragedy,
mentions the correction and refinement of the passions, pity,
terror, &c. as a useful *effect* of Tragic representations. But he no
where, either in his definition, where we might surely have expected him to be explicit, or in any other part of his book, calls
that effect the *end* of Tragedy. All his expressions prove, that *his*
end, both of Tragic and Epic Poetry, was *pleasure*; though, with
respect to Tragedy, he asserts, (by way, as I have before sug-
gested, of obviating Plato's objections to it,) that the pleasure
arising from it was so far from being pernicious, that it was even
useful; so far from *inflaming* the passions of men, that it tended,
on the contrary, to purify and moderate them in common life.

In spite of what Twining says about the success of rational criticism in exploding the utility doctrine, his was a
relatively small opposition party. "Rational critics,"
in the historical sense of the phrase, if not in his absolute
sense, constituted "the government," and behaved very
much as if no explosion had occurred. The eighteenth
century, on the whole, like the sixteenth and seventeenth
centuries, thought that the proper function of tragedy was
delightful teaching.

1. See *Poetics*, XXVI, 7.

CHAPTER VI

Poetic Justice

THE belief that delightful teaching is the proper function of tragedy is closely related to the further belief in the necessity of meting out poetical justice in tragedy, but in the eighteenth century it did not follow that because a man accepted the first belief he also accepted the second. Some thought that poetical justice was instructive, and some that it was not. According as they did or did not think so critics aligned themselves for or against it, although there were other arguments that determined opinion.

The issues were drawn early in the century by Addison and Dennis. These two advanced the only arguments on either side that the century managed to think of. After them, critics simply chose one side or the other and made use of the same old weapons that the first two champions had bequeathed to them. Dennis [1] issued the challenge to battle in 1701:

> *I conceive that every Tragedy ought to be a very solemn Lecture, inculcating a particular Providence, and showing it plainly protecting the good, and chastizing the bad, or at least the violent: and that if it is otherwise, it is either an empty amusement, or a scandalous and pernicious Libel upon the government of the world.*

1. *The Advancement and Reformation of Modern Poetry*, sig. A6ᵛ.

Addison [1] accepted the challenge on April 16, 1711:

The *English* Writers of Tragedy are possessed with a Notion, that when they represent a virtuous or innocent Person in Distress, they ought not to leave him till they have delivered him out of his Troubles, or made him triumph over his Enemies. This Error they have been led into by a ridiculous Doctrine in Modern Criticism, that they are obliged to an equal Distribution of Rewards and Punishments, and an impartial Execution of Poetical Justice.

On Addison, since he was the innovator, lay the burden of proof. He made seven contentions, the first five in *The Spectator*, No. 40 (April 16, 1711), and the sixth and seventh in *The Spectator*, No. 548 (November 28, 1712):

1. It is a modern doctrine.
2. It was not observed in the practise of the ancients. [2]
3. It is contrary to nature and reason.
4. It is contrary to the experience of life.
5. It is inimical to the raising of pity and terror.
6. Since no man is perfectly virtuous, his punishment is always justifiable.
7. The punishment of "a Man who is virtuous in the main of his Character" is more instructive and moral "than when he is represented as Happy and Triumphant."

1. *The Spectator*, No. 40.
2. "Who were the first that established this Rule I know not; but I am sure it has no Foundation in Nature, in Reason, or in the Practice of the Ancients." In *The Spectator*, No. 40, also, however, in condemning Tate's adaptation of *King Lear*, he writes: "At the same time I must allow, that there are very noble Tragedies, which have been framed upon the other Plan, and have ended happily; as indeed most of the good Tragedies, which have been written since the starting of the above-mentioned Criticism, have taken this Turn: As the *Mourning Bride*, *Tamerlane*, *Ulysses*, *Phaedra* and *Hyppolitus*, with most of Mr. *Dryden*'s. I must also allow, that many of *Shakespear*'s, and several of the celebrated Tragedies of Antiquity, are cast in the same Form. I do not therefore dispute against this way of writing Tragedies, but against the criticism that would establish this as the only Method; and by that Means would very much cramp the *English* Tragedy, and perhaps give a wrong Bent to the Genius of our Writers."

He made only one concession to his opponents: he granted [1]
that "there are many Men so Criminal that they can have
no Claim or Pretence to Happiness. The best of Men may
deserve Punishment, but the worst of Men cannot deserve
Happiness."

In 1701 Dennis had anticipated Addison's seventh contention by maintaining that not to observe poetic justice
in a tragedy is to make it *"either an empty amusement, or
a scandalous and pernicious Libel upon the government of
the world."* [2] Again in 1711, apparently before he had read
The Spectator, No. 40, he repeated the argument in his
essay, *On the Genius and Writings of Shakespear*. [3] Here he
defends his adaptation of *Coriolanus* to meet the requirements of poetic justice. He says, further, that "the Good
and the Bad . . . perishing promiscuously in the best of
Shakespear's Tragedies, there can be either none or very
weak Instruction in them: For such promiscuous Events
call the Government of Providence into Question, and by
Scepticks and Libertines are resolv'd into Chance."

When he had read *The Spectator*, No. 40, he prepared his
formal answer, in a letter "To the Spectator, upon his
Paper on the 16th of April." [4] His arguments, in the order
that they appear in the letter, are as follows:

1. It is not a modern doctrine, but was established by Aristotle in the *Poetics*, XIII.

2. It is founded in reason and nature, and "is it self the
Foundation of all the Rules, and ev'n of Tragedy itself. For
what Tragedy can there be without a Fable? or what Fable with-

---

1. *The Spectator*, No. 548 (November 28, 1712).
2. *The Advancement and Reformation of Modern Poetry*, sig. A6ᵛ.
3. In Smith, pp. 29–30.
4. *Original Letters* (1721), I, 409–415.

out a Moral? or what Moral without poetical Justice? What Moral, where the Good and the Bad are confounded by Destiny, and perish alike promiscuously." (Here he implies a denial of Addison's second contention.)

3. We cannot say with certainty that it is contrary to the experience of life, because we do not know men well enough. Men are punished for their passions, which the wicked "dissemble and conceal," but which the virtuous alone "command," so that the seemingly virtuous who are punished may really deserve punishment. The writer of tragedy, however, is omniscient, and knows whom to punish and whom to reward.

4. Men in real life, moreover, if they are not punished in this life will be punished hereafter; "but the Creatures of a poetical Creator are imaginary and transitory; they have no longer Duration than the Representation of their respective Fables; and consequently, if they offend, they must be punish'd during that Representation."

Dennis does not meet Addison's fifth and sixth contentions at all here. He emits a vast cloud of critical incense and invokes the name of Aristotle, but when the incense has floated away and the invocation is over, Addison and the spirit of evil still leer from the pulpit. The letter, indeed, is thoroughly disingenuous — either that or stupid. The thirteenth chapter of the *Poetics* is as clear a condemnation of the principle of poetic justice as one can imagine. Dennis's second argument is circular: the moral lesson taught by poetic justice is the foundation of tragedy, because the foundation of tragedy is a moral lesson. The third is a statement of the theory that underlay trial by fire: if your hand burns, you are guilty. The fourth, though it cannot be refuted, is unamiable; Jonathan Edwards would have considered it conclusive. The companion proposition to the fourth, Dennis stated in a letter to Sir Richard Blackmore, on December 5, 1716:[1] "That He who does good, and perseveres in it, shall always be Rewarded."

So far as progress in the controversy is concerned, the case might have rested with this last remark of Dennis's, or earlier still, with his "Letter to the Spectator." But it dragged wearily on to the end of the century. Richard Steele, to hark back for a moment, really deserves credit for taking up Dennis's gauntlet before his friend Addison did. On October 18, 1709, he wrote[2] that when the fortune of dramatic characters is disposed according to poetic justice, "an intelligent spectator, if he is concerned, knows he ought not to be so; and can learn nothing from such a tenderness, but that he is a weak creature, whose passions cannot follow the dictates of his understanding." Having furnished Addison with his seventh argument, he handed over the gauntlet to the abler warrior. After Dennis and Addison had retired from the dispute, Sir Thomas Hanmer (1736)[3] announced his "satisfaction" with Addison's sixth argument. A certain Craig, writing in *The Mirror*[4] for February 1, 1780, enlarged upon the instructiveness of the unhappy but virtuous hero (Addison, 7): "Even when he is cut off by premature death," Craig concludes, "we follow his memory with the greater admiration; and our respect and reverence for his conduct are increased so much the more, as all our prayers for his happiness in this life are disappointed." William Hodson (1780)[5] thought (Addison, 4 and 5) "that an unhappy catastrophe, not

---

1. *Original Letters* (1721), I, 7.
2. *The Tatler*, ed. Aitken (1898–1899), No. 82.
3. *Some Remarks on the Tragedy of Hamlet*, p. 60.   4. No. 77.
5. "Observations on Tragedy," bound with *Zoraida*, p. 81 n. On the same page Hodson says that he "acted against his own conviction" when he gave his own *Zoraida* a happy catastrophe.

only holds up a truer mirror of life (the great duty of the drama) but has the additional advantage of exciting terror, and pity, in a superior degree." In 1783 Hugh Blair [1] wrote (Addison, 4) that poetic justice "has been long exploded from Tragedy; the end of which is, to affect us with pity for the virtuous in distress, and to afford a probable representation of the state of human life, where calamities often befal the best, and a mixed portion of good and evil is appointed for all." In 1789 Belsham,[2] besides repeating Addison's fourth and seventh arguments, judiciously allowed that whether a tragedy should end happily or unhappily depends on the circumstances. More interesting is Belsham's training one of Dennis's guns against the Dennis party itself. When a virtuous hero "finally sinks under the pressure of accumulated misfortune," he wrote, " . . . we are inevitably induced to cherish the sublime idea, that a future day of retribution will arrive, when he shall receive not merely poetical but real and substantial justice." Aside from this old idea turned to a new use no one had anything to add to Addison's original arguments.

The other faction was equally unresourceful. Gildon (1718),[3] as one should expect, considered Dennis's "Letter" of 1711 "a perfect Confutation of so fundamental an Error in *Tragedy*," although he admitted [4] that a tragedy with a happy ending "is not the most perfect sort of *Tragedy*, either in its Use or Pleasure, since a *Tragedy* with an unfortunate Catastrophe is more delightful and more instructive," an admission that must have displeased Dennis. Hume (1742) [5] took a position well over toward the

1. *Lectures on Rhetoric and Belles Lettres*, II, 503.
2. *Essays Philosophical and Moral*, etc. (2nd ed., 1799), II, 559–560.
3. *The Complete Art of Poetry*, I, 196.   4. I, 189.
5. *Of Tragedy*, in *Essays*, ed. Green and Grose (1898), I, 265.

Dennis side. "The mere suffering of plaintive virtue, under the triumphant tyranny and oppression of vice," he
thought, "forms a disagreeable spectacle, and is carefully
avoided by all masters of the drama. In order to dismiss
the audience with entire satisfaction and contentment, the
virtue must either convert itself into a noble courageous
despair, or the vice receive its proper punishment." *The
Universal Magazine,*[1] in 1753, thought it a "defect" in
Edward Moore's *Gamester* that "the punishment of the
villain" was uncertain. The author of *An Essay upon the
Present State of the Theatre* (1760)[2] said of tragedy that
"the finest lesson which this most grave and moral of all
poems can teach mankind, is, that virtue, though long
crossed and persecuted, will at last triumph over all ob-
stacles and enemies." Dr. Johnson (1765)[3] was grieved
to see that Shakespeare "sacrifices virtue to convenience,
and is so much more careful to please than to instruct, that
he seems to write without any moral purpose." Thomas
Davies (1784)[4] commended Johnson's view, and, of course,
strongly disapproved of Addison's. A close student of
Aristotle might have been expected to feel most at home
in the camp of Addison, but the "feelings" of Henry James
Pye (1792)[5] were precisely what made him rejoice in "a
sudden revolution of fortune quite unexpected and yet not
improbable." In its review of Pye's *Commentary, The
Monthly Review* (1795) shows as well as could be shown how
far even the late eighteenth century sometimes was from
understanding Aristotle. It comes to grief on the thirteenth chapter of the *Poetics*, as Dennis had come to grief

1. XII, 88.   2. P. 75.
3. *Preface to Shakespeare*, in *Johnson on Shakespeare*, ed. Raleigh, pp. 20-21.
4. *Dramatic Micellanies* (*sic*) (2nd ed., 1785), II, 264-265.
5. *A Commentary Illustrating the Poetic of Aristotle*, p. 266.

more than three-quarters of a century earlier. But whereas Dennis had interpreted it as a formulation of the doctrine of poetic justice, *The Monthly Review* looked upon it as a denial of the doctrine, with which opinion we should have no fault to find if the *Review* had not chosen to attack the statement that "the downfall of the utter villain" should not be exhibited.[1] Aristotle, as anyone should be able to see, objects to this sort of plot *simply* because "it would inspire neither pity nor fear," not because he wishes to be kind to villains. The *Review*,[2] however, came blundering to the defense of poetic justice: "This rule would tend to banish retribution from the theatre, to preserve the tyrant whose villainy has molested us with habitual anxiety, and, by prohibiting poetical justice, to abolish that solution of the plot which has apparently the merit of being the most instructive." No further evidence is necessary to prove that, at least with respect to this doctrine, the end of the eighteenth century could still produce neo-classicists of the least admirable kind. The foregoing samples of opinion should make it clear also that the followers of Dennis were no more original than the followers of Addison. They were if anything less original. They were certainly more numerous.

Nahum Tate's version of *King Lear*, which appeared in 1681, observed poetic justice to the letter. It became a balm to the easily tortured feelings of the eighteenth century. Addison (April 16, 1711) [3] stood almost alone in preferring the play as Shakespeare wrote it. The original, he said, "is an admirable Tragedy . . . but as it is reformed according to the chymerical Notion of Poetical Justice, in

---

1. *Poetics*, XIII, 2.   2. XVIII, second series, 129.
3. *The Spectator*, No. 40.

my humble Opinion it has lost half its Beauty." The only other adverse comment on Tate's version that I have seen in eighteenth-century criticism appeared in a review of Davies' *Dramatic Miscellanies* in *The Monthly Review* [1] for 1784. It is brief and temporizing: "In the catastrophe, Tate has some merit; though we wonder that Garrick, who hazarded an alteration of Hamlet, never attempted a restoration of the conclusion of Lear, a scene which he, of all men, was most equal to exhibit; a scene which contains touches equal to any from the hand of Shakespeare." Davies himself, who knew the theatre well, probably did not wonder at all. If Garrick, who could do practically what he liked with an audience, did not dare to play the original version, the reason was that not even the great Roscius could make it palatable to the just and moral eighteenth-century audience.

Forty-one years after Addison's strictures upon the altered version *The Gentleman's Magazine* (1752) [2] remembered and took exception to them. Dr. Johnson (1765),[3] in a note on *Lear*, granted the possible goodness of a play that represented prosperous wickedness and unfortunate virtue, but he could not "easily be persuaded, that the observation of justice makes a play worse; or, that if other excellencies are equal, the audience will not always rise better pleased from the final triumph of persecuted virtue." Johnson's conviction may help to explain Garrick's unwillingness to restore the original catastrophe. The just distribution of rewards and punishments in Tate's version, especially the bestowing of Cordelia on Edgar, immensely

---

1. LXX, 459.
2. XXII, 254. The correspondent signed himself "A. B."
3. *Johnson on Shakespeare*, ed. Raleigh, p. 161.

pleased Francis Gentleman (1770).[1] "The old king's consent, with Gloster's and Kent's hearty blessing," he thought, "shed a brilliance on TATE's last scene, highly pleasing to every good and tender mind; it adds great force to the old king's restoration, and furnishes, to our apprehension, as satisfactory and compleat a catastrophe as any in the whole scope of dramatic composition." Edward Taylor (1774),[2] like Dr. Johnson, admitted the verisimilitude of unhappy catastrophes, but he eagerly welcomed[3] a happily ending *Lear*. "Such, if practicable," he said, "should be the winding up of all dramatic representations, that mankind may have the most persuasive allurements to all good actions: for although virtue depressed may be amiable, virtue triumphant must be irresistable." Mrs. Griffith (1775),[4] who had so much difficulty finding morals in Shakespeare, thought Tate's ending the best of all logically possible endings. It not only "fulfilled Horace's precept of *utile dulci*" but also raised pity and terror as well as any other "Play that ever was written." Her "feelings" more than her reason taught her to prefer it. The feelings of a writer for *The Critical Review* (1784)[5] taught him the same preference: "Lear has derived little advantage from the efforts of those who endeavoured to remove its imperfections; but we still prefer the happy conclusion: reason opposes it, while the tortured feelings at once decide the contest."

The support that the authority of the feelings lent to the doctrine of poetic justice is particularly interesting, for, in-

1. *The Dramatic Censor*, I, 367.
2. *Cursory Remarks on Tragedy*, pp. 48–49.
3. Pp. 46–47.
4. *The Morality of Shakespeare's Drama*, p. 351.
5. LVIII, 58–59.

spite of the fact that poetic justice was a characteristic neo-classic conception, the feelings tended to usurp the position of reason, which was the faculty that the neo-classicists began by defending against all intruders, and especially against emotion. To maintain that tragedy instructed best when it distributed poetic justice, while also maintaining that poetic justice was opposed to reason, was a paradox. Dennis had at least realized that the paradox needed a resolution. The fact that Mrs. Griffith and *The Critical Review* freely admitted the opposition between the feelings and the reason without seeming to have been aware of the paradox shows what strides had been taken since 1711. Whether the strides were forward or backward it is difficult for the twentieth century to say. It would doubtless have been equally difficult for the late eighteenth century. In any event, the strides had been taken, and one could espouse a neo-classic cause without having a neo-classic reason for doing so.

CHAPTER VII

The Characters of Tragedy

ALTHOUGH the eighteenth century was not unanimous in saying that tragedy should instruct, or that the wicked should be punished and the virtuous rewarded, it was virtually unanimous about the character of the tragic hero. Aristotle's opinion that the tragic hero should be neither eminently good nor eminently bad, but should rather be a medium between these extremes, was also the opinion of the eighteenth century. The author of *An Essay upon the Present State of the Theatre* (1760),[1] it is true, wrote that "the hero of a piece should never be faulty; nay, there should be in him no appearance of evil. If he has a bad side, the poet should hide it, and paint his face in profile." The opinion, however, appears to have been unique.

Even so, there was some disagreement, not about the character of the hero, but about the reason for giving him that character. Again it was Dennis and Addison who, chronologically speaking, led the two schools of thought. The unimportance of the disagreement may be measured by the fact that no one became ill-tempered — not even Dennis, although at the time he was angry with Addison on another score. Dennis's reason for believing as he did about the tragic hero appears in the letter "To the Spectator, upon his Paper on the 16th of April" (1711),[2] and con-

1. P. 58.   2. *Original Letters* (1721), I, 415.

sists merely in a paraphrase of Aristotle's reason, namely, that the hero should represent neither extreme, because for him to do so would be to preclude the possibility of the tragedy's raising pity and fear in the audience. Gildon (1718),[1] in complete accord with Dennis, simply repeated Aristotle. "The only objection I find to Aristotle's account of tragedy," wrote Lord Kames (1762),[2] "is, that he confines it within too narrow bounds, by refusing admittance to the pathetic kind." By the pathetic kind he meant "a poem, whether dramatic or epic, that hath no tendency beyond moving the passions and exhibiting pictures of virtue and vice."[3] But, after all, the objection is fairly serious. It seems to reveal that Kames, though he may have agreed with Aristotle's view of the hero, did not fully appreciate what that agreement entailed, that is to say, the impossibility of pathetic tragedy according to Kames's own definition. William Cooke (1775)[4] also, but not too clearly, was on Dennis's side, as were William Hodson (1780),[5] James Harris (1781),[6] Belsham (1789),[7] and Pye (1792).[8]

The other school, not exactly in opposition to the first, was represented by Addison, Alexander Gerard, Hugh Blair, and doubtless others who have escaped notice. They believed in the medium hero because he was "natural," a man obviously drawn from the life. "Our Goodness being of comparative, and not an absolute Nature," wrote Addi-

---

1. *The Complete Art of Poetry*, I, 243–244.
2. *The Elements of Criticism* (2nd ed., 1763), III, 257.
3. III, 247.
4. *The Elements of Dramatic Criticism*, p. 31.
5. "Observations on Tragedy," bound with *Zoraida*, pp. 87–88.
6. *Philological Inquiries*, p. 153 n.
7. *Essays Philosophical and Moral*, etc. (2nd ed., 1799), II, 558.
8. *A Commentary Illustrating the Poetic of Aristotle*, p. 247.

son (November 28, 1712),[1] "there is none who in strictness can be called a Virtuous Man. Every one has in him a natural Alloy, tho' one may be fuller of Dross than another: For this Reason I cannot think it right to introduce a perfect or a faultless Man upon the Stage; not only because such a Character is improper to move Compassion, but because there is no such thing in Nature." To say this, of course, is only to carry the reasoning of the school of Dennis one step further back — to give the reason of a reason. When Gerard (1759)[2] asserts that "imperfect and mixt characters are, in all kinds of writing, preferred to faultless ones, as being juster copies of real nature," he is again simply explaining why such characters move compassion. "They display emotions and passions," writes Blair (1783),[3] "which we have all been conscious of"; that is to say, we are affected through empathy. Essentially, then, the two schools differed only in the thoroughness with which they carried through the analysis of their reasons for equipping the tragic hero with a character that was midway between moral extremes. Both schools, it may be said in their favor, were in the Aristotelian tradition; and the second was even more explicitly analytical than Aristotle himself.

Agreement went no further, however. With regard to the rank of the hero and of the other characters of tragedy there was a sharp divergence. Here again two schools developed, one of which was an un-Aristotelian survival from the Renaissance that continued to thrive until at least 1781. The opinion of this group was crystalized in the definition of tragedy that appeared in the first edition of

1. *The Spectator*, No. 548.   2. *An Essay on Taste*, p. 54.
3. *Lectures on Rhetoric and Belles Lettres*, II, 504.

the *Encyclopædia Britannica*,[1] published in 1771: "TRAG-EDY, a dramatic poem, representing some signal action per-formed by illustrious persons, and which has frequently a fatal issue, or end." The definition was reprinted in all editions of the *Encyclopædia* until 1842, the date of the seventh edition. Not until the eighth edition did it disap-pear. In this dictionary fossil one easily recognizes the Renaissance misreading of Aristotle's statement that the tragic hero should be a man of "moral nobility." To many eighteenth-century minds the statement continued to mean that the hero and the other characters of tragedy should be of noble rank.

Those who thus misread Aristotle fell into two sub-groups. The first misread him because of their moral bias. Like Shaftesbury (1711)[2] they thought it necessary to rep-resent "the disorders and misery of the great" in order that "those of a lower condition may be taught the better to content themselves with privacy, enjoy their safer state, and prize the equality and justice of their guardian laws," or, as Gildon (1718)[3] said, in order to teach "the Uncer-tainty of this World, and on what weak Foundation the gilded Palaces of Princes are built." John Upton (1746),[4] too, thought that "it might be likewise deserving notice, how finely Shakespeare observes that rule of tragedy, to paint the miseries of the great. . . . The lesson to be learnt by the lower people is, acquiescence in the ease of a private station, not obnoxious to those disorders, which attend greatness in the stage of the world." Aristotle's *katharsis* and "moral nobility" are here thoroughly corrupted.

1. III, 901. The second edition appeared in 1778–1783, the third in 1797.
2. *Characteristics*, ed. Robertson, I, 143.
3. *The Complete Art of Poetry*, I, 63.
4. *Critical Observations on Shakespeare*, pp. 56–57.

The second sub-group preferred persons of quality because of their superior efficacy in "moving" or "affecting" the audience. Such was Gildon's [1] opinion (1718), and he deserves credit for being so productive of reasons for his preference. Gildon did not think, however, that kings were necessary, and he had a good English reason for not thinking so: "'Tis true, that in all the *Greek* Tragedies, the Principal Persons are Kings: But then first we must remember, that they were but Petty Monarchs, and scarce attended with the Magnificence of our Noblemen." Otway's *Orphan*, with its noble but unroyal characters, he thought a sufficient proof of his contention. Since the exciting of pity and terror is the end of tragedy, Bishop Hurd (1757) [2] thought that the inclusion of persons of *"principal rank and dignity"* followed of necessity:

For the actions of these are, both in *themselves* and in their *consequences*, most fitted to excite passion. The *distresses* of private and inferior persons will, no doubt, *affect* us greatly; and we may give the name of *tragedies*, if we please, to dramatic representations of them: as, in fact, we have several applauded pieces of this kind. Nay, it may seem, that the fortunes of private men, as more nearly resembling *those* of the generality, should be most *affecting*. But this circumstance, in no degree, makes amends for the loss of other and much greater *advantages*. For, whatever be the *unhappy incidents* in the story of private men, it is certain, they must take faster hold of the *imagination*, and, of course, impress the heart more forcibly, when related of the higher characters in life. . . . Kings, Heroes, Statesmen, and other persons of great and public authority, influence by their *ill-fortune* the whole community, to which they belong. The attention is rouzed, and all our faculties take an alarm, at the apprehension of such extensive and important wretchedness. And, besides, if

1. *The Complete Art of Poetry*, I, 244.
2. *A Dissertation on the Provinces of the Drama*, in *Works* (1811), II, 34–36.

we regard the *event* itself, without an eye to its *effects*, there is still the widest difference between the two cases. Those ideas of awe and veneration, which opinion throws round the persons of princes, make us esteem the very *same event* in their fortunes, as more august and emphatical, than in the fortunes of private men. In the *one*, it is ordinary and familiar to our conceptions; it is singular and surprising, in the *other*. The fall of a *cottage*, by the accidents of time and weather, is almost unheeded; while the ruin of a *tower*, which the neighbourhood hath gazed at for ages with admiration, strikes all observers with concern. So that if we chuse to continue the absurdity . . . of planning *unimportant action* in our tragedy, we should, at least, take care to give it this foreign and extrinsic *importance* of great *actors*: Yet our passion for the *familiar* goes so far, that we have tragedies, not only of private action, but of *private persons*; and so have well nigh annihilated the noblest of the two dramas amongst us. On the whole it appears, that as the proper object of tragedy is *action*, so it is *important* action, and therefore more especially the action of *great and illustrious men*. Each of these conclusions is the direct consequence of our idea of its *end*.

Hurd's statement scarcely needed improvement. When Hurd expressed an opinion, he expressed it not only at length but well. He overlooked only one consideration, which William Cooke later supplied. The miseries of the great may somehow be more affecting than are those of the lower sort, but can the man in the street believe the poet's story? We can enjoy vicariously the misery of the man who loses a million dollars, but can we believe that anyone has a million dollars to lose? Yes, answered Cooke (1775),[1] but only if the story is one about millionaires. "The greatness of eminent men render [*sic*] the action great, and their reputation makes it credible; a foot soldier may shew more courage and prudence in the day of battle than his general,

1. *The Elements of Dramatic Criticism*, p. 42.

yet the victory will be ascribed to the latter, on account of the superiority of his station, and the probability of the cause."

Gildon, serving as a liaison officer, was at home both among those who believed that noble characters were desirable for their instructive value, and among those who found the miseries of the great more moving than the miseries of private men. Because of the basically friendly relations existing between the two groups, Gildon could maintain his position without ambiguity or danger of being arraigned for treason. James Harris (1781),[1] on the other hand, stood in a sort of critical no-man's land, and was a fair target, not only for the two groups that Gildon linked, but for the enemies of that whole point of view. His sympathies lay ambiguously with both lines of possible marksmen. He spoke with warm approval of "that capital Play," Lillo's *Fatal Curiosity*, and his encomium carried the implication that he approved of domestic tragedy in general. But in the following passage,[2] where he is discussing the difference between tragedy and comedy, he makes the traditional neo-classic distinction between the two *genres*, which commits him automatically to the neo-classic view that exalted personages are necessary to tragedy: "THE DIFFERENCE between them *only lies* in the *Persons* and the *Catastrophe*, inasmuch as (contrary to the usual practice of *Tragedy*) THE COMIC PERSONS are mostly either of *Middle* or *Lower* Life, and THE CATASTROPHE for the greater part from *Bad* to *Good*." Divided critical personalities like Harris's were rarities in eighteenth-century England. The normal thing was for a man to know what

1. *Philological Inquiries*, p. 154.
2. Pp. 159–160.

he thought, and to think only one thing at a time. Some men, like Gildon and Hurd, thought that the characters of tragedy had to be kings or noblemen, and some, as we shall see, thought that there was no such necessity, but no one except Harris seems to have tried to think both things at once.

The century as a whole, however, was capable of more than one thought. It was capable, indeed, as should already be apparent, of thinking diametrically opposite thoughts. Lounsbury [1] is clearly wrong, for example, when he says that "the belief in the necessity of preserving unimpaired the dignity of tragedy by excluding from it all men of the baser sort prevailed generally in the critical literature of the eighteenth century." The belief, on the contrary, was exactly balanced by its opposite.

As early as May 16, 1710, Steele [2] contradicted everyone of the reasons that were advanced to support the belief that only persons of quality were fit for tragedy. His words deserve full quotation:

When unhappy catastrophes make up part of the history of princes, and persons who act in high spheres, or are represented in the moving language and well-wrought scenes of tragedians, they do not fail of striking us with terror; but then they affect us only in a transient manner, and pass through our imaginations, as incidents in which our fortunes are too humble to be concerned, or which writers form for the ostentation of their own force; or, at most, as things fit rather to exercise the powers of our minds, than to create new habits in them. Instead of such high passages, I was thinking it would be of great use (if anybody could hit it) to lay before the world such adventures as befall persons not exalted above the common level. This, methought,

1. *Shakespeare as a Dramatic Artist*, p. 145.
2. *The Tatler*, ed. Aitken (1898–1899), No. 172.

Steele

would better prevail upon the ordinary race of men, who are so prepossessed with outward appearances, that they mistake fortune for nature, and believe nothing can relate to them that does not happen to such as live and look like themselves.

His observation was not a compliment, perhaps, to the Queen Anne audience, but it was what a contemporary honestly thought about that audience, and about the sort of inappropriate entertainment that neo-classic tradition was trying to impose upon it. Steele distinctly denies that for such an audience royal tragedy is moving, credible, or instructive, the three qualities that were claimed for it. What he considered the qualities of a really instructive tragedy he made clear two years later, in some flattering remarks on Ambrose Philips's *Distressed Mother*. "The Persons," he said,[1] "are of the highest Quality in Life, even that of Princes; but their Quality is not represented by the Poet with Direction that Guards and Waiters should follow them in every Scene, but their Grandeur appears in greatness of Sentiments, flowing from Minds worthy their Condition. To make a Character truly Great, this Author understands that it should have its Foundation in superior Thoughts and Maxims of Conduct." In other words, the instructiveness of a tragedy will be proportionate to the superiority of its thought and conduct, not to the superiority of the rank of its characters. On August 23, 1788, "Timothy Touchstone" said[2] once more what Steele had said in 1710, that because "the exploits of high life" are so far removed from the experience of the spectator of exalted tragedy "those performances . . . in which the duties of private life are delineated, are the most instructive."

1. *The Spectator*, No. 290 (February 1, 1712).
2. *The Trifler*, No. 13.

Those who said that royal tragedy was less moving than domestic tragedy were much more numerous than those who said it was less instructive. "Our poets might consider," wrote the Earl of Orrery (1759),[1] "that we feel not so intensely the sorrows of the higher powers, as we feel the miseries of those who are nearer upon a level with ourselves. The revolution and fall of empire affect us less than the distresses of a private family." The advocates of royal tragedy would have done well to ponder this observation, coming as it did from a nobleman. The Reverend Thomas Franklyn, in *A Dissertation on Ancient Tragedy* (1760),[2] considered tragedy dealing with "the humbler walk of private life . . . more interesting to the generality of mankind." Mrs. Montagu (1769),[3] whom some have unjustly thought unworthy of her subject, favorably contrasted Shakespeare's effective, if sometimes indecorous, language of passion, "which in all ranks of men is much alike," with the decorous and formal language of French tragedy, which, she thought, had been emasculated by a meticulous respect for rank and form. Francis Gentleman (1770)[4] "wished that tragic writers would rather bend their thoughts to familiar circumstances in life, than those which concern elevated feelings and abstract passions." Because it is more difficult for the ordinary man to feel the fate of "the exalted characters of heroic tragedy," Edward Taylor (1774)[5] argued in favor of plays representing the fortunes

---

1. "Preface" to *The Greek Theatre of Father Brumoy*, translated by Mrs. Charlotte Lennox and others, I, xxvi.

2. (2nd ed., London: 1768), p. 80 n. *The Critical Review* (X, 34–41) reviewed the first edition in 1760.

3. *An Essay on the Writings and Genius of Shakespear*, p. 38.

4. *The Dramatic Censor*, I, 131.

5. *Cursory Remarks on Tragedy*, pp. 100–103.

of humbler characters. Hugh Blair (1783),[1] with whom we shall conclude, well represented the case for domestic tragedy:

It has been thought, by several Critics, that the nature of Tragedy requires the principal personages to be always of illustrious character, and of high, or princely rank; whose misfortunes and sufferings, it is said, take faster hold of the imagination, and impress the heart more forcibly, than similar events happening to persons in private life. But this is more specious, than solid. It is refuted by facts. For the distresses of Desdemona, Monimia, and Belvidera, interest us as deeply as if they had been princesses or queens. The dignity of Tragedy does, indeed, require, that there should be nothing degrading, or mean, in the circumstances of the persons which it exhibits; but it requires nothing more. Their high rank may render the spectacle more splendid, and the subject seemingly of more importance, but conduce [*sic*] very little to its being interesting or pathetic; which depends entirely on the nature of the Tale, on the art of the Poet in conducting it, and on the sentiments to which it gives occasion. In every rank of life, the relations of Father, Husband, Son, Brother, Lover, or Friend, lay the foundations of those affecting situations, which make man's heart feel for man.

The upshot was, from the point of view of Blair and those of his opinion, but in the words of Samuel Foote (1747),[2] that "if the Incidents are truly interesting, and the Story affecting the Rank and Quality of the *Personae* are of no great Consequence." To embellish a tragedy, said another writer,[3] in 1760, with "the names of princes and kings . . . to give an air of grandeur to the subject . . . though not amiss, does not appear by any means necessary." Certainly to depend entirely upon the rank of the

---

1. *Lectures on Rhetoric and Belles Lettres*, II, 502–503.

2. *The Roman and English Comedy Consider'd and Compar'd* (London), pp. 6–7.

3. Anonymous, *An Essay upon the Present State of the Theatre*, p. 3.

characters for effect, Dr. Johnson (May 28, 1751) [1] thought, was not enough. After Blair's raking broadside in 1783 all was quiet. The neo-classicists had presumably had enough. By this time kings were becoming unpopular in reality as well as in the theatre.

The related doctrine of "manners" also remained vigorous until about the same time, and then the untenable portions of it were discarded. Eighteenth-century neo-classicists, like their precursors, continued to explain that characters should be good, like (or agreeable), convenient (or suitable), and equal (or even). There was no reason why they should not have said that characters should be equal, because "equal" simply meant "consistent," which was Aristotle's word (τὸ ὁμαλόν),[2] and conveyed a legitimate idea. Aristotle may be interpreted as concurring with them in requiring also that characters be like, or agreeable. "*Like* relates only to known and publick Persons, whose Characters are in History, with which the Poetick Characters must agree," wrote Gildon [3] in 1709; "that is, the Poet must not give a Person any Quality contrary to any that History has given him." In 1718 he added [4] that the characters given to particular men by "establish'd Fiction" likewise should not be violated. "The poet being an imitator, like a painter or any other artist," says Aristotle,[5] "must of necessity imitate one of three objects, — *Things as they were or are, things as they are said or thought to be*, or things as they ought to be."

1. *The Rambler*, No. 125.
2. *Poetics*, XV, 4.
3. *An Essay on the Art*, etc., in Rowe's Shakespeare (2nd ed., 1714), IX, xxxviii.
4. *The Complete Art of Poetry*, I, 221.
5. *Poetics*, XXV, 1.   The italics are mine.

Later in the same chapter [1] he says that "in general, the impossible must be justified by reference to artistic requirements, or to the higher reality, *or to received opinion.*" Since Aristotle in these two passages is simply exhausting certain logical possibilities that the artist should be aware of, and does not specifically mention character, it is perhaps safest to say merely that these passages *may* have been the source of the idea expressed by Gildon. The idea was not peculiarly neo-classical, and is not dead yet. "Historians may indict a hero or whitewash a villain at their leisure; but to the dramatist a hero must be (more or less) a hero, a villain (more or less) a villain, if accepted tradition so decrees it." These words are not Aristotle's or Gildon's, but William Archer's.[2]

Of the two other qualities that it was thought every character should possess — goodness and convenience, or suitableness — the first was usually defined in such a way as to conflict with Aristotle's meaning. When Aristotle said that a character should be good he meant morally good,[3] but Gildon [4] and Cooke,[5] for example, meant poeti-

1. *Poetics*, XXV, 17.   The italics are mine.
2. *Play-Making, a Manual of Craftsmanship* (Boston: 1923), p. 157.
3. *Poetics*, II, 1.
4. *An Essay on the Art*, etc. (1709), in Rowe's Shakespeare (2nd ed., 1714), IX, xxxviii: "*Good* is when they are mark'd; that is, when the Discourse of the Persons makes us clearly and distinctly see their Inclinations, and what good or evil Resolutions they are certain to take."
5. *The Elements of Dramatic Criticism* (1775), pp. 49–50: "The *goodness* which belongs to poetical manners, being to make them appear such as they are, it is necessary to observe, what are the things which discover to us the inclinations of the personages: and first, the speeches and actions; 'there are manners in a poem, (says Aristotle) if, as we said, the speeches and actions discover to us any inclination;' so that these two things are wholly owing to the poet, who makes his personages speak and act as he pleases, and they are the foundation of all the rest; when the manners are well expressed after this way, they are denoted purely and simply by the term *good*, and this *goodness* makes their first and principal

cally good, or "well-marked." Theirs was an old Renaissance error in the interpretation of Aristotle. John Upton (1746),[1] however, managed to combine Aristotelianism with neo-classicism, by saying that when a character is good he is "not only strongly marked and distinguished, but *good* in a moral sense, as far forth as the character will allow." Fortunately not many critics of the eighteenth century felt that the point was worth laboring. The idea would probably have died from the lack of attention paid to it, but Twining[2] mercifully and scornfully spared it any lingering agonies by putting it to the sword in 1789.

The history of the neo-classic notion that the poet should preserve "the type" has been briefly sketched in the Introduction.[3] Some eighteenth-century critics perpetuated the notion. They said, with Gildon (1709),[4] that the "manners" of a character should be "*Convenient*, that is, these must be agreeable to the *Age*, *Sex*, *Climate*, *Rank*, and *Condition* of the Person that has them." According to Gildon (1718),[5] it was particularly necessary to make the manners of women agreeable. "Thus," he said, "*Valour* is properly a moral Virtue, but it is extremely disagreeable to a *Woman*, for that Sex ought neither to be *Bold*, nor *Valiant*. *Chastity* is agreeable to Woman, and that Poet who robs the Sex of it in any Character fit for Tragedy, gives *Manners* to them, which are disagreeable,

---

qualification. Aristotle places it in the front of all the rest, that it may be the more exactly observed; and Horace gives the same lesson with his usual accuracy and knowledge.
    '*Notandi sunt tibi mores.*'"

1. *Critical Observations on Shakespeare*, p. 78.
2. *Aristotle's Treatise on Poetry*, pp. 325–330.
3. See above, pp. 34–35.
4. *An Essay on the Art*, etc., in Rowe's Shakespeare (2nd ed., 1714), IX, xxxviii.   5 *The Complete Art of Poetry*, I, 247.

and so offend against this Rule." A woman should not be introduced "arguing on Physical Notions, unfit for her Capacity, and unbeseeming her character." She ought not to be credited with "abstruse Knowledge, which the Ladies are by no means esteem'd capable of." [1] No one else seems to have been the extremist that Gildon was, but several others agreed with him in the main.[2] The rule was justified, at least by Dennis,[3] on the familiar ground that types of men, because they are universal, or allegorical, are more instructive than particular men. But it too would have died of inanition. As Alexander Gerard (1759)[4] said, the taste that supported the rule was afflicted with "false delicacy," which was not a natural English growth. After 1784 everyone seems to have entered into a conspiracy to maintain silence on this venerable rule.

---

1 I, 250.

2. Compare Cuthbert Constable, *An Essay Towards a New English Dictionary* (ca. 1720), in *Shakespeare and Shakespeareana* (London: Maggs, No. 434 [1923]), p. 251; John Upton, *Critical Observations on Shakespeare* (1746), p. 82; William Cooke, *The Elements of Dramatic Criticism* (1775), p. 49; William Hodson, "Observations on Tragedy," bound with *Zoraida* (1780), pp. 88–89; James Beattie, *Dissertations Moral and Critical* (1783), I, 223; Hugh Blair, *Lectures on Rhetoric and Belles Lettres* (1783), II, 507; William Richardson, *On the Faults of Shakespeare*, in *Essays on Shakespeare's Dramatic Characters* (1784), pp. 128–130.

3. See *Reflections Critical and Satyrical*, etc. (1711), in Durham, pp. 250–252; but particularly *The Stage Defended*, etc. (1726), pp. 7–8: "For as when *Æsop* introduces a Horse, or a Dog, or a Wolf, or a Lion, he does not pretend to shew us any singular Animal, but only to shew the Nature of that Creature, as far as the Occasion where it appears admits of; so when a Dramatick Poet sets before us his Characters, he does not pretend to entertain us with particular Persons, tho' he may give them particular Names; but proposes to lay before us general and allegorical Fantoms, and to make them talk and act as Persons compounded of such and such Qualities, would talk and act upon like Occasions, in order to give proper Instructions."

4. *An Essay on Taste*, p. 132: "The nicety of *Rymer* is disgusted with the cunning and villany [*sic*] of *Iago*, as unnatural and absurd, soldiers being commonly described with openness and honesty of character. To critics of this class, *Homer's* low similitudes, and simple manners, or *Shakespear's* irregularities and unharmonious numbers, are intolerable faults."

In brief, then, the eighteenth century agreed with Aristotle that the tragic hero should not be eminently good and just, on the one hand, or simply villainous, on the other. Some gave the Aristotelian reason that the misfortunes of an extreme character do not arouse pity or terror, while others went behind this reason by saying that perfectly good characters, if not perfectly villainous ones, are unnatural. Two distinct opinions, however, were entertained concerning the neo-classic conception that tragic characters should be of kingly or noble rank. According to the first, royal or noble characters were necessary because their miseries are more instructive, more moving, and more credible than the miseries of less exalted persons. According to the second, humbler characters were necessary for exactly the same reasons. It was also widely believed that characters should be well-marked and typical, but between 1780 and 1790 this belief seems to have faded from the critical consciousness. During the last quarter of the century, though the old neo-classic ideas regarding the characters of tragedy still had their exponents, they were vigorously opposed. Strictly speaking, it should be said, only the requirements that tragic characters should be royal or noble, well-marked, and typical were of neo-classic extraction; and only these have altogether ceased to be requirements.

CHAPTER VIII

Elements Incompatible with Tragedy

A. *Comedy*

FOR the neo-classicist, tragedy was a delicate art, and he admonished the poet to walk delicately in its precincts. The passions that it raised were the most powerful within the range of human experience, but they were also easily dampened if brought into juxtaposition with alien emotions. Hence the neo-classicist frowned upon the mixture of mirth and melancholy in a play that pretended to be tragedy. To the eighteenth century, as to the Restoration period, a play that contained this mixture was known as a tragi-comedy. If it afforded light pleasure it was a tragi-comedy no matter how calamitous its conclusion might be.[1] On the other hand, at least those who championed poetic justice, as well as some who did not, believed with Hugh Blair (1783)[2] that "it is not essential to the Catastrophe of a Tragedy, that it should end unhappily. In the course of the Play, there may be sufficient agitation and distress, and many tender emotions raised by the sufferings and dangers of the virtuous, though, in the end, good men are rendered successful." The Elizabethan distinction between tragedy, a play that ends unhappily, and comedy, a play that ends happily, in

1. Compare Dr. Johnson, *Preface to Shakespeare* (1765), in *Johnson on Shakespeare*, ed. Raleigh, p. 17.
2. *Lectures on Rhetoric and Belles Lettres*, II, 494.

both of which tears and laughter may be mingled, had long since been given up.[1]

Some eighteenth-century neo-classicists were content with hurling bad adjectives at tragi-comedy, such as "grotesque," "low," and "vulgar." But most writers who disliked it gave reasons, and one of the commonest was that comic circumstances "degrade the Majesty and Dignity of Tragedy."[2] The Elizabethan, who knew not dignity, had obviously enjoyed the "puerilities" and vulgarities of Shakespeare, but the neo-classicist was not amused. "It must be acknowledged," wrote Edward Taylor (1774),[3] "that Shakespear abounds in the true sublime; but it must be allowed that he abounds likewise in the low and vulgar. And who is there, that after soaring on eagle wings to unknown regions and empyreal heights, is not most sensibly mortified to be compelled the next moment to grovel in dirt and ordure." The scene of the gravediggers in *Hamlet*, especially, was a stench in neo-classic nostrils. It "is certainly real life, or as it is vulgarly termed, highly natural," Taylor admitted,[4] "yet how misplaced, how unworthy the tragedian." Sensitiveness to undignified scenes was part and parcel of the sensitiveness to the

1. In the first edition, 1771, of the *Encyclopædia Britannica* tragi-comedy is defined as "a dramatic piece partaking of the nature both of tragedy and comedy; the event whereof is not bloody or unhappy, and wherein is admitted a mixture of less serious characters." The same definition was repeated in the second edition, 1778–1783. In the third edition, 1797, the definition is more clearly neo-classic: "a dramatic piece, partaking both of the nature of tragedy and comedy; in which a mixture of merry and serious events is admitted."

2. Sir Thomas Hanmer (?), *Some Remarks on the Tragedy of Hamlet* (1736), p. 24. Compare Dennis, *On the Genius and Writings of Shakespear* (1711), in Smith, p. 26: "For want of this Poetical Art, *Shakespear* has introduced things into his Tragedies, which are against the Dignity of that noble Poem, as the Rabble in *Julius Caesar*, and that in *Coriolanus*."

3. *Cursory Remarks on Tragedy*, p. 42.   4. P. 40.

indecorous generally. Such scenes were bad for the same reason that it was bad to involve "inferior agents," however natural, in great events.[1] The degree to which decorum and dignity ruled the English stage may be judged from Thomas Davies' remark (1784)[2] on Garrick's conservative managership of Drury Lane: "In the more advanced state of the stage, Mr. Garrick would not risk the appearance of half, or even disordered, dress, though extremely proper, and what the incident of the fable and situation of the characters seemed to require." There was small chance, then, that a buffoon who broke a jest or a grave-digger who spit on his hands should be looked upon with favor.

A more serious objection was that tragedy and comedy arouse emotions that jar upon each other. If "Grief and Laughter," said Gildon (1709),[3] were joined in the same painting, the combination "wou'd be monstrous and shocking to any judicious Eye. And yet this Absurdity is what is done so commonly among us in our *Tragi-Comedies*; this is what our *Shakespear* himself has frequently been guilty of." These plays, said James Ralph (1731),[4] blend Sorrow and Mirth so cunningly together, that a Man does not know whether to cry or laugh, without he could play *Heraclitus*

1. Compare William Richardson, *On the Faults of Shakespeare*, in *Essays on Shakespeare's Dramatic Characters* (1784), pp. 128–132.

2. *Dramatic Micellanies (sic)* (1783), II, 157.

3. *An Essay on the Art*, etc., in Rowe's Shakespeare (2nd ed., 1714), IX, vii. Compare Cuthbert Constable, *An Essay Towards a New English Dictionary (ca. 1720)*, in *Shakespeare and Shakespeareana* (London: Maggs, No. 434 [1923]), p. 251: "There is no Theatre in the world that has any thing so absurd as the English tragi-comedy, tis a drama of our own invention, and fashion of it is enough to proclaim it so, here a course of mirth, there another of sadness and passion; a third of Honour a fourth a duel; in two hours we run through all the fits of Bedlam."

4. *The Taste of the Town*, pp. 57–58.

and *Democritus* at the same time. These Cubs of POETRY, that have never been lick'd into any true Form, can neither be call'd *Tragedies*, *Comedies*, nor *Tragi-Comedies*; they are no real Manufacture, but a Sort of Linsy-Woolsy Entertainment; where a Man of Sense is at a Loss how to settle his Looks, unless he could new coin his Face, and let one Side wear the Stamp of Grief, and t'other that of Joy: Nay, so sudden are the Changes from one to the other, that his right Eye must look grave, and the left smile at the same time, lest he should be surpriz'd into a wrong Behaviour before the Scene is half out.

Kames (1762) [1] thought it "a solid objection to tragi-comedy" that it raised "discordant passions," which "are unpleasant when jumbled together." Francis Gentleman (1770) [2] said that it filled "the imagination with a chaos of idea," and turned "the most serious feelings into laughter."

The last phrase of Gentleman's introduces a still more serious objection, that is to say, that the laughter of comedy not only fails to harmonize with the emotions proper to tragedy, but actually destroys them. It was for this reason that Addison (April 16, 1711) [3] called tragi-comedy "one of the most monstrous Inventions that ever entered into a Poet's Thoughts. An Author might as well think of weaving the Adventures of *Aeneas* and *Hudibras* into one Poem, as of writing such a motly Piece of Mirth and Sorrow." Comic circumstances not only degraded the dignity of tragedy, thought Hanmer (1736),[4] but also destroyed "the Effect of the Intention which the Spectators had in being present at such Representations; that is, to acquire that pleasing Melancholy of Mind, which is caus'd

1. *The Elements of Criticism* (2nd ed., 1763), III, 281.
2. *The Dramatic Censor*, I, 90.
3. *The Spectator*, No. 40.
4. *Some Remarks on the Tragedy of Hamlet*, p. 24.

by them, and that Satisfaction which arises from the Consciousness that we are mov'd as we ought to be, and that we consequently have Sentiments suitable to the Dignity of our Nature." Is it not evident, asked William Cooke (1775),[1] that "*compassion*" will be destroyed if it is mixed with "mirth" and "low humour"? Writer after writer agreed that it was.[2] Hurd (1751)[3] attempted to demonstrate the curious fact that although tears might be inopportunely dried by laughter, laughter could not be drowned in tears:

It is true, in one sense, the *tragic* muse has *veniae minus*; for though grave and pleasant scenes may be indifferently represented, or even mixed together, in comedy, yet, in tragedy, the serious and solemn air must prevail throughout. Indeed, our Shakespear has violated this rule, as he hath, upon occasion, almost every other rule, of just criticism: Whence, some writers, taking advantage of that idolatrous admiration which is generally professed for this great poet, and nauseating, I suppose, the more common, though juster, forms of literary composition, have been for turning his very transgression of the principles of common sense, into a standing precept for the stage. 'It is said, that, if comedy may be wholly *serious*, why may not tragedy now and then be indulged in being *gay*?' If these critics be in earnest in putting this question, they need not wait long for an answer.

1. *The Elements of Dramatic Criticism*, p. 120.
2. See the review of Cumberland's *Mysterious Husband* in *The Critical Review*, LV (1783), 151; also William Richardson, *On the Faults of Shakespeare*, in *Essays on Shakespeare's Dramatic Characters* (1784), p. 133: "As the tendency of these dissonant emotions is to destroy one another, the mind, during the contest, is in a state of distraction"; H. J. Pye, *A Commentary Illustrating the Poetic of Aristotle* (1792), p. 127: "The mixing the serious and the comic, in one piece, tends to destroy the efficacy of both, and is therefore a fault"; John Penn, *Letters on the Drama* (1796), pp. 55–56, and Notes to Calsabigi's *Letter on Tragedy*, in *Critical and Poetical Works* (1797), p. 92.
3. Note on l. 169 of Horace's *Epistle to Augustus*, ed. Hurd, in *Works* (1811), I, 386–387.

The *end* of comedy being *to paint the manners*, nothing hinders . . . but 'that it may take either character of *pleasant* or *serious*, as it chances, or even unite them both in one piece:' But the end of tragedy being *to excite the stronger passions*, this discordancy in the subject breaks the flow of those passions, and so prevents, or lessens at least, the very effect which this drama primarily intends.

How it came about that sorrow, without danger to itself, could pacifically fraternize with mirth in that species of drama in which mirth was usually, if not always, predominant, but could not do so in tragedy, where the serious and strongest passions were uppermost, was a problem in psychological "moments" the solution of which would be a severe test of any science of critical mechanics, and was clearly too severe for Hurd's.

Criticism was on safer ground when it gave the explanation, as did Addison (April 16, 1711),[1] that the tragic "Tide of Sorrow" was broken by the double plot of many tragi-comedies. The same explanation, for example, was given by *The Gentleman's Magazine* (1752)[2] for the weakness of Southerne's *Oroonoko*: "By introducing an under plot of the comic kind, though complete in all its parts, by exhibiting mirth in one scene and distress in another, our attention is too much diverted from the main story, and our concern for those who suffer too much weakened by such quick transitions." The logical Lord Kames (1762),[3] as one should expect, based his objection on this ground, as did also the equally logical William Cooke (1775),[4] who pointed out that the two plots were frequently so nearly

1. *The Spectator*, No. 40.
2. XXII, 163.
3. *The Elements of Criticism* (2nd ed., 1763), III, 280–281.
4. *The Elements of Dramatic Criticism*, pp. 119–120.

parallel that the two sets of characters "keep their distances like the *Mountagues* and *Capulets*, and seldom begin an acquaintance till the last scene of the fifth act, when they all meet upon the stage to wind up their own stories." Anyone should have been willing to admit that a comic plot that serves only as a distraction is bad. In 1792 Pye [1] insisted upon its badness, and in 1796 John Penn [2] commended his predecessor's position.

In one place Gildon (1709) [3] is even more formal than any of this last group of critics, for, he says, adhering to the inspired letter of the *Poetics*, since "a Tragedy is the Imitation of some one grave Action, but not all the Actions of a Man's Life . . . it is plain, that there is no place in Tragedy for any thing but grave and serious Actions." The proposition has the inescapableness of all tautology. In 1789 a writer for *The European Magazine* [4] advanced a somewhat similar argument:

The true principle of objection to that species of composition which we call Tragi-comedy, is not the mixture of tragic and comic action; for the drama is the mirrour of life; and we know that in real life calamitous events are often produced by those which are pleasant or ludicrous. The fault arises from the difficulty of interweaving two plots so, that they shall mutually promote each other, and terminate in one catastrophe; and this difficulty is peculiarly insurmountable in tragedy, from the simplicity of its fable and the rapidity of its action, it being an imitation of men's actions, comedy of their characters.

In this passage, it is clear, the writer is precariously balancing himself on a knife-edge. The slightest suspicion

1. *A Commentary Illustrating the Poetic of Aristotle*, pp. 127–128.
2. *Letters on the Drama*, p. 53.
3. *An Essay on the Art*, etc., in Rowe's Shakespeare (2nd ed., 1714), IX, xxiii.   4. XVI, 15.   The writer signed himself "J. G."

that the fable of a tragedy need not be *quite* simple would have tumbled him groveling into the dirt of tragi-comedy.

On one side this last writer touches the formal Gildon, and on the other certain logically transitional figures, who bridge the gap between the opponents and the defenders of tragi-comedy. Like Gildon he believes that tragi-comedy inevitably violates the unity of action, but unlike Gildon he can see no harm in tragi-comedy *per se*. He differs from John Upton (1746) only in believing that the tragi-comic action must necessarily be double, for Upton,[1] though he disliked the "preposterously jumbled" plots of Southerne's *Oroonoko* and Dryden's *Spanish Friar*, found Shakespeare's skilful blend of the comic and tragic refreshing. According to Frederic Pilon (1777)[2] — who, to be sure, was not thinking of separate tragic and comic plots — in the fifth act of *Hamlet* the connection between the "low ribaldry" and the "striking beauties" is so intimate "that it would be impossible to expunge the one without losing the other." Another writer, in Anderson's *Bee* (1793),[3] who was no friend to "scenes of ribaldry," thought that Shakespeare had handled "low characters, and ludicrons [*sic*] scenes with the same unrivalled propriety as the sublime and the pathetic." Critics like these applied the pragmatic test, and said, in effect, that if tragi-comedy worked it was good. They seemed naturally inclined to reject it as "low."

At the opposite extreme of natural temperament was Fielding (1749),[4] who professed to find the word "low"

1. *Critical Observations on Shakespeare*, p. 106.

2. *An Essay on the Character of Hamlet, as performed by Mr. Henderson* (2nd ed., London: 1777), p. 22.

3. "Critical Remarks on Some Celebrated Authors," *The Bee*, ed. Anderson, XVI, 274.   4. *Tom Jones*, V, i.

meaningless. "Hath any one living," he exclaimed, "attempted to explain what the modern judges of our theatres mean by that word *low*; by which they have happily succeeded in banishing all humour from the stage, and have made the theatre as dull as a drawing-room!" Strangely enough, in a discussion of the first part of *Henry IV*, Mrs. Montagu (1769),[1] who was ordinarily squeamish, and who granted that "perhaps correct taste may be offended with the transitions from grave and important, to light and ludicrous subjects, and more still with those from great and illustrious, to low and mean persons," was sufficiently of Fielding's opinion to defend the tragi-comedy of the play against "the pedantry of learning" and "its dogmatical rules." "Foreigners," she said, "unused to these compositions will be much disgusted at them. The vulgar call all animals that are not natives of their own country, monsters, however beautiful they may be in their form, or wisely adapted to their climate and natural destination. The prejudices of pride are as violent and unreasonable as the superstitions of ignorance." She came pretty close to turning the tables by a near identification of pride with vulgarity and lowness. A reviewer (1795)[2] of Pye's *Commentary* likewise appeals to *Henry IV* in defending tragi-comedy against Pye's charges, but his defense rests mainly on the argument that in domestic tragedy the ludicrous and low may successfully be mingled with the pathetic. Here was good evidence that the word "low," if not meaningless, was a relative term, and that the comic was not inherently inimical to the tragic.

That the tragi-comic mixture was not only not an un-

1. *An Essay on the Writings and Genius of Shakespear*, p. 101.
2. *The Monthly Review*, 2nd series, XVIII, 123.

natural concoction but, on the contrary, highly natural
was, it should be especially emphasized, the opinion of Dr.
Johnson. At first he had thought otherwise. In *The
Rambler*, No. 125 (May 28, 1851), he congratulated his
own age for not having made the mistake "of the last Century," which, he thought, had "polluted its most serious
Interlocutions with Buffoonery and Meanness," and had
indulged in "unseasonable Levity." Later in the same
year [1] he announced his semi-conversion to tragi-comedy.
The mixture was probably in accordance with the laws of
nature. "Impartial Reason" could not condemn it. "The
Impropriety of suppressing the Passions before we have
raised them to the intended Agitation, and of diverting the
Expectation from an Event which we keep suspended only
to raise, it may indeed be speciously urged. But will not
Experience," he asked, "confute this Objection?" He himself at this time could not utter a whole-hearted yes. He
was not yet sure but that "we might have been more interested in the Distresses of his [Shakespeare's] Heroes,
had we not been so frequently diverted by the Jokes of
his Buffoons." Fourteen years afterward, however, his
last doubt had vanished. His study of Shakespeare had
done its work, and in his *Preface* (1765) [2] he acknowledged
his final conversion:

Shakespeare's plays are not in the rigorous and critical sense
either tragedies or comedies, but compositions of a distinct kind;
exhibiting the real state of sublunary nature, which partakes of
good and evil, joy and sorrow, mingled with endless variety of
proportion and innumerable modes of combination; and expressing the course of the world, in which the loss of one is the gain of

1. *The Rambler*, No. 156 (September 14, 1751).
2. *Johnson on Shakespeare*, ed. Raleigh, pp. 15–17.

another; in which, at the same time, the reveller is hasting to his wine, and the mourner burying his friend; in which the malignity of one is sometimes defeated by the frolick of another; and many mischiefs and many benefits are done and hindered without design.

Lastly

Tragi-comedy, he now thought, was as instructive as tragedy and comedy together, "because it includes both in its alterations of exhibition and approaches nearer than either to the appearance of life." Moreover, "daily experience" proved that it was moving, "though it must be allowed that pleasing melancholy be sometimes interrupted by unwelcome levity."

Johnson's voice was the most authoritative raised in favor of the mixed drama, but it was not so "solitary" as Lounsbury [1] would have us believe. In 1749, two years before Johnson's semi-conversion, Fielding had cast suspicion on the favorite word of the enemies of tragi-comedy. In 1761, four years before the *Preface*, George Colman, although he expressed his dislike for certain "Scenes of a low and gross nature" in Massinger and for "the Buffoonry [*sic*] in Venice Preserved," [2] had "allowed" the naturalness of the grave-diggers and of Polonius in *Hamlet* and of the nurse in *Romeo and Juliet*; [3] and in 1765 he was prepared to praise the *Preface* for its "very sensible and spirited vindication of the mingled drama of Shakespeare, and the interchange of serious and comick scenes in the same play." [4] *The Monthly Review* (1765),[5] also, in its criticism of the *Preface*, despite its failure to feel the force of

---

1. *Shakespeare as a Dramatic Artist*, p. 156.
2. *Critical Reflections on the Old English Dramatick Writers*, in *Prose on Several Occasions* (1787), II, 142.   3. II, 113.
4. *Notes on the Preface to Mr. Johnson's Edition of Shakespeare*, in *Prose on Several Occasions* (1787), II, 63.   5. XXXIII, 290.

Johnson's "reasoning," thought that the critics had "condemned this kind of drama too severely." In the same year Horace Walpole, in the "Preface" to the second edition of *The Castle of Otranto*,[1] justified the introduction of smile-provoking domestics into his novel by asserting that his "rule" had been "Nature." But he had had "higher authority" than his own for his practise, he said:

> That great master of nature, *Shakespeare*, was the model I copied. Let me ask if his tragedies of *Hamlet* and *Julius Caesar* would not lose a considerable share of their spirit and wonderful beauties, if the humour of the grave-diggers, the fooleries of *Polonius*, and the clumsy jests of the *Roman* citizens were omitted, or vested in heroics? Is not the eloquence of *Antony*, the nobler and affectedly-unaffected oration of *Brutus*, artificially exalted by the rude bursts of nature from the mouths of their auditors? These touches remind one of the *Grecian* sculptor, who to convey the idea of a Colossus within the dimensions of a seal, inserted a little boy measuring his thumb.

Johnson, it appears, only precipitated a feeling that was already in the atmosphere.

After 1765 the esteem in which tragi-comedy was held mounted steadily, rising with Shakespeare's reputation. The moral Mrs. Griffith (1775) [2] called his plays "a more natural species of composition than either" tragedies or comedies. Their comic portions, said *The Universal Magazine* (1787),[3] afford a relaxation of which "Nature herself" approves. "In Shakespeare alone of all poets," wrote *The Analytical Review* (1789) [4] of his mixing "buffoonery"

1. Pp. viii–ix. 2. *The Morality of Shakespeare's Drama*, p. 172.
3. LXXXI, 243.
4. V, 568. For other defenses of tragi-comedy, in the last quarter of the century, see John Berkenhout, *Biographia Literaria* (1777), quoted in *The Monthly Review*, LVII (1777), 194; *The Mirror*, No. 100 (April 22, 1780); *The Critical Review*, LVII (1784), 107, a review of William Richardson's *Essays on Shakespeare's Dramatic Characters* (1784).

with "sublimity," "is man represented as he really is: and he is the greatest of dramatic poets, because his works afford the truest representation of human life." Tragicomedy, from having been considered his most serious "blemish," had risen here, if only by inadvertent implication, to the position of being the explanation of his greatness, a position that Johnson, it is certain, would have refused to recognize. If the thermometer of Shakespeare's glory was graduated to the end of time, the mingled drama was consequently destined to have a long and brilliant future.

The discord of opinion among those of "critic learning," however, was drowned out by the concord of applause that issued from the pit of the theatre. The learned of all ages might dispute the merit of tragi-comedy; the unlearned vulgar had never been in doubt about it. Too much weight could not be attached, thought Berkenhout (1777),[1] to the fact that "at least a part of the audience" for whom Shakespeare had written had liked what "modern delicacy" considered "too low or vulgar." It was "the common mistake" of the Elizabethan age to admire tragi-comedy, said Rowe (1709),[2] but he had to admit that the mistake was perennial: "tho' the severer Critiques among us cannot bear it, yet the generality of our audiences seem to be better pleas'd with it than with an exact Tragedy." In 1761 Colman[3] could not remember that any "critical Catcall" had ever greeted the indecorums "in our darling Shakespeare." On the whole, it appeared that if, as a writer for

---

1. *Biographia Literaria*, quoted in *The Monthly Review*, LVII, 194.
2. *Some Account of the Life &c. of Mr. William Shakespear*, in Smith, p. 10.
3. *Critical Reflections on the Old English Dramatick Writers*, in *Prose on Several Occasions* (1787), II, 113.

The Universal Magazine (1787) [1] believed, "the judgment of true criticism, and the voice of the public, when once un-prejudiced and dispassionate, will never fail to coincide at last," the coincidence must be effected by a concession from criticism.

The Reverend Martin Sherlock (1786),[2] like many an-other critic before and since, charged Shakespeare with having sacrificed his taste to the desire of making a fortune. But Shakespeare and his contemporaries had not been the only ones to visit the altar. The Restoration writers had followed their profitable example. Indeed, said Thomas Davies (1784),[3] "the politest people in Europe" had been obliged "to tack a diverting petite pièce to make a tragedy palatable to the audience." In his adaptation of *Coriolanus* Dennis (1711)[4] made so shameless a sacrifice that he felt the need for apology:

I know very well that you will be surpriz'd to find, that after all that I have said in the former Part of this Letter against *Shakespear*'s introducing the Rabble into *Coriolanus*, I have not only retain'd in the second Act of the following Tragedy the Rabble which is in the Original, but deviated more from the *Roman* Customs than *Shakespear* had done before me. I desire you to look upon it as a voluntary Fault and a Trespass against Conviction: 'Tis one of those Things which are *ad Populum Phalerae*, and by no means inserted to please such Men as you.

It would have made Dennis feel very humble indeed to hear Boileau remark, as he does in one of Lord Lyttelton's dialogues (1765),[5] that "a great Genius ought to guide, not

---

1. LXXXI, 4.   2. *A Fragment on Shakespeare*, p. 37.
3. *Dramatic Micellanies* (*sic*), I, 240.
4. *On the Genius and Writings of Shakespear*, in Smith, p. 45.
5. *Dialogues of the Dead* (4th ed., London), p. 126. This remark did not appear in the third edition of 1760. I have not seen the first and second editions.

servilely follow, the Taste of his Contemporaries." Whatever a great genius ought to do, it is clear that a prudent theatre manager in 1772 should not have produced *Hamlet* with the grave-diggers left out, as Garrick expensively discovered.[1] Thriftier men than Garrick, whether they adapted Shakespeare or produced plays of their own, catered to the pleasure of the groundlings.[2] The eighteenth-century audience held the whip, as audiences always do, so that tragi-comedy had no need to fear its adverse critics. Theoretical support, besides, it had from Dr. Johnson, Walpole, and others, who, *ex cathedra*, tendered genteel applause, which mingled with the handclapping and vulgar laughter of the pit.

B. *Admiration*

To object to the inclusion of comic and undignified scenes in tragedy was normal neo-classic behavior, in the seventeenth century as well as in the eighteenth. To say that tragedy ought to excite admiration for its personages had been common among seventeenth-century critics, and to observe the precept in practise had been common among seventeenth-century playwrights, but in the eighteenth century, critics and playwrights alike were nearly unanimous in rejecting the doctrine. Almost nothing, indeed, was said about admiration during the eighteenth century. Cuthbert Constable, whose *Essay Towards a New English Dictionary* (*ca.* 1720)[3] is a quite irresponsible hodge-podge

1. See Lounsbury, *Shakespeare as a Dramatic Artist*, pp. 168–169, 172–173.
2. See *The Critical Review*, LV (1783), 151, for a criticism of Cumberland's *Mysterious Husband*.
3. In *Shakespeare and Shakespeareana* (London: Maggs, No. 434 [1923]), p. 252.

of trite theory, did say that a tragic action ought to be "admirable," and he apparently meant the word in its old sense, but he cannot be taken seriously. If anyone agreed with Constable he kept his own counsel. Gildon's belief (1709)[1] that admiration "is a Passion too weak to have the Effect of *Tragedy*" was presumably the belief of most other critics. In 1783 Hugh Blair,[2] for example, granted that the epic, the object of which is "to elevate the imagination," may properly "excite our admiration," but he maintained that for tragedy to do so is to "disappoint" its "main effect," which is the moving of the heart. That the practise of the century gave some reason for so late a revival of the subject in criticism had been indicated three years before by William Hodson, in his *Observations on Tragedy* (1780).[3] Hodson's objection to admiration was the same as Gildon's and Blair's: it is, he said, a "reflective," not an "instinctive," or "natural," passion, and therefore more fitting in the epic than in tragedy. On this ground, then, he condemned the dramas of Corneille,[4] "Ben Johnson's and Thomson's tragedies, with Comus, Charactacus, and variety of other beautiful pieces of composition, which do infinite honour to their authors as poets," but "flag in representation."[5] No one came to the defense. The old question was allowed to drop.

C. *Love*

Love, which had been the companion emotion to admiration in the heroic plays, continued to suffer critical disapproval during the eighteenth century, though there

1. *An Essay on the Art*, etc., in Rowe's Shakespeare (2nd ed., 1714), IX, xxxiii. See also Gildon, *The Complete Art of Poetry*, I, 199, 237–238.
2. *Lectures on Rhetoric and Belles Lettres*, II, 480.
3. Bound with *Zoraida*, pp. 70–71.   4. P. 84.   5 . P. 71 n.

were some men in whose eyes it found favor. Constable (*ca.* 1720) [1] belatedly announced that "an Heroick play ought to be an imitation (in little) of an Heroick poem, and consequently that love and valour ought to be the subject of it." In 1774 Edward Taylor [2] argued that since love is a natural, pleasing, and, in some circumstances, an instructive passion, it is a fitting object for tragic imitation. William Hodson,[3] in 1780, defended its employment in tragedy by saying that if a poet wishes to make use of a foreign story, in the treatment of which he is likely to render the manners of his characters either improper to them or unintelligible to his audience, his only course is "to lay its foundation, as much as possible, on universal manners, so that its leading features may be independent of time, or place, intelligible, and interesting, to all. This it is scarce possible to effect, by any other means than making love the basis of the fable, which, being circumscribed by no bounds of climate or education, if painted with the vivid tints of nature, makes (wherever the scene is laid) sometimes the most terrible, sometimes the most amiable, and at all times the most interesting picture of all the passions." Taylor and Hodson, however, were love's only wholehearted friends.

Several half-hearted friends it had, nevertheless. William Cooke (1775),[4] like Hodson, said that if the tragic poet ought to imitate "passions of which men are susceptible," there could be no reason for his avoiding the passion of love, "which is confessedly the most general of all."

1. *An Essay Towards a New English Dictionary*, in *Shakespeare and Shakespeareana* (London: Maggs, No. 434 [1923]), p. 250.
2. *Cursory Remarks on Tragedy*, pp. 78–79.
3. "Observations on Tragedy," bound with *Zoraida*, p. 91.
4. *The Elements of Dramatic Criticism*, p. 45.

He should, however, exercise moderation, and not allow it to decline, as it too often did, into "the fooleries and intrigues of a *drawing-room*." William Mason's view (1751) [1] was similar to Cooke's. In his judgment love, because of "the universality of its influence," was "a passion very proper for tragedy," provided that it did "not degenerate into episodical gallantry," but made "the foundation of the distress." Joseph Warton (1756),[2] Francis Gentleman (1770),[3] Hugh Blair (1783),[4] and the author of *An Essay upon the Present State of the Theatre* (1760) [5] agreed with Mason that love, if used at all, should be central, not episodic. On the other hand, it was frequently objected by the lukewarm supporters of love that it was the subject of too many tragedies. If you are going to write a love play, they said, make love the chief theme, but if you are going to write more than one play, let some, or even most, of them deal with other subjects. Love, said Joseph Warton (December 4, 1753) [6] again, had usurped too much attention in the theatre:

One of the most remarkable differences betwixt ancient and modern tragedy, arises from the prevailing custom of describing

1. "Letters Concerning the Following Drama," prefixed to *Elfrida, a Dramatic Poem* (2nd ed., 1752), p. iii. Compare Hanmer, *Some Remarks on the Tragedy of Hamlet* (1736), p. 5: "Love will always make a great Figure in Tragedy, if only its chief Branches be made use of; as for instance, Jealousy (as in *Othello*) or the beautiful Distress of Man and Wife (as in *Romeo* and *Juliet*) but never when the whole Play is founded upon two Lovers desiring to possess each other: And one of the Reasons for this seems to be, that this last Species of that Passion is more commonly met with than the former, and so consequently strikes us less."

2. *An Essay on Pope*, I, 262–265.

3. *The Dramatic Censor*, I, 454, a criticism of the "incongruous" and "insipid love scenes" in Addison's *Cato*; his approval of Tate's adaptation of *Lear* (I, 353–354) is inconsistent with this passage, however.

4. *Lectures on Rhetoric and Belles Lettres*, II, 506.

5. P. 17.   6. *The Adventurer*, No. 113.

only those distresses that are occasioned by the passion of love; a passion, doubtless, which, from the universality of its domin- ion, may justly claim a large share in representations of human life; but which, by totally engrossing the theatre, hath contrib- uted to degrade that noble school of virtue into an academy of effeminacy.

Blair (1783) [1] and Pye (1792) [2] were of the same opinion.

Others thought that love was entirely out of place in tragedy. This view, indeed, had been dominant ever since the time of Rymer, because love was inconsistent with the rationalistic standards of neo-classicism. As of old the French [3] and the women [4] were held ultimately responsible for the whole silly business. They had no sense of dignity, and it was against the dignity of tragedy, among numerous other things, that the love-plot sinned. Love, said Gildon (1718),[5] "is directly opposite to that Majesty which this Poem requires." The soft passion, being universal, is necessarily "below the dignity of this drama," Hurd (1757) [6] maintained. The action of modern tragedy, he said, "when stripped of its accidental ornaments and re- duced to the *essential fact*, is nothing more than what might as well have passed in a cottage, as a king's palace." Straighter thinking, it might appear, would simply have in- ferred from this evidence that rank is unnecessary to tragedy, since love, which is common to all ranks, may be tragic. The truth was that it was impossible for men of

1. *Lectures on Rhetoric and Belles Lettres*, II, 506.
2. *A Commentary Illustrating the Poetic of Aristotle*, pp. 250–251.
3. See Mrs. Elizabeth Montagu, *An Essay on the Writings and Genius of Shakespear* (1769), pp. 43–47. *The Monthly Review* (XLI [1769], 134), in its re- view of the *Essay*, agreed with Mrs. Montagu in blaming the French.
4. See John Upton, *Critical Observations on Shakespeare* (1746), pp. 32–33.
5. *The Complete Art of Poetry*, I, 199.
6. *A Dissertation on the Provinces of the Drama*, in *Works* (1811), II, 34.

Hurd's opinion to make such an inference, for they reasoned from definitions to characteristics. Upton (1746),[1] therefore, could rule love out of tragedy by simply defining it as "a comic passion," although Upton, curiously enough, did not dislike comic scenes in tragedy.

Since the characters of tragedy, according to the neo-classicist, had to be dignified personages of high rank, their motives, or frailties, had to be characteristic of noble minds. Ambition was such an infirmity; love was not. To represent love as ruling where ambition should have ruled was therefore "*absurd in Physicks*," said Dennis (1701).[2] "*For Ambition makes a man a Tyrant to himself, as well as it does to others; and where it once prevails, enslaves the Reason, and subdues all other Passions.*" In other words, the poet who showed really tragic heroes in love, that is, noble heroes, violated decorum, and destroyed "the Beauty of the Sentiments, because no Sentiment can be beautiful, which is improper in him who speaks it." [3] For the same general reason women, Gildon (1718) [4] thought, should not be depicted as too amorous, for it seemed to him "a little inconsistent with that Character of Modesty, which is essential to the Sex." In brief, wrote Dr. Johnson (1765),[5] modern dramatists, who introduced nothing but love as the motive of tragic action, violated probability, and misrepresented life. Tragedy of this sort, of course, could not delight.

---

1. *Critical Observations on Shakespeare*, p. 15.
2. *The Advancement and Reformation of Modern Poetry*, sig. a3^r. See also Dennis, *On the Genius and Writings of Shakespear* (1711), in Smith, p. 25.
3. Dennis, "To Judas Iscariot, Esq." (May 25, 1719), in *Original Letters* (1721), I, 72.
4. *The Complete Art of Poetry*, I, 200.
5. *Preface to Shakespeare*, in *Johnson on Shakespeare*, ed. Raleigh, p. 13.

A more important defect, perhaps, was its failure to instruct. If to show women violently in love was inconsistent with their modesty, was it not likely also that it would prove "injurious to the Virtue of a Virgin" who sat in the audience? Gildon (1718) [1] believed so. Toward the end of the century a writer for *The Lounger* (August 6, 1785) [2] eloquently gave voice to the same belief. Love-tragedy was dangerous, he thought, to the young of both sexes.

The moral consequences of such a drama it is unnecessary to question. Even where this passion is purified and refined to its utmost degree, it may be fairly held that every species of composition, whether narrative or dramatic, which places the only felicity of life in successful love, is unfavourable to the strength and purity of a young mind. It holds forth that single object to the ambition and pursuit of both sexes, and thus tends to enfeeble and repress every other exertion. This increases a source of weakness and corruption, which it is the business of a good instructor to correct and overcome, by setting before the minds of his pupils other objects, other attainments, of a nobler and less selfish kind. But in that violence, in that tyranny of dominion, with which Love is invested in many of our tragedies, it overbears every virtue and every duty. The obligations of justice and of humanity sink before it. The king, the chief, the patriot, forgets his people, his followers, and his country; while parents and children mention the dearest objects of natural attachment only to lead them in the triumph of their love.

The latent implication of such arguments was that love was so powerful that it was liable to obscure the other, more instructive, passions of tragedy. Some writers, however, gave an exactly contrary reason for wishing to exclude love from serious plays. It was too weak for tragedy,

1. *The Complete Art of Poetry*, I, 201.
2. No. 27.

they said. Dennis (May 25, 1719) [1] went so far as to assert that it moved the passions "least." Everything considered, wrote Johnson (1765),[2] "it has no great influence upon the sum of life." Modern tragedy, complained Mrs. Montagu (1769),[3] because of its preoccupation with love, was "melting away in the strains of elegy and eclogue," and she begged [4] her countrymen not to let French "example teach us to fetter the energy, and enervate the noble powers of the British muse."

In spite of contradictions, it is evident that love-tragedy found little favor among the critics of the eighteenth century. Except for Taylor and Hodson and the insignificant Cuthbert Constable everyone criticized it with greater or less severity. In this respect eighteenth-century criticism was at one with Rymer and the early formalists. In the theatre itself, nevertheless, a thaw was in progress, as Mrs. Montagu noted for reproof, and here and there a critic was thawing too.

D. *Violence*

If love was too weak to excite the tragic emotions, violence and bloodshed, on the contrary, were too strong. The overwhelming majority of eighteenth-century critics coincided in the opinion that murder and torture were not so much pitiable and terrible as horrible and shocking. Even Orestes' murder of Clytemnestra behind the scenes raised too much horror in the imagination for Rowe's (1709) comfort.[5] But as a critic he was more sensitive than most, for

1. "To Judas Iscariot, Esq." in *Original Letters* (1721), I, 72.
2. *Preface to Shakespeare*, in *Johnson on Shakespeare*, ed. Raleigh, p. 13.
3. *An Essay on the Writings and Genius of Shakespear*, pp. 40–41.
4. P. 42.
5. *Some Account of the Life &c. of Mr. William Shakespear*, in Smith, pp. 18–19.

it was pretty generally agreed that any amount of cruelty could be legitimately perpetrated back-stage. "All cruel Objects ought to be hid, as that of *Medea's* murdering her Children . . . yet beautiful Descriptions of these done with Force and Life will please the Ear, and the Mind, which seeing not the Fact, never examines into its Credibility or Cruelty." [1] These words of Gildon's expressed the conviction of almost everyone. To show the same objects on the stage, however, was considered extremely bad art — the cutting off of hands, for example, as in *Titus Andronicus*; [2] "the extrusion of *Gloucester's* eyes" [3] in *Lear*; or the smearing of the stage "with mingled brains and gore," [4] as in Rowe's *Ambitious Stepmother*. A reviewer (1753) [5] of Edward Moore's *Gamester* condemned even "self-murder, a crime which ought to be looked upon with horror, and never brought upon a stage, but to shew a detestation of it." Pity and terror, which were widely accounted incongruous with laughter, were still more widely accounted incongruous with the tears of agony. [6]

1. Gildon, *The Complete Art of Poetry* (1718), I, 255.

2. Gildon, I, 245.

3. Dr. Johnson, Note on *King Lear* (1765), in *Johnson on Shakespeare*, ed. Raleigh, p. 160.

4. Hume, *Of Tragedy* (1742), in *Essays*, ed. Green and Grose (1898), I, 265.

5. *The Universal Magazine*, XII, 88. Compare Lounsbury, *Shakespeare as a Dramatic Artist*, p. 175: "A character in the tragedy could be permitted to kill himself, whether he did it by poison or steel."

6. Other critics besides those already mentioned who condemned violence on the stage because it was "shocking" are Shaftesbury, *Characteristics* (1711), ed. Robertson, II, 315; Hurd, note on l. 185 of Horace's *Art of Poetry* (1749), ed. Hurd, in *Works* (1811), I, 143–145; Lord Chesterfield, letter to his son (January 23, 1752), in *The Letters of Philip Dormer Stanhope, 4th Earl of Chesterfield*, ed. Dobrée, V, 1820; the Earl of Orrery, "Preface" to *The Greek Theatre of Father Brumoy*, translated by Mrs. Charlotte Lennox and others (1759), p. xxvi; Mrs. Montagu, *An Essay on the Writings and Genius of Shakespear* (1769), p. 41; Francis Gentleman, *The Dramatic Censor* (1770), I, 362, II, 55; and Mrs. Elizabeth Griffith, *The Morality of Shakespeare's Drama* (1775), pp. 403–404.

Some men were opposed to violence on the stage, not merely because it was shocking, but because the shock destroyed the illusion of the theatre. When we read a description of suffering, said Addison (June 30, 1712),[1] we are pleased by "the secret Comparison which we make between our selves and the Person who suffers," but when we actually see the sufferer in agony, "the Object presses too close upon our Senses, and bears so hard upon us, that it does not give us Time or Leisure to reflect on our selves. Our Thoughts are so intent upon the Miseries of the Sufferer, that we cannot turn them upon our own Happiness." Addison seems not to have had tragedy specifically in mind here, but Kames (1762),[2] when he wrote to the same effect, did have it in mind.

Violent action ought to be excluded from the stage. While the dialogue runs on, a thousand particulars concur to delude us into an impression of reality, genuine sentiments, passionate language, and persuasive gesture: the spectator once engaged, is willing to be deceived, loses sight of himself, and without scruple enjoys the spectacle as a reality. From this absent state, he is roused by violent action: he wakes as from a pleasing dream, and gathering his senses about him, finds all to be a fiction.

He thought, indeed, that the French overlooked the most substantial objection when they urged only that violence "is barbarous, and shocking to a polite audience." If you wish merely to be shocked, he said,[3] reminding us of Rowe, listen to the recital of Clytemnestra's murder by Orestes. "I appeal to every person of feeling, whether this scene be not more horrible, than if the deed had been committed in sight of the spectators upon a sudden gust of passion."

1. *The Spectator*, No. 418.
2. *The Elements of Criticism* (2nd ed., 1763), III, 281–282.
3. III, 283.

In complete agreement with Kames, Dr. Johnson (1765) [1] asserted that "the extrusion of *Gloucester*'s eyes" compelled "the mind to relieve its distress by incredulity." Dying, William Cooke (1775) [2] believed, was an expert act, "which none but a Roman Gladiator could naturally exhibit on the stage, when he did not imitate, but actually perform it; therefore, 'tis better to omit the representation." One who had no real experience in dying would be sure to bungle the act, so that "when we see death thus represented, we are convinced it is but fiction." It is interesting to find Kames and Johnson, two of the clearest thinkers of the century, both using this purely neo-classic argument. It is particularly interesting to find Johnson using it, because in the *Preface* he denies the possibility of delusion. [3]

A select few compromised on the question of stage violence. Addison (April 20, 1711) [4] said that there was "generally something ridiculous in it," but that it was "almost as ridiculous" to do as the French did, and never perform an execution or commit a murder within sight of the audience. "The *French* have therefore refined too much upon *Horace*'s Rule, who never designed to banish all Kinds of Death from the Stage: but only such as had too much Horror in them, and which would have a better Effect upon the Audience when transacted behind the Scenes." Pye (1792) [5] was exactly of Addison's opinion. He thought it likely that "the general stabbing scene, in Titus Andronicus, if represented, would hardly be less risible than the

---

1. Note on *King Lear*, in *Johnson on Shakespeare*, ed. Raleigh, pp. 160–161. This note, of course, was written before the *Preface*.
2. *The Elements of Dramatic Criticism*, pp. 108–109.
3. See below, pp. 209–211.   4. *The Spectator*, No. 44.
5. *A Commentary Illustrating the Poetic of Aristotle*, p. 207.

catastrophe of Tom Thumb," but he had little sympathy with the "delicacy of the French," [1] and named certain stabbings that had "a very fine theatrical effect." [2] Thomas Hanmer (1736),[3] too, admitted that there was "a great deal of Justice" in the complaints about blood-spilling, but felt kindly toward milder scenes that conduced "to the Beauty of the Piece."

Only three critics, one of them a foreigner, seem to have had stomachs strong enough for unmitigated violence. The hearty James Ralph (1731) [4] scorned the "puny Appetites and weak Desires" of the French. For him "shocking" and "agreeable" were synonyms:

We *English* scorn such trifling Kick-shaws; what is substantial, alone charms us; and, when we feed, it must be Knuckle-deep in a Sirloin. Let not then the Forms of their Romantick Love and Honour, regulate our Taste. We are convinc'd, that the more naturally things are represented on the Stage, the more shocking, or agreeable they prove, according to the Heinousness, or Innocence of the Fact. How can we shew a just Abhorrence of that Crime we sleep over, when 'tis told? Let the Representation be faithful, and every Passion is rous'd; the Sight blows up the Coals of Indignation, and Rivets a Detestation in our Souls. Thus the wise *Spartans* made their Slaves get drunk, that their Children might imbibe the truest Idea of, and fix'd Aversion for that beastly Vice.

The Englishmen who sat for Lewis Riccoboni's flattering picture (1738) [5] were obviously not the sirloin-gorging

1. P. 203.
2. Pp. 206–207. *The Monthly Review* (2nd series, XVIII [1795], 122–123), in its review of the *Commentary*, apparently agreed with Pye.
3. *Some Remarks on the Tragedy of Hamlet*, p. 61.
4. *The Taste of the Town*, p. 65.
5. *A General History of the Stage. . . . Translated from the Eminent Lewis Riccoboni. . . . To which is Prefixed an Introductory Discourse concerning the Present State of the English Stage and Players* (2nd ed. of the translation, London: 1754), pp. 171–172. The first edition of the translation appeared in 1741.

Anglo-Saxons whom Ralph had painted seven years before — either that, or one or both of the artists had failed to catch a true likeness of the sitters. Both pictures, however, served to justify hair-raising scenes on the stage.

The principal Character of the *English* is, that they are to be plunged in Contemplation. . . . It is owing to this their pensive Mood, that the Sciences of the most sublime Nature are by the Writers of that Nation handled with much Penetration, and that Arts are carried to that Pitch of Perfection which they are now arrived at; because their native Melancholy supplies them with that Patience and Exactness which other Countries have not.

To pursue my Reasoning; I believe that were there to be exhibited on their Stage, Tragedies of a more refined Taste, that is, stript of those Horrors that sully the Stage with Blood, the Audience would perhaps fall asleep. The Experience which their earliest Dramatic Writers had of this Truth, led them to establish this Species of Tragedy, to raise them out of their contemplative Moods, by such bold Strokes as might awaken them.

Kindness and ingenuity like this deserved royal recognition. Not until 1789, when Twining published his edition of Aristotle, did anyone else come out uncompromisingly in favor of violence. Twining [1] denied that Greek practise furnished authority for the delicate decorum that was insisted upon by the French. In Sophocles, he said, there is the most vivid "*description* of Oedipus tearing out his own eyes."

But Sophocles did not confine himself to *description*. Oedipus himself immediately appears upon the stage, and exhibits the shocking spectacle of his bloody eyes to the audience. Certainly, the French rule, "de ne pas ensanglanter le Theatre," was not *much* more strictly observed here by Sophocles, than it was by Shakspeare in his LEAR, where Gloster's eyes are *trodden out*, ἐν φανερῳ, upon the stage.

1. *Aristotle's Treatise on Poetry*, pp. 289–290.

With the exception of Twining and Ralph, however, English critics were all more or less of the French, or neo-classic, opinion in this matter.[1] Concerning the advisability of scenes of bloodshed and violence there was less change of critical opinion during the eighteenth century than there was concerning comic scenes or love-plots. Addison may have been right when he said that there is something ridiculous in most stage fights and murders. It is certainly true that the fight between Macduff and Macbeth seldom fails to raise a titter in the audience, and one is inclined to agree with Pye that the lopping off of hands in *Titus Andronicus* would probably be more risible than tragic.

1. See Lounsbury, *Shakespeare as a Dramatic Artist*, pp. 174–208, for an account of the discrepancy between theory and practise during the eighteenth century. Two passages from the letters of Lord Chesterfield to his son perfectly illustrate what happened when plays that observed the neo-classic rule about bloodshed attempted to invade the theatre. The passages concern Philip Francis's "classical" *Eugenia*, which was produced in Drury Lane on the night of February 17, 1752. On February 20 Chesterfield wrote as follows (*Letters*, ed. Dobrée, V, 1836): "Francis's *Cénie* has been acted twice with most universal applause; to-night is his third night, and I am going to it. I did not think it would have succeeded so well, considering how long our British audiences have been accustomed to murder, racks, and poison, in every tragedy; but it affected the heart so much, that it triumphed over habit and prejudice. All the women cried, and all the men were moved." On March 2 he had a different story to tell (V, 1839): "Francis's *Eugenia*, which I will send you, pleased most people of good taste here; the boxes were crowded till the sixth night, when the pit and gallery were totally deserted, and it was dropped. Distress, without death, was not sufficient to affect a true British audience, so long accustomed to daggers, racks, and bowls of poison; contrary to Horace's rule, they desire to see Medea murder her children upon the stage. The sentiments were too delicate to move them; and their hearts are to be taken by storm, not by parley."

CHAPTER IX

The Unities

A S EARLY as Pierre de Laudun's *L'Art Poétique François* (1598) [1] the unities had become the target
of critical fire, and seventeenth-century critics
on both sides of the Channel had now and then
discharged volleys of adverse comment. In England even
Rymer had been only a lukewarm friend. Among eighteenth-century English critics the great majority, for one
reason or another, were hostile to the unities — especially,
and indeed almost exclusively, to the unities of time and
place.

These minor unities, of course, received some encouragement. A handful of writers gave them complete, if somewhat vague and general, approval. [2] A few others defended

1. See above, p. 48.
2. For example: Cuthbert Constable, *An Essay Towards a New English Dictionary* (*ca.* 1720), in *Shakespeare and Shakespeareana* (London: Maggs, No. 434
[1923]), p. 251: "In the mecanick Beauties of ye plot, which are the Observations
of the 3 unities, time, place and action, both Shakespear & Fletcher are deficient
but Shakespear most." William Mason, "Letters Concerning the Following
Drama," prefixed to *Elfrida* (2nd ed., 1752), p. ii: "Good sense, as well as antiquity, prescribed an adherence to the three great Unities; these therefore were
strictly observed." Lord Chesterfield's letter to his son (January 23, 1752), *Letters*, ed. Dobrée, V, 1820: "The English ought to give up their notorious violations of all the unities." *The Universal Magazine*, XII (1753), 86: "Those, who
judge best, say the unities of action, time, and place, are essential." Henry Boyd,
"An Essay on French Tragedy," *Anthologia Hibernica*, I (1793), 288: "It is indeed objected to the French tragedies in general, that their rigorous adherence to
the doctrine of the Unities has introduced into their drama, a spirit of complicated intrigue. This, however, has its advantages, as it gives an animation to the
action, inversely proportioned to the length of the time."

them with definite and specific arguments. Gildon (1718) [1] represents Tyro as reasoning in the manner that was made familiar by Farquhar in 1702 and that became even more familiar as the years passed:

If we must take a *Barry* for a *Lucrece*, and a *Goodman* for an *Alexander*, or destroy the Representation, I think we may as well admit other Impositions that equally advance and enlarge the Pleasure. If we may suppose that while we sit still, our Stage moves from Place to Place, tho' the different Places be never so contiguous; as for Example, out of one Room into another of the same House; we may with equal Probability suppose the Stage may move twenty, nay a thousand Miles. In like manner, if we can suppose that twenty-four Hours pass while we sit in the Theatre no more than three or four, I can see no reason but that we may as well imagine that fifty Years may have pass'd in the same Time; and if fifty, five hundred; for in Impossibilities, there are no degrees of more or less.

Gildon,[2] through the mouth of Laudon, shows Tyro his mistake:

You are highly deceiv'd to think that there is the least Imposition on your Understanding, or on Truth, in the *Tragic* Representation, for that is absolutely false. Who ever that went to see a Play imagin'd that he must suppose *Barry* a *Lucrece*, or *Goodman* an *Alexander*? No, we go to see the Picture of some Action either of *Alexander*, *Achilles*, *Lucrece*, or others represented by the Actors. . . .

But you say farther, that if we can suppose a Stage before us moving from place to place while we sit still, we may as justly suppose it to travel five hundred Miles, as to pass from one Room into another, tho' in the same House. I grant it, and therefore all that can be drawn from your Objections is, that there is a

1. *The Complete Art of Poetry*, I, 228–229. Compare Farquhar, *A Discourse upon Comedy*, in Durham, pp. 282–285.
2. I, 230–231.

necessity that the *Unity of Place* be preserv'd, to avoid shocking your Reason. For indeed, if you once pass the Bounds of *Truth* and *Probability*, I see not where you can stop, and why you should stop any where. But, Sir, the Antients never were guilty of this Absurdity, but the Place where your Play open'd, continu'd to the conclusion of your *Fable*.

The same thing may be said of the Unity of Time; and what you observe is certainly true, you may as well extend it to 500, nay 5000 Years, as to 24 Hours.

A moment later [1] Laudon concedes that if more time is necessary for the fictive action than may be accounted for in the representation, it "should be cast into the Intervals of the Acts, because that Deception is not so obvious, and easily observ'd by the Audience, as hap'ning out of Sight." Although Gildon denies that the audience takes Barry for Lucrece, or that its understanding is imposed upon in any way, his use of the word "deception" reveals that he entertains the old neo-classic delusion-theory in spite of himself. His advice about the disposal of excess time, moreover, amounts to a desertion of the unity of time.

Until after 1765 Gildon's defense of the strict unity of place was the last of any importance. It received a good deal of casual encouragement, such as William Guthrie's [2] praise of Ben Jonson for having observed "the unities of place and characters," but of reasoned defense there was almost none. Strict unity of time was in no better case. Guthrie's assertion that Jonson's plays were "so complete in the unity of time, that they are acted upon the stage in the same time which the same story would have taken up in real life," serves only to reveal the writer's sympathies.

1. I, 233. Compare Gildon, *An Essay on the Art*, etc., in Rowe's Shakespeare (2nd ed., 1714), IX, xxix, xxx.

2. *An Essay upon English Tragedy* (*ca.* 1747), p. 6.

Joseph Warton, by criticizing Addison's *Cato* [1] and Rowe's *Jane Shore* [2] for their violation of the unity of time, which was the same, he thought, as a violation of probability, accomplished no more than Guthrie. Johnson's *Preface* (1765), with its critique of the unities and its concomitant denial of the theory of delusion, stimulated a few late and mostly incomplete and confused efforts to justify the minor unities, the discussion of which, however, must for the moment be postponed.

The major unity of action was in no danger, for almost everyone saw that it was essential. Daniel Webb (1762) [3] was one of the few to find fault with it — on the same old grounds that Englishmen had always criticized French tragedy:

> As no one simple and confined action can furnish many incidents, and those, such as they are, must tend to one common point, it necessarily follows, that there must be a sameness and uniformity in the sentiments. What must be the result of this? Why, narration is substituted in the place of the action; the weakness in the manners supplied by elaborate descriptions; and the quick and lively turns of passion are lost in the detail, and pomp of declamation.

William Hodson (1780) [4] also preferred a double plot, except when a single plot could be made "sufficiently vari-

1. *An Essay on Pope* (1756), I, 265.
2. I, 273.
3. *Remarks on the Beauties of Poetry* (London: 1762), p. 105.
4. "Observations on Tragedy," bound with *Zoraida*, p. 78. Compare Martin Sherlock, *A Fragment on Shakspeare* (1786), p. 35, who objected to all three unities on this ground, and represented Shakespeare as saying to Jonson: "I will sacrifice the unities, to which one cannot submit but at the expence of action." Also "Critical Remarks on the Othello of Shakespear," *The Bee*, ed. Anderson, I (1791), 61: "To be scrupulously attentive to the unities of time and place, confines the genius of the writer, makes the work barren of incidents, and consequently less interesting." The "Remarks" are subscribed "W. N."

ous, and implex," for in his judgment anything was "preferable to the apathy produced by want of incident." Samuel Foote (1747) [1] *implies* that the unity of action may be dispensed with when he praises Shakespeare for having succeeded so often while observing only the unity of "Character." In its review of Johnson's *Preface*, *The Monthly Review* (1765) [2] was outspoken in its rejection of the strict observance of the primary unity:

> The unity of action is sufficiently observed when a single end is proposed, to which all the means made use of, in the piece, effectually tend. These means, consisting of subordinate actions, may accordingly be few or many, provided their several directions converge to one point, in which they unite and are concentrated.

Like Foote, this writer [3] set unity of character above the other three. The opinion of the critics here mentioned, however, was not the normal one. Iconoclasm usually stopped short of smashing the idol of unified action.

It is true that when critics made fun of or seriously condemned the three unities, they may be said to have meant to include the unity of action, but "the three unities" was a petrified phrase, and those who used it meant generally, if not always, the two unities of place and time — even, it should seem, when action was specifically named. This loose inclusion of the chief unity in the ridicule or damnation of the other two occurred only in the vaguer, more

---

1. *The Roman and English Comedy Consider'd and Compar'd*, p. 21.
2. XXXIII, 377–378.
3. XXXIII, 378. Compare William Richardson, *On the Faults of Shakespeare*, in *Essays on Shakespeare's Dramatic Characters* (1784), pp. 132–133: "There is a certain consistency of passion, emotion, and sentiment, to be observed in fine writing; not less important than unity of action, and of much greater consequence than the unities either of time or of place." Richardson (pp. 142–143), however, was friendly to the unities.

uncritical disparagements. When Steele,[1] in a comment upon Powell's operas, playfully tells us that he has provided himself "with the works of above twenty French critics, and shall examine (by the rules which they have laid down upon the art of the stage) whether the unity of time, place and action, be rightly observed in any one of this celebrated author's productions," we may be reasonably sure that the word "action" is used simply because it was part of a traditional phrase. So also, unless he had never read, or had forgotten, *Othello* and other unified Shakespearean plays, "Tragicomicus"[2] cannot be taken to have wished to include the unity of action when he said that if Shakespeare had observed the three unities "he wou'd have flown like a *Paper-Kite*, not *soar'd like an Eagle*." In most celebrations of Shakespeare's successful violation of the unities, which was commonly hailed as a victory of nature over art,[3] it was his violation of time and place that received the emphasis.

> When Shakespear leads the mind a dance,
> From France to England, hence to France,
> Talk not to me of time and place;
> I own I'm happy in the chace.
> Whether the drama's here or there,
> 'Tis nature, Shakespeare, every where.

Robert Lloyd (1760),[4] who wrote these lines, may have been happy also in the chase of one of Shakespeare's double

1. *The Tatler*, ed. Aitken, No. 115 (January 3, 1709/1710).
2. *The Covent-Garden Journal*, ed. Jensen, No. 62 (September 16, 1752). Jensen (II, 259) says that "Tragicomicus" is "probably not a pen-name of Fielding's."
3. Compare the Earl of Orrery, "Preface" to *The Greek Theatre of Father Brumoy* (1759), pp. ix–x; Berkenhout, *Biographia Literaria* (1777), quoted in *The Monthly Review*, LVII (1777), 193–194; *The Universal Magazine*, LXXXI (1787), 243.
4. Robert Lloyd, "Shakespeare," in *The Poetical Works* (1774), I, 78–79.

plots, but he does not say so. Those who did formally say
that they were happy in such a chase give the impression,
on the whole, that their greatest happiness came from
being wafted through time and space, not from being
plunged into the confusion of a multiplicity of plots.

In the more definite arguments against the unities the
emphasis was unmistakably on those of time and place.
Of these arguments perhaps the most damaging was the
historical one that the unities had been necessary on the
Greek stage only because of the presence of the chorus, a
line of reasoning that was apparently not used by anyone
until 1760, when it appeared in *An Essay upon the Present
State of the Theatre*. The anonymous author of this important contribution to the controversy was by no means
wholly opposed to the unities, parts of his essay being
reminiscent of Gildon himself. The writer's trouble was
that he knew all that could be said against the unities, but,
while feeling the force of his knowledge, was unwilling to
accept the conclusion toward which it pushed him. He
destroyed the unities with regret in his heart, though in his
historical argument [1] regret does not appear:

The Chorus . . . laid the poet under a necessity of observing
the continuity of the action; for, if it was to be interrupted, there
could be no reason to imagine, that the Chorus which met merely
on its account, should continue upon the stage. It was this likewise, that made the observation of the Unity of Place inviolable
with the antients; for since the Chorus was to continue upon the
stage, from the beginning to the end of the piece, it could not,
without a manifest absurdity, be supposed to pass from Europe
to Asia, from Thebes to Athens, &c. The Unity of Time as well
as that of place, took its rise from the Chorus; for, if the poet had
given his tragedy the extent of a week, a month, or a year, how

1. Pp. 119–120.

could he have made the spectators believe, that so many persons, who had not disappeared for a moment, had passed all that time, without his ever seeing them eat, drink, or sleep? Hence it follows, that the Unities so rigorously insisted upon by the critics, were observed by the antients only because the Chorus made them necessary; and, that the moderns may be allowed to dispense with them, since the invention of a variety of scenes makes the strict observation of Unity of Place unnecessary; and, since the intervals between the acts allow the poet whatever latitude he thinks proper, with regard to Time.

After the appearance of the *Essay* the historical explanation became fairly common property. Lord Kames used it in 1762, Dr. John Brown in 1763, Maurice Morgann in 1777, and Hugh Blair in 1783.[1]

The argument from history, however, was hardly more damaging than certain others based upon logic, or at least upon common sense. In 1718 Gildon had been forced to say that there must be an exact correspondence between the time of action and the time of representation, for he had recognized that if any discrepancy was admitted, there was no limit to which the playwright might not go.[2] Farquhar (1702)[3] first explicitly raised this objection to the unity of time.

Now for another Impossibility; the less rigid Criticks allow to a Comedy the space of an artificial Day, or Twenty Four Hours; but those of the thorough Reformation, will confine it to the natural or Solar Day, which is but half the time. Now admitting this for a Decorum absolutely requisite: This Play begins when it is exactly Six by your Watch, and ends precisely at Nine,

1. Kames, *The Elements of Criticism* (2nd ed., 1763), III, 300–303; Brown, *A Dissertation on the Rise*, etc., pp. 42, 114–115; Morgann, *An Essay on Falstaff*, in Smith, p. 251; Blair, *Lectures on Rhetoric and Belles Lettres*, II, 482–483.
2. See above, pp. 195–196.
3. *A Discourse upon Comedy*, in Durham, pp. 282–283.

which is the usual time of the Representation. Now is it feazible in *rerum Natura*, that the same Space or Extent of Time can be three Hours, by your Watch, and twelve Hours upon the Stage, admitting the same Number of Minutes, or the same Measure of Sand to both. I'm afraid, Sir, you must allow this for an Impossibility too; and you may with as much Reason allow the Play the Extent of a whole Year; and if you grant me a Year, you may give me Seven, and so to a Thousand. For that a Thousand Years shou'd come within the Compass of three Hours is no more an Impossibility, than that two Minutes shou'd be contain'd in one. *Nullum minus continet in se majus*, is equally applicable to both.

Farquhar, of course, went too far, because, in spite of the contrary evidence of such a play as *The Winter's Tale*, unity of character does put some limit upon the time. The other writers who adopted Farquhar's reasoning were more moderate. The restraint of Johnson's [1] statement of it was usual: "He who can multiply three Hours into twelve, or twenty-four, might image with equal Ease a greater Number." Twining (1789) [2] insisted upon the evident absurdity of forcing Aristotle's "single revolution of the sun" to mean strict unity of time. If Aristotle had meant this, wrote Twining, he would have said it. Pye (1792),[3] besides stressing the contradiction that such an interpretation reads into Aristotle, pointed out that the neo-classic rule could not have been based upon Greek practise, as Aristotle says that his was, for Greek trage-

---

1. *The Rambler*, No. 156 (September 14, 1751). Compare Hanmer (?), *Some Remarks on the Tragedy of Hamlet* (1736), p. 52; *The Monthly Review*, XIII (1755), 494–495; anonymous, *An Essay upon the Present State of the Theatre* (1760), pp. 96–97; "Critical Remarks on the Othello of Shakespear," *The Bee*, ed. Anderson, I (1791), 61–62. All of these writers take essentially the same position as Johnson.

2. *Aristotle's Treatise on Poetry*, p. 227.

3. *A Commentary Illustrating the Poetic of Aristotle*, pp. 130–131.

dians did not always confine the time of action to the time of the representation.

When a Greek, French, or English dramatist did manage to make the two exactly correspond, ran another argument, he usually did so at the expense of probability, in the interest of which the neo-classic rule had originally been invented. In *Tristram Shandy* (1759) [1] Sterne poked fun at those who took "probability of time" too seriously. "The idea of duration, and of its simple modes," he said, "is got merely from the train and succession of our ideas, — and is the true scholastic pendulum, — and by which, as a scholar, I will be tried in this matter, — abjuring and detesting the jurisdiction of all other pendulums whatever." Such a pendulum may have satisfied the requirements of an unorthodox novelist like Sterne, but critics of the drama, unorthodox and more or less orthodox alike, felt the need for a more precise timepiece. Daniel Webb (1762),[2] who may be classed as unorthodox, was one who desired greater precision:

When the action is confined to the time of the representation, the Poet must often bring events together within the space of four hours, which, in the natural course of things, would have taken up as many days. Thus, by a strange kind of management, he commits a violence on nature, in order to come nearer to truth.

Pye (1792),[3] also, as one should expect, said that the breach of this moral unity of time was worse than the breach of strict unity. In 1719 Dennis,[4] who was fundamentally orthodox, had taken the same unorthodox position:

1. II, viii.
2. *Remarks on the Beauties of Poetry*, p. 106.
3. *A Commentary Illustrating the Poetic of Aristotle*, p. 131.
4. "To Judas Iscariot, Esq.," in *Original Letters* (1721), I, 73.

Another of *Shakespear*'s Faults is the Length of Time em-ploy'd in the carrying on his Dramatick Action. The present Spectators are extreamly shock'd at this in a modern Tragedy, but at the same time approve of those in which the Unity of Time is preserved by offending all Common Sense.

Everyone saw the point — even Edward Taylor, and it is amusing to watch him use this deadly argument in an at-tempt to reveal the absurdity of Johnson's belief that there is nothing unreal about representing the preparations for a war in the first act and the event of the war in the fifth.[1] It is all very well, reasoned Taylor (1774),[2] to say that there is nothing unreal about this; but

the question is not about the reality, but the seeming possibility of the action represented. Now it is possible that some prepara-tions for war might be made in the space of three hours; but it is not possible that the preparations for war, and that the event of the war should take place in so limited a time.

The only catch here is that Johnson was not talking about an action of only three hours, so that in trying to rescue the unity of time Taylor knocked it, instead of its assailant, on the head. Taylor, however, was uncommonly obtuse. Other men, after achieving this stage of enlighten-ment, realized that it was probably too late to defend strict unity of time in a play as a whole, although many rightly insisted upon unity within the act.[3]

1. See Johnson, *Preface to Shakespeare* (1765), in *Johnson on Shakespeare*, ed. Raleigh, p. 27.

2. *Cursory Remarks on Tragedy*, p. 4.

3. Other critics to object to the breach of the moral unity of time were the anonymous author of *An Essay upon the Present State of the Theatre* (1760), p. 95; Lord Kames, *The Elements of Criticism* (1762) (2nd ed., 1763), III, 319–320; the reviewer of Johnson's *Preface* in *The Monthly Review*, XXXIII (1765), 380; Sher-lock, *A Fragment on Shakespeare* (1786), pp. 34–35.

Rigid formalism led also to the violation of the moral unity of place. It was often just as absurd to have everything happen in the same place as it was to have it happen in three hours. French drama, as Englishmen delighted in pointing out, was particularly marred by this absurdity. From unity of place, wrote *The Monthly Review* (1755),[1]

the *French* dramatic writers seldom or never depart; for, say they, it is absurd to suppose ourselves transported from one place to another, whilst we actually remain in the same house. — Very true; but the nature of the theatre is such, that whilst we are endeavouring to avoid one absurdity, we certainly fall into another. The *French* poet, in compliance with this rule, is frequently obliged to introduce his personages under very disadvantageous circumstances. If he lays his scene in the street, his fine full-dressed ladies are obliged to hold long conversations in the open air. If, on the contrary, we are all the while to suppose ourselves spectators of what passes in a particular apartment, as it is impossible that every necessary thing should be transacted there, he is obliged to have recourse to description of events, the *sight* of which would have given us much more pleasure.

The Greek dramatists, said Blair (1783),[2] had had to struggle with the same absurdity, but upon them the struggle had been forced by the presence of the chorus. With the chorus gone, except in such deliberate archaisms as *Elfrida* and *Caractacus*, modern dramatists were under no necessity to burden themselves with the ancient restrictions.

The logical, or common-sense, argument concerning the inferences that could be drawn from any discrepancy be-

1. XIII, 496 n.
2. *Lectures upon Rhetoric and Belles Lettres*, II, 485–486. Other critics to object to the breach of the moral unity of place were Dennis, "To Judas Iscariot, Esq." (1719), in *Original Letters* (1721), I, 73–74; Kames, *The Elements of Criticism* (1762) (2nd ed., 1763), III, 316–319; Beattie, *Dissertations Moral and Critical* (1783), I, 226–227; Pye, *A Commentary Illustrating the Poetic of Aristotle*, p. 131.

tween the time of action and the time of representation, together with the arguments concerning the moral unities of time and place, though strong, were secondary to the psychological arguments, if they may be so called, regarding the possibility or reality of delusion. Neo-classic theory asserted that the unities of time and place were necessary if the audience was to *believe* that it was actually present at the time and place of representation, and that if this belief were shattered, theatrical illusion vanished. The eighteenth century began early to undermine the old theory. The esteem in which imagination and fancy came to be held weakened the older rationalistic position, for men had begun to see more and more clearly that the imagination perversely accepted what the reason recognized as absurd. Decorum and regularity, said the rationalists, must be maintained at all hazards. But, said Farquhar,[1] in 1702,

we can expect no more Decorum or Regularity in any Business, than the Nature of the thing will bear; now if the Stage cannot subsist without the Strength of Supposition, and Force of Fancy in the Audience; why shou'd a Poet fetter the Business of his Plot, and starve his Action, for the nicety of an Hour, or the Change of a Scene; since the Thought of Man can fly over a thousand Years with the same Ease, and in the same Instant of Time, that your Eye glances from the Figure of Six, to Seven, on the Dial-Plate; and can glide from the *Cape of Good-Hope* to the *Bay of St. Nicholas*, which is quite cross the World, with the same Quickness and Activity, as between *Covent-Garden Church*, and *Will's Coffee-House*.

1. *A Discourse upon Comedy*, in Durham, p. 285. Compare Fielding, *Tom Jones* (1749), V, i: "Who ever demanded the reasons of that nice unity of time or place which is now established to be so essential to dramatic poetry? What critic hath been ever asked, why a play may not contain two days as well as one? Or why the audience (provided they travel, like electors, without expense) may not be wafted fifty miles as well as five?"

The volant "Thought of Man," stimulated by the poet's magic, could put a girdle round the earth in much less than Puck's forty minutes. In *The Tatler* (April 29, 1710),[1] a dogmatic fop having found fault with a comedy because its author had violated the unity of place, Addison, through the mouth of an intelligent woman, replied:

> It is a pretty kind of magic . . . the poets have, to transport an audience from place to place without the help of a coach and horses. I could travel round the world at such a rate. 'Tis such an entertainment as an enchantress finds when she fancies her self in a wood, or upon a mountain, at a feast, or a solemnity; though at the same time she has never stirred out of her cottage.

The human imagination, men had rediscovered, was capable of more than the formalists had given it credit for. The theme announced by Farquhar and Addison was embroidered by critic after critic.

In 1736 Sir Thomas Hanmer [2] said that to assume that "our Imagination will not bear a strong Imposition" is to leave a great deal of indubitable imposition unaccounted for. Our imagination is certainly deluded, he said, when, in the theatre, it permits all nations to speak fluent English, believes a London stage to be Rome, and Wilks to be Hamlet, — all of which are "as great Impositions" as the violation of time and place. "No Rules are of any Service in Poetry, of any kind," he wrote, "unless they add Beauties, which consist (in Tragedy) in an exact Conformity to Nature in the Conduct of the Characters, and in a sublimity of Sentiments and nobleness of Diction." He did admit, however, that delusion is impossible when the poet defies reason. If not defied, reason assisted in the decep-

---

1. No. 165.
2. *Some Remarks on the Tragedy of Hamlet*, pp. 52–54.

tion. John Upton,[1] in 1746, welcomed the "magical operations" of the poet, which help on "an innocent deceit," and
impose on the spectator to his delight. "Dramatic poetry
is the art of imposing," he wrote; [2] "and he is the best poet,
who can best impose on his audience; and he is the wisest
man, who is easiest imposed on." Fourteen years before his
Preface Johnson (September 14, 1751) [3] said that "since it
will frequently happen that some Delusion must be admitted, I know not where the Limits of Imagination can be
fixed." The author of *An Essay upon the Present State of
the Theatre* (1760),[4] although he was inclined to stand firm
on the unity of time, believed that "change of scenes" con-
tributed to the "illusion." Lord Kames (1762),[5] who has
sometimes been given more credit for originality than he
deserves, simply elaborated what Farquhar had said sixty
years before. Because of its bearing on what Johnson said
three years later, however, one remark of Kames's [6]
merits special attention:

Where the representation is suspended, we can with the greatest facility suppose any length of time or any change of place.
The spectator, it is true, may be conscious, that the real time and
place are not the same with what are employ'd in the representation, even including the intervals: but *this is a work of reflection*; and by the same reflection he may also be conscious, that
Garrick is not King Lear, that the playhouse is not Dover cliffs,
nor the noise he hears thunder and lightning.

1. *Critical Observations on Shakespeare*, p. 74.
2. P. 73.
3. *The Rambler*, No. 156.
4. P. 97.
5. *The Elements of Criticism* (2nd ed., 1763), III, 304–306. In 1773 *The Macaroni and Theatrical Magazine* reprinted Kames's chapter on the unities, and William Cooke also took it over in *The Elements of Dramatic Criticism* (1775).
6. III, 305. The italics are mine.

The italicized clause reveals that Kames did not hold that the spectator willingly suspended his disbelief, but rather that, in order to disbelieve, the spectator had to make a kind of conscious effort. The theory of real delusion was never carried further.

By the time of Johnson's *Preface* (1765) all of the arguments against the unities that anyone has ever been able to think of had been used.[1] Johnson, consequently, could at best have done no more than restate the old ones. Apparently he chose not to do so, for he ignored them all except one, which he himself, following Hanmer, had used in 1751: if the imagination, he wrote,[2] recapitulating a familiar idea, can suffer one imposition, such as taking the stage "for the palace of the *Ptolemies*," it can suffer any number of impositions; for "delusion, if delusion be admitted, has no certain limitation." He accepted the conclusion to which this reasoning led, namely, that the unities of time and place are unnecessary, but he no longer accepted the reasoning. Like Farquhar, Hanmer, and Kames, he believed[3] that "supposition" could extend times and annihilate space; he said that "time is, of all modes of existence, most obsequious to the imagination"; but he denied theatrical delusion. He denied that the mind of an audience wandered "in extacy," or that the spectator suffered from a "calenture of the brains." "The truth is," he said, "that the spectators are always in their senses, and know, from the first act to the last, that the

---

1. Unless the discovery by Twining, in 1789 (*Aristotle's Treatise on Poetry*, pp. 226–227), that the unities of time and place did not have the authority of Aristotle may be considered an argument. In 1792 Pye (*A Commentary Illustrating the Poetic of Aristotle*, p. xi) confirmed the discovery of Twining.

2. *Preface to Shakespeare*, in *Johnson on Shakespeare*, ed. Raleigh, p. 26.

3. Pp. 26, 27.

stage is only a stage, and that the players are only players."
Any extent of space might be traversed and any length of
time consumed without undeceiving the audience, for it
was not deceived to begin with. To the question, If the
drama is not "credited," how does it move the audience?
he answered: [1]

It is credited with all the credit due to a drama. It is credited,
whenever it moves, as a just picture of a real original; as representing to the auditor what he would himself feel, if he were to
do or suffer what is there feigned to be suffered or to be done.
The reflection that strikes the heart is not, that the evils before
us are real evils, but that they are evils to which we ourselves
may be exposed. If there be any fallacy, it is not that we fancy
the players, but that we fancy ourselves unhappy for a moment;
but we rather lament the possibility than suppose the presence
of misery, as a mother weeps over her babe, when she remembers
that death may take it from her. The delight of tragedy proceeds
from our consciousness of fiction; if we thought murders and
treasons real, they would please no more.

This explanation of the effect that a play has upon an
audience looks very much like "rationalization." After
denying theatrical illusion, Johnson had to find something
to take its place. If we are not deceived about the reality
of the business transacted before us on the stage, if we are
not deluded even in the slightest degree, then some theory
must be invented to account for the evident pleasure that
we feel in dramatic exhibitions. The pleasure, Johnson
said, is that of recognizing the similarity between the imitation and the reality, or truth, imitated; or that of being
reminded of reality by the evident verisimilitude of the
imitation. At first glance Johnson's argument has the
appearance of good neo-classic doctrine, which had always

1. P. 28.

insisted that only the verisimilar is pleasing, and it would have been good if it had not been put to an unholy use. Johnson's making it serve, however, as a substitute for the theory of real delusion was sacrilegious, for in the old time verisimilitude had been the handmaid of delusion, and the unities of time and place, in their turn, had been the servants of verisimilitude. The neo-classic system had had many ironic jokes played on it, but none more ironic than this.

The contribution of Johnson's *Preface*, then, to the age-long dispute consisted in a denial of theatrical illusion, a denial that was of dubious value. So far as the unities were concerned, the *Preface* was important mainly because of its influence on later writers. *The Critical Review* (1765) [1] was perhaps the first to assert that the remarks on the unities were "worthy of Mr. Johnson's pen." Speaking of the edition as a whole, *The Gentleman's Magazine* (1765) [2] said that "all commendation is precluded by the just celebrity of the author." The discussion of the unities was approved by Mrs. Montagu (1769), Twining (1789), and Joseph Warton (1797).[3] It was restated, in more or less fullness, by Beattie (1783), Sherlock (1786), and a certain "J. G.," in *The European Magazine* (1789); also by Belsham (1789) and a writer for *The Bee* (1791).[4] Apparently the last critic of the century to give Johnson's argument full statement

---

1. XX, 330.   2. XXXV, 479.

3. See Mrs. Montagu, *An Essay on the Writings and Genius of Shakespear*, pp. 14–15; Twining, *Aristotle's Treatise on Poetry*, p. 230; *The Works of Alexander Pope*, ed. Warton, I, 213.

4. See Beattie, *Dissertations Moral and Critical*, I, 227–228; Sherlock, *A Fragment on Shakspeare*, pp. 34–35; *The European Magazine*, XVI, 14–15; Belsham, *Essays Philosophical and Moral*, etc. (2nd ed., 1799), II, 551–552; *The Critical Review*, New Arrangement, IV (1792), 139, which approved of Belsham; *The Bee*, ed. Anderson, I, 141.

was Henry James Pye (1792),[1] who concluded his observations with the quotation of the following important sentence of the *Preface*: "It is false that any representation is mistaken for reality; that any dramatic fable, in its materiality, was ever credible, or, for a single moment, was ever credited." Whether Johnson was as important in his generation as he has come, in ours, to seem to have been, some have disputed; but the influence that his *Preface* wielded during the last thirty-four years of the century was certainly very great.

The *Preface* did not meet with universal approval, however. George Colman (1765),[2] although he was favorably impressed by it, and agreed in the main with what it said about the unities, thought, nevertheless, that Johnson had gone too far. "All liberties," he wrote, "may be carried to an excess, and the violation of these Unities may be so gross as to become unpardonable." Essentially, Colman's judgment was also that of *The Monthly Review* (1765),[3] which criticized the *Preface* at great length. The unities of time and place in their strict interpretation, said the reviewer, may be disregarded, but in their looser interpretation they are essential, for they guarantee the unities of action and character. The writer was very much annoyed [4] by what Johnson had said about delusion:

1. *A Commentary Illustrating the Poetic of Aristotle*, p. 137; see Johnson, *Preface*, in *Johnson on Shakespeare*, ed. Raleigh, p. 26.
2. *Notes on the Preface to Mr. Johnson's Edition of Shakespeare*, in *Prose on Several Occasions* (1787), II, 67. The *Notes* appeared in 1765 in *The London Magazine* (vol. XXXIV) and, in part, in *The Scots Magazine* (vol. XXVII). On the unity of time Francis Gentleman (*The Dramatic Censor* [1770], II, 167) was of much the same opinion as Colman: "We are by no means advocates for that pinching limitation which so disadvantageously fetters modern composition; imagination will indulge several trespasses of liberty, but must be offended when all the bounds of conception are arbitrarily trodden under foot."
3. XXXIII, 296, 381.   4. XXXIII, 298.

We do not pretend to say that the spectators are not always in their senses; or that they do not know (if the question were put to them) that the stage is only a stage, and the players only players. But we will venture to say, they are often so intent on the scene, as to be absent with regard to every thing else.

The man who could write these words deserved more attention than he got. He granted that the understanding was not deceived, but insisted that the "passions" were. That he was no supporter of the older neo-classic delusion-theory is perfectly clear, however: [1]

The ingenious Abbé Batteux, in treating of this subject, observes, that "if the place of the dramatic action be changed, or the time of it prolonged, the spectator must necessarily perceive there is some artifice used; after the discovery of which deceit, he can no longer be brought to believe any thing that passes, and consequently nothing in the representation will be capable of affecting him." It is notorious, however, as hath already been observed, that the spectator is affected, and yet believes nothing at all of the actual distress of the scene, or as our Editor calls it, the *materiality* of the fable.

What really happens in the theatre, he said,[2] anticipating Coleridge, is that "the understanding enters into a compact, as it were, to keep holiday, while the passions are amusing themselves within the ordinary bounds of sentiment, or what is usually called common sense." His was certainly a sounder view than Johnson's, if Johnson really meant what he seems to have meant.

Two other writers also disagreed with Johnson. William Hodson (1780) [3] did not explicitly deny what Johnson had said about delusion, but his own position on the subject of the minor unities is an implicit denial:

1. XXXIII, 374–375.   2. XXXIII, 376.
3. "Observations on Tragedy," bound with *Zoraida*, p. 76.

I cannot therefore help dissenting in this point from a celebrated writer, when he reasons thus: If I can suppose the stage
in the first scene one apartment, and in the second another, why
may I not suppose one scene in England, and the next in France?
Because, though a small change of place adds to probability and
interest, a greater change has a quite opposite effect.

He wished to restrict the time to "the diurnal revolution
of the sun, the period prescribed by Aristotle." Concerning the same passage in the *Preface* to which Hodson here
referred, John Penn (1796),[1] with his characteristic lack of
clarity, wrote:

This is at least certain, that supposing us to transport ourselves in imagination to the first, it is possible for us to conceive
the absurdity of any place's being, at once, the same and different, whatever force there be in this idea. It is not less improbable, that the time and place should be varied between the
acts; for we, in a manner, see through the curtain.

In several other places, so far as one can make out his
meaning, Penn seems to favor the strict observance of the
unities. He says,[2] for example, that

extreme perspicuity is only to be had by a strict adherence to the
unities of time and place. Where they are, observed there is a
perpetual key to the story; the mind no longer having occasion
to enter into itself to develope any part of it. Thus if perspicuity
be a quality of the least value in composition, these unities
are not, as Johnson represents them, superfluous, or rather a
blemish.

In one breath he speaks [3] disrespectfully of "the cavils of
French dogmatism," and in the next praises [4] the unities
for giving the drama the privilege "of being regulated by

1. *Letters on the Drama*, p. 22.
2. P. 49.   3. P. 47.   4. Pp. 49–50.

precise invariable rules, drawn from the nature of things."
His stand on delusion is marked by the same absence of
perspicuity: [1]

> The skilful development of the plot, the effect of theatrical
> spectators, as exhibited in the chorus, and that perspicuity,
> which I shall speak more of, resulting from the unities of place
> and time, and owing to the equal connection of all the parts of
> regular tragedy, seem to produce a more vivid conception of the
> event passing before our eyes, mistaken, I imagine, for that
> belief, which it would naturally accompany. The more there is
> of this vivid conception so produced, and unattended by belief,
> the more pleasure do we derive from tragedy.

Does this mean that the spectator, when he enjoys a
"vivid conception" of a fictitious event represented upon
the stage, mistakes that conception for belief in the reality
of the event? If so, what difference does it make whether
we call it "vivid conception" or "belief"? Or does it
mean simply that the spectator does not believe in the
reality of the event? If Penn was following Pye, as he says
he was, he succeeded only in making very obscure what
Pye and Johnson had made very clear.

James Harris (1781),[2] who was apparently not thinking
of Johnson, may be said to have retained the old delusion-
theory. When he saw Garrick act he could not help
thinking, he said, that he was "in *Denmark* with HAMLET,
or in *Bosworth* Field with RICHARD." He clearly rejected
the strict unities, nevertheless, although he would have
confined the place of action to a single city, and the time
to "*a Day or two.*" [3] Harris, however, could "endure" a

1. P. 27.
2. *Philological Inquiries*, p. 108.
3. P. 219.

play that violated these restrictions if it was good in other respects. Edward Taylor (1774) could not. His support of the strict unity of time was no more muddled and disastrous than his support of the strict unity of place. To Johnson's denial that the spectator really believes that his walk to the theatre "has been a voyage to Egypt" Taylor replies: [1]

But the objection is not only to the impossibility, but to the impropriety of changing the place; for the spectator does not imagine that he is at Alexandria, he knows he is in a theatre; and whilst he is there, if he knows he is not at Alexandria, he must know à fortiori that he cannot be at Alexandria and at Rome too; if the stage cannot represent Venice, à fortiori, it cannot represent Venice and Cyprus too; if the stage is but one, the place cannot be more than one. The objection to removing the scene of action from one place to another arises from the disgust we feel at being presented with one palpable impossibility upon another.

The argument does not make the slightest sense, but it convinced Taylor that the stage must always represent the same place. For him there was no doubt about the reality of delusion, or about the unfortunate effect that a violation of the unities would have upon it. The dramatic rules, he said,[2] are "consonant to reason, and calculated to deceive the spectator into a persuasion, that he is interested in a real event, whilst time, place, and action, conspire to strengthen the delusion." It is a curious thing that Taylor should have been able to take such a line so late in the day. It testifies to the strength of the old dominion of the rules.

1. *Cursory Remarks on Tragedy*, pp. 6–7.
2. P. 33. Presumably *The Critical Review* (XXXVIII [1774], 119) was of the same opinion, for it approved of the *Remarks*.

Johnson's *Preface* stirred up a good deal of opposition, but with the exception of Taylor no one wanted to reestablish the ancient state of things in its entirety. So far as theory was concerned, the forces of revolt had triumphed even before Johnson had come to their assistance, although in the theatre itself the old allegiance lived stubbornly on. [1]

Great credit for this revolution must be given to the writers who preceded Johnson and Kames. In 1702 Farquhar demonstrated that the time of action and the time of representation must correspond exactly or not at all. In 1719 Dennis insisted upon the superiority of the moral unities of time and place. And in 1760 *An Essay upon the Present State of the Theatre* pointed out that the absence of the chorus in modern drama was all the excuse that a writer needed for neglecting the minor unities. Kames and Johnson added only the weight of their authority.

Mr. T. M. Raysor [2] is right in saying that Lounsbury "inclines to give Dr. Johnson and Lessing the credit which really belongs in large part to their predecessors." Johnson, to be sure, had more influence than any one of the earlier critics — even more than Kames; but his contribution to theory was negligible — not through any inherent lack of originality, but simply because, when he appeared on the scene, all the work had been done. Lessing, great as he was in criticism, suffered the same historical misfortune as Johnson. The forty-fifth and forty-sixth numbers of his *Hamburgische Dramaturgie* were not written until 1767, so that his observations on the origin of the

1. Compare Lounsbury, *Shakespeare as a Dramatic Artist*, p. 90.
2. "The Downfall of the Three Unities," *M. L. N.*, XLII (1927), 5. See Lounsbury, *Shakespeare as a Dramatic Artist*, pp. 74–82, 87–91.

unities in the Greek chorus [1] and on Voltaire's violation of the moral unity of time in *Mérope* [2] were a little belated. Lounsbury [3] himself, of course, names a number of men who preceded Lessing in their condemnation of plays that crowd too much action into three hours. What Lessing did, of course, he did well; but in 1767 it was not new. Moreover, he had no influence in England until late in the century, as Lounsbury admits.[4] In short, the downfall of the theory of the unities in England was mainly due to English critics who wrote before 1762, but it is almost certain that the great body of Englishmen would have remained in ignorance of this revolution if it had not been for *The Elements of Criticism* and the *Preface to Shakespeare*. There can be little doubt, either, that the collapse of the theory would have taken a much longer time to affect theatrical practise if it had not been for the popularity of Shakespeare's plays on the eighteenth-century stage.

1. *Hamburgische Dramaturgie* (Hamburg: 1769), No. 46 (October 6, 1767).
2. No. 45 (October 2, 1767).
3. *Shakespeare as a Dramatic Artist*, p. 80. He names Racine, La Place, and Lord Chesterfield.
4. P. 87. In 1780 T. Winstanley (*Aristotelis de Poetica* [Oxford], p. 278) referred to the *Hamburgische Dramaturgie*. In 1789 Twining (*Aristotle's Treatise on Poetry*, pp. xviii–xix) said that he first learned of the book's existence through Winstanley's reference, and that he had only just read it in a French translation, since he did not know German, and had not been aware of the translation until it was sent to him by a friend. He praised Lessing very highly. In 1792 Pye (*A Commentary Illustrating the Poetic of Aristotle*, p. xv) wrote as follows: "From the Dramaturgie of M. Lessing I have occasionally inserted large extracts, as it is a work not generally known, nor yet translated into our language, though abounding with just and original criticism."

CHAPTER X

The Minor Rules

THE only one of the "mechanic rules" to retain any vitality in the eighteenth century was that of the three unities. The minor rules were regarded by most men as merely historical curiosities. The question whether a chorus is desirable in tragedy generated more heat than any of the other subordinate issues — more, indeed, than it had any right to generate, considering that the chorus had really been cold in its grave since the time of the *Ars Poetica*. William Mason, who impressed its gibbering ghost to serve in his *Elfrida* (published, 1751; acted, 1772) and *Caractacus* (published, 1759; acted, 1764, 1776), was certain of its desirability. Ordinary "Play-makers may have gain'd by rejecting the Chorus," he wrote (1752),[1] but, he went on ingenuously, "the true Poet has lost considerably by it. For he has lost a graceful and natural resource to the embellishments of Picturesque Description, sublime allegory, and whatever else comes under the denomination of *pure Poetry*." Its value as embellishment had been highly appreciated some twenty years before by James Ralph (1731),[2] who called it "the noblest Ornament of the *Stage*"; in 1760 Dr. Thomas Franklyn [3] said that the chorus had been "absolutely

1. "Letters Concerning the Following Drama," prefixed to *Elfrida* (2nd ed., 1752), p. xi.
2. *The Taste of the Town*, p. 118.
3. *A Dissertation on Ancient Tragedy* (2nd ed., 1768), p. 32.

necessary on the ancient stage, and that it might be rendered useful and ornamental even on our own"; and John Penn,[1] in 1796, praised it for "its effect in improving the spectacle" and for its increment of song. The esthetic effect of tragedy was also heightened in another way by the chorus, Mason [2] and Penn [3] agreed, for the emotions it manifested served to augment the pathos felt by the audience.

Its instructiveness was more important than the pleasure that it gave, in the opinion of Hurd and Mason, who were both clergymen. "Nothing can compensate," said Hurd (1749),[4] for its absence on the modern stage:

For it is necessary to the truth and decorum of characters, that the *manners*, bad as well as good, be drawn in strong, vivid colours, and to that end that immoral sentiments, forcibly expressed and speciously maintained, be sometimes *imputed* to the speakers. Hence the sound philosophy of the chorus will be constantly wanting to rectify the wrong conclusions of the audience, and prevent the ill impressions that might otherwise be made upon it.

Only the chorus was fit for such a purpose, thought Mason.[5] For

in those parts of the Drama, where the judgment of a mixt audience is most liable to be misled by what passes before its view, the chief actors are generally too much agitated by the furious passions, or too much attach'd by the tender ones, to think

1. *Letters on the Drama*, pp. 38–39.
2. "Letters Concerning the Following Drama," prefixed to *Elfrida* (2nd ed., 1752), pp. xiii–xvi.
3. *Letters on the Drama*, pp. 23–24.
4. Note on l. 193 of Horace's *Art of Poetry*, ed. Hurd, in *Works* (1811), I, 146–147.
5. "Letters Concerning the Following Drama," prefixed to *Elfrida* (2nd ed., 1752), pp. xii–xiii.

cooly, and impress on the spectators a moral sentiment properly. A Confidant or Servant has seldom sense enough to do it, never dignity enough to make it regarded. Instead therefore of these, the antients were provided with a band of distinguish'd persons, not merely capable of seeing and hearing, but of arguing, advising, and reflecting; from the leader of which a moral sentiment never came unnaturally, but suitably and gracefully; and from the troop itself, a poetical flow of tender commiseration, of religious supplication, or of virtuous triumph, was ever ready to heighten the pathos, to inspire a reverential awe of the Deity, and to advance the cause of *honesty* and of truth.

For these two moralists the chorus was another means of persuading the *dulce* to walk amicably with the *utile*.

Three other reasons, not mentioned by Mason, were given for believing in the desirability of the chorus in tragedy. Hurd,[1] Joseph Warton (1756),[2] who quotes from "the excellent Brumoy," and Penn [3] all considered it indispensable to the probability of a play. Their reasoning was based on the assumption that the characters of tragedy should be royal, or noble, and therefore public, personages, to whom the most natural accidents that can happen are such things as revolutions and other unfortunate affairs of state. Events like these, of course, take place before witnesses, who are represented in tragedy by the chorus, so that to make them take place as if in private is to go contrary to the nature of things. Warton,[4] or rather Brumoy, from whom he quotes, added the supplementary argument that the chorus insures the moral unity of place, since it forbids the crowding of too many actions on the stage, which the spectator is asked to consider a public

1. Note on l. 193 of Horace's *Art of Poetry*, ed. Hurd, in *Works* (1811), I, 146.
2. *An Essay on Pope*, I, 74–77.
3. *Letters on the Drama* (1796), p. 23.
4. *An Essay on Pope*, I, 76.

area. Finally, said Warton (or Brumoy), the continuous presence of the chorus effects a continuity of action that is altogether lacking in the modern drama.

That the chorus had this last effect no one seems to have denied, but the other claims that were made for it were contradicted by many writers. Of Mason's remarks on its poetic advantages Thomas Gray (1751) [1] had a low opinion:

> Here are we got into our tantarums! It is certain that pure poetry may be introduced without any chorus. I refer you to a thousand passages of *mere* description in the Iambic parts of Greek tragedies, and to ten thousand in Shakespeare, who is moreover particularly admirable in his introduction of pure poetry, so as to join it with pure passion, and yet keep close to nature.

The banishment of the chorus, in Gray's judgment,[2] was not only not an esthetic loss but a positive gain, for it made many subjects available to the tragic writer that the chorus rendered unfit for use, and it afforded him an opportunity to introduce a greater richness of intrigue. With Mason's other esthetic argument, that the sight of the emotion of the chorus heightens the emotion of the audience, *The Gentleman's Magazine* (1752),[3] in a review of *Elfrida*, disagreed strongly:

> A chorus is purely artificial, and wholly foreign to every natural event; it is only an expedient which was used to assist the

1. "Mr. Gray's Remarks on the Letters prefixed to Mason's Elfrida," in *The Works of Thomas Gray*, ed. Mitford (1858), IV, 3.

2. IV, 1–2.

3. XXII, 224. The reviewer goes on to refute each of Mason's arguments. Compare "Tragicomicus," *The Covent-Garden Journal*, ed. Jensen, No. 62 (September 16, 1752); Robert Lloyd, "Shakespeare" (1760), in *The Poetical Works* (1774), I, 81–82; Blair, *Lectures on Rhetoric and Belles Lettres* (1783), II, 485–486; Richard Cumberland, *The Observer*, No. 111 (1788).

representation before a better was discovered; for nothing surely can be more absurd than to admit the reality of a company of women, who are not only present to every incident, but make and sing an extemporary ode on the occasion: whenever this *Chorus* is present, the power of fancy is at an end, the hero and the palace vanish, and the theatre and the actors rush upon the mind.

Many critics, moreover, thought that the chorus was as ill adapted to the uses of instruction as it was to the uses of pleasure. George Colman (1783) [1] was one, and Pye (1792) another. "If the poet has drawn vice amiable, and virtue contemptible or repelling," said Pye,[2] "it is in vain for him to endeavour to alter the impression by a chorus." The creation of delight through beauty and the promotion of goodness through moral instruction might or might not be equally desirable, but, it was generally believed, neither the one nor the other could be effected by this ancient means.

The reason that most writers reached the same conclusion as Pye is contained in the passage that has just been quoted from *The Gentleman's Magazine*. The chorus was considered absurd and improbable, destructive of theatrical illusion. The Earl of Orrery (1759), in his "Preface" to Brumoy's *Greek Theatre*,[3] explained the nature of the improbability:

Delusion may compel us to imagine ourselves at Athens, or at Thebes, it may conjure up ghosts and goblins to our eyes, and may even transport us into the Elysian fields; but no delusion

1. Note on l. 288 of *The Art of Poetry: an Epistle to the Pisos. Translated from Horace. With Notes*, ed. George Colman (London), pp. xxiii–xxv.
2. *A Commentary Illustrating the Poetic of Aristotle*, p. 232. Compare Morgann, *An Essay on Falstaff* (1777), in Smith, p. 255.
3. P. xi.

can ever render us sufficiently inchanted to suppose fifteen people capable of keeping a secret, and, which is still as extraordinary, fifteen people of the same mind, thought, voice, and expression. Yet, this is the jury, without whose verdict the laws of the ancient drama cannot be put in force.

The explanation given by "Ideus Dactylus" (1777) [1] was more usual: "We have been much told about the justice and probability of a chorus, and that there always must be spectators in all scenes; but it seems to me absurd to suppose, that the principal persons of a tragedy would conduct their affairs so badly as to have all their thoughts exposed to the public eye." In other words, the presence of the chorus makes it inevitable that the dramatist should violate the moral unity of place, for in every play at least one thing is bound to happen within sight and hearing of the chorus that one would naturally expect to happen in private. The chorus and the unities were inextricably entangled with one another, and to revive the first, said Lord Kames (1762),[2] would be "to revive the Grecian slavery" of the others. The arguments against the revival had been so many and so powerful that by 1797 Joseph Warton,[3] who, forty-one years earlier, had approvingly quoted Brumoy's assertion of the probability of the chorus, announced that his "conviction of its utility and propriety" had been shaken. With regret he joined the number of those who thought it best finally to lay this ancient ghost.

1. *The Gentleman's Magazine*, XLVII, 64. Compare Chesterfield's letter to his son (January 23, 1752), in *Letters*, ed. Dobrée, V, 1821; Dr. John Brown, *A Dissertation on the Rise*, etc. (1763), p. 233 n.; Blair, *Lectures on Rhetoric and Belles Lettres* (1783), II, 485–486; *The European Magazine*, XVI (1789), 14; *The Monthly Review*, 2nd series, XVIII (1795), 121.

2. *The Elements of Criticism* (2nd ed., 1763), III, 314.

3. Note on "Two Chorus's to the Tragedy of Brutus," in *The Works of Alexander Pope*, ed. Warton, I, 158.

In 1797 John Penn must have found his own loyalty a lonely one.

One of the reasons for favoring the chorus had been that it insured the continuity of action and scene, but it was possible to believe in the necessity of the *liaison des scènes* without believing in the necessity of the chorus. In 1693 Dennis [1] could find no justification for the chorus in modern drama, but on May 25, 1719, he criticized [2] Shakespeare for frequently "breaking the Continuity of the Scenes." Lord Kames (1762),[3] also, while ruling out the chorus, thought it "an essential requisite, that during an act the stage be always occupied; for even a momentary vacuity makes an interval." Hugh Blair (1783) was another who rejected the one [4] and accepted the other: [5]

> During the course of one Act, the Stage should never be left vacant, though but for a single moment; that is, all the persons who have appeared in one scene, or conversation, should never go off together, and be succeeded by a new set of persons appearing in the next Scene, independent of the former. This makes a gap, or total interruption in the representation, which, in effect, puts an end to that Act. For, wherever the Stage is evacuated, the Act is closed.

Aside from these three remarks, however, there was almost complete silence on the subject of *liaison* during the eight-

1. *The Impartial Critic*, in *Critical Essays of the Seventeenth Century*, ed. Spingarn, III, 148, 183.
2. "To Judas Iscariot, Esq.," in *Original Letters* (1721), I, 73.
3. *The Elements of Criticism* (2nd ed., 1763), III, 322. "French writers, generally speaking, are extremely correct in this particular," he wrote (III, 323). "The English, on the contrary, are so irregular as scarce to deserve a criticism: actors not only succeed each other in the same place without connection; but, what is still worse, they frequently succeed each other in different places."
4. See *Lectures on Rhetoric and Belles Lettres*, II, 485–486.
5. II, 497.

eenth century, an indication that most men consented to the persistent English practise of breaking scenes. Two men explicitly approved the English practise. The reviewer of Johnson's *Preface* in *The Monthly Review* (1765) [1] gave a pertinent example of the sort of absurdity to which *liaison* sometimes led the older French dramatists:

> The French, indeed, in support of the unity of place, maintain that the stage never should be empty during the act; in consequence of their observance of this rule, however, they are guilty of much greater absurdities than would arise from shifting the scene. It is mentioned, as an instance of consummate skill in Corneille, that he hath provided, in one of his plays, for keeping the stage full, while one of the characters goes to the field to fight, and returns conqueror. Now had this supposed combat passed during the interval between the acts, or even during the shifting of the scene, it had not transgressed the bounds of dramatic probability, because it then had passed during the interlude of the imagination; but the audience would not fail of perceiving the improbability of a combat's being fought while they had been listening to some twenty or thirty lines, spoken by the persons of the stage.

Such conduct of the action was a violation of the moral unity of time. "The antient continuity of scene," wrote William Hodson (1780), [2] also precluded the possibility of action in such plays as those of Corneille. If the same scene had to be maintained throughout an entire act, the dramatist, Hodson apparently thought, without much reason, would be hard put to it to find excuses for bringing much action upon the stage. Fortunately not many critics considered the issue sufficiently alive to warrant either sup-

1. XXXIII, 381.
2. "Observations on Tragedy," bound with *Zoraida*, p. 84.

port or attack, and a dull subject was allowed to pass into oblivion.

Horace's rule that every play should be divided into five acts also had few eighteenth-century admirers. Gildon (1718),[1] however, exercised his ingenuity in an attempt to justify it:

> The first Act contains the Matter or Argument of the Fable, and the introducing the principal Characters. . . . The *second* brings the Affairs or Business into Act. The *third* furnishes Obstacles and Difficulties. The *fourth* either shews how these Difficulties may be remov'd, or finds new in the Attempt. The *fifth* puts an End to them all, in a fortunate Discovery, and settles the whole Matter according to Reason and Probability.

William Guthrie (*ca.* 1747) [2] and William Cooke (1775) [3] also came to its defense. But these three were the only faithful ones. Everyone else either ignored or condemned it, and on September 14, 1751, Johnson [4] gave it the lie circumstantial:

> By what Accident the Number of Acts was limited to five, I know not that any Author has informed us, but certainly it is not determined by any Necessity arising either from the Nature of Action or the Propriety of Exhibition. An Act is only the Representation of such a Part of the Business of the Play as proceeds in an unbroken Tenor without any intermediate Pause. Nothing is more evident than that of every real, and, by Consequence, of every dramatick Action, the Intervals may be more or fewer than five; and indeed the Rule is upon the *English* Stage, every Day broken in Effect, without any other Mischief than that

1. *The Complete Art of Poetry*, I, 266. The discussion concerns comedy, but he presumably thought the same thing of tragedy.
2. *An Essay upon English Tragedy*, p. 6.
3. *The Elements of Dramatic Criticism*, p. 40.
4. *The Rambler*, No. 156. Compare his *Preface to Shakespeare* (1765), in *Johnson on Shakespeare*, ed. Raleigh, p. 57.

which arises from an absurd Endeavour to observe it in Appearance. For whenever the Scene is shifted the Act ceases, since some Time is necessarily supposed to elapse while the Personages of the Drama change their Place.

An occasional critic had been impolite to the rule before these words were written,[1] but afterwards, except for Cooke, everyone became insulting.[2] After 1775 it was completely dishonored.

Of all the ancient rules, that which forbade the simultaneous presence of more than three speaking persons on the stage received least consideration during the eighteenth century. William Cooke (1775)[3] appears to have been its unique defender. This rule, he said, "should be almost universally attended to," because when only two or three persons engage in a dialogue, "we then come to be closer judges of their characters, are more interested and more readily find out the merit, or demerit of the poet." In the catastrophe he was willing to allow some licence, but he recommended "this licence to be used sparingly, and only where the plot is better elucidated with it than without it." Dr. Johnson (September 14, 1751)[4] and Joseph Warton (1756)[5] condescended to pay the rule the passing tribute of a sneer. Others reserved their contempt for less unworthy objects.

1. See Leonard Welsted, *A Dissertation Concerning the Perfection of the English Language*, etc. (1724), in Durham, p. 370; and Fielding, *Tom Jones* (1749), V, i.

2. See *The Gentleman's Magazine*, XXII (1752), 163; J. Warton, *An Essay on Pope* (1756), I, 128; anonymous, *An Essay upon the Present State of the Theatre* (1760), p. 105; Beattie, *Dissertations Moral and Critical* (1783), I, 225–226; Blair, *Lectures on Rhetoric and Belles Lettres* (1783), II, 490–491; Pye, *A Commentary Illustrating the Poetic of Aristotle* (1792), pp. 215–216.

3. *The Elements of Dramatic Criticism*, pp. 106–107.

4. *The Rambler*, No. 156.

5. *An Essay on Pope*, I, 128.

Concerning eighteenth-century opinion on the proper style for tragedy little need be said. There had never been a neo-classic rule on this subject for the tragic dramatist to follow — nothing comparable, that is, to the rule of the unities, for example. The eighteenth century, however, developed some stylistic rules of its own. From the latter years of the seventeenth century it accepted the judgment that rime was a "monstrous ornament,"[1] a "true Gothic livery,"[2] with which no Englishman would think of decking out a tragedy, for rime was frivolous and undignified. Lack of dignity, if not frivolity, was an objection that was brought against prose tragedy as well.[3] George Colman, in a prologue to one of William Hayley's rimed comedies, *The Two Connoisseurs* (1784),[4] represents Bays as saying that he has

> Ne'er tried aught so *low*, or so *sublime*,
> As Tragedy in Prose, or Comedy in Ryme.

---

1. Shaftesbury, *Characteristics* (1711), ed. Robertson, II, 320; see also II, 321.

2. Mrs. Montagu, *An Essay on the Writings and Genius of Shakespear* (1769), p. 5. The objection to rimed tragedies was universal.

3. See especially *The Universal Magazine*, XII (1753), 87, a review of Moore's *Gamester*: "The diction is next to be considered. It is here prose, and, in many places, excellent prose; the language is often fine and nervous, but sometimes trifling and much below the dignity of tragedy: A circumstance, which cannot but happen in prose tragedies. And, when we consider we are not cramped to write in rhime, but have so excellent a medium as blank verse (a medium scarce any language but our own can boast of) I see no necessity for innovations, except the author thought genteel prose more natural to persons in middle life; which I can scarce allow, since many men speak blank verse without knowing it, and our language is so adapted to that, as we can hardly say any thing above common discourse, but it will insensibly run into feet. It is true, as Mr. Garrick and Mr. Mossop speak, they make many words sound well, which a common reader would not, and, by their attention to proper pointing, you cannot find much difference: But we should consider we cannot always have them on the stage, never in our closets, nor can every reader make up that deficiency to himself; so that, on the whole, I cannot but look on prose as much beneath the dignity of tragedy."

4. Quoted by Lounsbury, *Shakespeare as a Dramatic Artist*, p. 212. The only editions of Hayley to which I have had access, *Plays and Poems* (London: 1784 and 1785), do not contain the prologue.

To imitate nature was a cardinal rule of art, but "tragedy in prose," John Penn (1796) [1] thought, approached "too near to deception to obtain our purpose." If it is legitimate to assume that Penn believed with Bays in the lowness of prose tragedy, his remark becomes hard to reconcile with eighteenth-century society's estimate of its own elevation.[2] Besides, it is contradicted by the popularity of such tragedies as *George Barnwell*, in which both the subject and the style were "low." Most critics, nevertheless, agreed that blank verse was as close an approach to the language of "common Use," [3] or "of nature," [4] as the dramatist dared to make. It was like prose, but more harmonious, more dignified,[5] and therefore more appropriate as a tragic medium; for, said Lord Chesterfield,[6] "tragedy must be something bigger than life, or it would not affect us." Blank verse was the perfect form. "It has," said Blair (1783),[7] "sufficient majesty for raising the Style; it can descend to the simple and familiar; it is sus-

1. *Letters on the Drama*, p. 28.
2. See Hodson, "Observations on Tragedy," bound with *Zoraida* (1780), p. 89: "In these times this latter part of the precept, which regards the management of under characters, is not the least difficult, or perplexing to the dramatic poet. In more early ages, while the language, and the audience were equally unpolished, and unrefined, the task was not very difficult; but now, when all uncultivated language on the stage, as well as in the closet (at least certainly in the latter) would be rejected with disdain, as savouring more of Comedy than Tragedy; to make the style so simple as to be natural for such characters (the sentiments being at the same time obliged to be more common, and trite) and yet avoid vulgarity, is a medium much easier to describe, than to execute."
3. Dennis, *On the Genius and Writings of Shakespear* (1711), in Smith, p. 25.
4. George Colman, *Critical Reflections on the Old English Dramatick Writers* (1761), in *Prose on Several Occasions* (1787), II, 135.
5. Dennis, *On the Genius and Writings of Shakespear* (1711), in Smith, p. 25. Compare Gildon, *An Essay on the Art*, etc. (1709), in Rowe's Shakespeare (2nd ed., 1714), IX, xliv.
6. Letter to his son (January 23, 1752), in *Letters*, ed. Dobrée, V, 1821.
7. *Lectures on Rhetoric and Belles Lettres*, II, 513.

ceptible of great variety of cadence; and is quite free from the constraint and monotony of rhyme." Consequently it was generally considered an unnecessary "Solæcism" to mingle blank verse and rime,[1] or blank verse and prose.[2] Lord Kames (1762)[3] occupied an exceptional position, for although he was glad that rime had been "banished" he deplored the prejudice that would exclude all prose:

However suitable blank verse may be to elevated characters and warm passions, it must appear improper and affected in the mouths of the lower sort. Why then should it be a rule, that every scene in tragedy must be in blank verse? Shakespear, with great judgement, has followed a different rule; which is, to intermix prose with verse, and only to employ the latter where the importance or dignity of the subject requires it. Familiar thoughts and ordinary facts ought to be expressed in plain language; and if it appear not ridiculous to hear a footman delivering a simple message in blank verse, a vail must be drawn over the ridiculous appearance by the force of custom. In short, the variety of characters and of situations, which is the life of a play, requires not only a suitable variety in the sentiments, but also the like variety in the language of the dialogue.

Shakespeare, once more, furnished the strongest argument for irregularity, but, on the whole, theory departed from his great example. Shakespeare packed the theatres, but he did so in defiance of the law and the prophets.

1. See Addison, *The Spectator*, No. 39 (April 14, 1711).
2. See John Penn, Notes to Ranieri di Calsabigi's *Letter to Count Alfieri, on Tragedy*, in Penn, *Critical and Poetical Works* (1797), p. 92.
3. *The Elements of Criticism* (2nd ed., 1763), III, 287–288.

CHAPTER XI

Conclusion

ENGLISH literature between 1660 and 1798 was predominantly a prose literature. Of the poets who wrote between those dates the names of a bare half dozen live in the memory. Dryden and Pope, moreover, we are apt to think of as critics rather than as poets — critics of society and institutions as well as of literature. Prose was the medium and criticism was the function of a great bulk of the memorable writing of these years. It is significant that the four great philosophers of the period — Hobbes, Locke, Berkeley, and Hume — were all of the critical type, in line with the dominant mood of their time. The philosophical skepticism of Hume matches the religious skepticism of Gibbon, and the satire of Fielding and Swift.

In the light of this critical and prose tradition it is easy to see the appropriateness of the neo-classic theory of tragedy. The hostility of the neo-classicist to unrestrained emotion and to the fancy and imagination found its counterpart in the hostility of Locke, Hobbes, Hume, and Gibbon to religious enthusiasm. A fine frenzy in the theatre was as undesirable as a religious frenzy in the chapel. To ravish applause from regular method rather than from irregular fancy was the dramatic poet's proper business, for his object was to deceive the *mind* of the audience, and make it accept the stage representation as reality. This deceit was innocent, of course, because it aimed at the instruction of the mind by way of delight, or, as it was sometimes put, at the delight of the mind by way of instruction. The function of tragedy, that is to say, nicely agreed with what tragedy was and represented.

But dependence on authority was as much a part of neoclassic tradition as was the intellectual and skeptical spirit, and the two things were irreconcilable. What Aristotle and Horace and their commentators had said about tragedy was for a long time accepted without question. At the same time, however, and occasionally by the same men, authority was being contradicted in other fields of learning. While Hume, for example, was defending "the rules of art" he was attempting to undermine the authoritative position on physical causation, and recording the fact that royal and religious authority was losing its hold on the people. Revolt was in the air, but theatrical decorum and regularity tyrannized in the study of the dramatic theorist. Kings might not have been safe on their thrones, but if the critics had had their way, royalty would have been safe on the stage.

Authoritarianism and skepticism worked at cross-purposes from within. Other forces tended to destroy the tradition from without. During the course of the eighteenth century, fancy, imagination, and emotion successfully reasserted their rights. The poets became interested in fancy-inspiring graveyards and grottos. They celebrated the pleasures of the imagination and of melancholy. William Collins considered superstitions and the passions proper subjects for poetry, and Joseph Warton, besides his *Ode to Fancy*, wrote *The Enthusiast: or the Lover of Nature*, which reveals that enthusiasm, poetic if not religious, was regaining caste. Some dramatic theorists granted that passion was good, and conceded that the function of tragedy was rather to delight than instruct. Even poetic justice, a neo-classic concept, came to be welcomed because it delighted the feelings, not because it instructed the mind. The appeal to taste, also, was ordinarily an appeal to the feelings, despite attempts by the rationalists to claim this test of artistic excellence as their own. Taste for many was a sixth sense, which was above and less fallible than reason; and the man of taste, like the man of feeling and the man of fancy, and even like many a rationalistic skeptic, doubted the value of the rules and compasses.

At the same time that emotion and imagination were again becoming respectable, as a natural concomitant there was springing up a romantic interest in the "Gothic origins" of early art. The eighteenth century turned to this rediscovered "world of fine fabling" with a relief that was obviously heartfelt. The turning was momentous, not only because it brought relief from the verisimilitude of "classical" art, but also because it taught that the verisimilitude of one age and country is bound to be different from that of another, and that the rules for attaining it vary from age to age and from country to country. The seventeenth century had suspected the truth, and such men as Thomas Warton, Bishop Hurd, and Bishop Percy confirmed the suspicion. The rules of tragedy suffered along with all the others, for they were the rules, it had long been thought, of the fifth-century Athenian stage, to which alone the chorus and the unities, for example, were natural. When it was further discovered that many of the dramatic rules did not have the authority of Aristotle and the Greek tragedians, their cause was as good as lost. The portions of

them that were applicable to modern conditions were retained, but the others were stricken from the canon.

Among the conditions of eighteenth-century England
that determined theatrical theory and practise none was
more important than the rise of the middle class. No
theory or theatre could survive that did not respect its
tastes and predilections. If Hume was right, this class was
losing its awe of kings and churches. Why, then, should it
have revered a merely academic theory? If it no longer
shouted "God save the King" with quite the old conviction, there was no reason why it should have insisted upon
royal tragedy or upon the decorum and etiquette that had
pleased Rymer and that gratified the "varnished snob-
bery" of Lord Chesterfield. The upper classes might enjoy the cultured restraint of *Elfrida* and *Caractacus*, but
the middle class preferred the emotion of *Fatal Curiosity*
and *George Barnwell*. It knew nothing about dramatic
theory, but it knew what it liked, and that was a good cry
over the misfortunes of men like themselves. Aristotle,
whom Mason probably thought that he was following,
would have understood its preference for Lillo.

By the end of the eighteenth century the neo-classic
theory of tragedy, although it was not quite dead, was
dying rapidly. If a few John Penns were left to say a kind
word for some of its clauses, no Gildons remained to defend
it as a whole.

INDEX OF AUTHORS AND TITLES

INDEX OF AUTHORS AND TITLES